David Bowie FAQ

David Bowie FAQ

All That's Left to Know About Rock's Finest Actor

Ian Chapman

Backbeat
Books

Guilford, Connecticut

Backbeat Books
An imprint of The Rowman & Littlefield Publishing Group, Inc.
4501 Forbes Blvd., Ste. 200
Lanham, MD 20706
www.rowman.com

Distributed by NATIONAL BOOK NETWORK

The FAQ series was conceived by Robert Rodriquez and developed with Stuart Shea.

Book design by Snow Creative Services

British Library Cataloguing in Publication Information available

Library of Congress Cataloging-in-Publication Data available

ISBN 978-1-61713-706-8-0 (paperback)
ISBN 978-1-4930-5140-3 (e-book)

∞™ The paper used in this publication meets the minimum requirements of American National Standard for Information Sciences—Permanence of Paper for Printed Library Materials, ANSI/NISO Z39.48-1992

For Ben, Mia, and Arlo

Contents

Foreword

When I was sitting in the dressing room at the Rainbow Theatre on the night of August 30, 1972, waiting to go onstage with the Spiders from Mars starring David Bowie, I could hardly imagine then that I would be asked to write a foreword for the book that Ian Chapman was producing in 2020!

I joined the Spiders as a last-minute substitute when the previous keyboard player was struck down with an illness two days before the performance. Indeed, when I got the phone call from Mr. Bowie, I hung up on him, thinking it was a pal hoaxing me!

It was my first professional gig, and boy was I nervous. I mean, to appear onstage with an artist who was riding high with a hit single ("Starman"), his concert was a sellout, and I was driving a bread van only two days before. Would you believe it?

But in the Dorchester Hotel on London's Park Lane before the gig, David (and the other members of the Spiders) put me entirely at ease and dispelled all my qualms.

Robin Lumley performing "Starman" with David Bowie on the BBC TV show *Top of the Pops*, July 6, 1972
Author's collection

David Bowie was indeed a gentleman in every sense of the word—quiet, polite, and with a wry sense of humor. He made me feel that I *belonged*! As time went by, I realized that this was no mere show on his part. He really *was* like that.

And as for his music, when I got to grips with the chord charts, I discovered very quickly that the construction of his songs was very complex and original. Sure, they might appear simple to a radio listener, but, in fact, they were far from it. Have you ever cast an audio eye across "Changes" or "Life on Mars," for example?

I can quite see how the author of this book has become a staunch Bowie fan over the years, and this is the second tome he has written on this superb artist. As for the "frequently asked questions" implied in the title, I trust that many of them will be answered as you read through *David Bowie FAQ*. The facts will "out," as they say, and you, as a Bowie aficionado, will gain much pleasure from this book.

David Bowie was an actor first and foremost, and any of his accomplishments came second to that. He "played" at being a musician and took the role of superstar as another of his "parts," but always he was an actor. The only thing he didn't "act" was himself. If you'd been as lucky as I was, you would have seen him up close and personal and come to know him. Nevertheless, I cannot claim to have been a close pal and wandered about in awe of his personal magnetism. But I can absolutely attest to his talents and warmth of character.

I cast my mind back to the pre-gig dressing room with the obligatory Campari and Soda (David's favorite tipple at the time) enjoyed by all the Spiders and ruefully muse on the fact that nearly all of us from 1972 are gone. So Ian Chapman's choice of a "foreword writer" was a bit limited! I am delighted to have been asked.

—Robin Lumley
Robin Lumley, keyboard player for David Bowie's Spiders from Mars in 1972 and subsequently Brand X and many other well-known acts and artists.

Rainbow STAGE PASS 14

30th August

"DAVID BOWIE"

The Rainbow Theatre
232 Seven Sisters Road London N4 telephone: 272 4485/6/7

Robin Lumley's Musician Stage Pass for Rainbow Theatre, August 30, 1972   *Robin Lumley Collection*

Introduction

When David Bowie passed away on January 10, 2016, it took almost the entire world by surprise. Shock waves reverberated across countries and continents. His death was announced on his official Facebook page with the following short message: "Jan. 10, 2016—David Bowie died peacefully today surrounded by his family after a courageous 18-month battle with cancer. While many of you will share in this loss, we ask that you respect the family's privacy during their time of grief."

Throughout his entire career, David Bowie was the master of detail and maestro of outward appearances and remained ever mindful of the separation between personal and public lives. He stage-managed all of his affairs superbly, right up until the last. Nobody has exited this mortal coil with more class and dignity than David Bowie did, the most interesting, intelligent, uber-cool, and always surprising rock star the world has ever seen. But, of course, and as this book hopes to demonstrate, he was far more than just a rock star.

As more and more facts became available in the days and weeks following his death, it became clear that nobody outside his small inner circle of family, closest friends, and a handful of musical collaborators ever knew that he had liver cancer—diagnosed in mid-2014—and, reportedly, even David Bowie himself did not know that the end was imminent until just a few months before he passed away. When his passing did occur, just two days after the release of his final album, the typically groundbreaking *Blackstar*, the world witnessed an outpouring of grief, love, admiration, and loss that went far beyond anything normally seen on the passing of a popular entertainer or celebrity. Tributes containing universally effusive praise flowed throughout all forms of traditional media, and social media platforms such as Facebook turned into the digital equivalent of a global fan tribute wall festooned with poignant and heartfelt messages. The reason for such unprecedented adoration? Simply, while David Bowie was indeed a popular entertainer and celebrity—one of the biggest—he was also far more than that. His intelligence, his artistic depth, and his influence across a broad range of disciplines marked him as an artist without precedent. Even more than *that*, through his enormous body of work, he influenced and impacted positively on generations of people, helping them make sense of the world in which they lived and thereby making their lives better in the process. Such a thing should be, of course, the ultimate and overriding role/aim of both art and artists. That a skinny, pale young Englishman could achieve such a thing on such an enormous global scale, rewriting as he did so the rule book for what artists could and couldn't be and do, is more than just remarkable. It was astounding. When he died, the world showed its understanding of that fact in its reaction.

When a pop-cultural icon dies, be he or she a rock star or a movie actor or any other kind of widely admired celebrity and/or artist, there is frequently a blaze of attendant public attention that soon fades away once the news of his or her demise becomes old. "Today's news is tomorrow's fish and chip wrapper," as the old English saying goes. This is not the case with David Bowie, who is today, four years after his death, as popular as ever. As a university music lecturer, I can report with confidence that each year's intake of new students at my university, whose ages sit mostly in the seventeen- to twenty-year range, has an awareness of David Bowie that is far and above that of almost all of the artists with whom he rubbed shoulders during his 1970s and 1980s heyday. This is no accident. David Bowie quite simply had more to offer, and his legacy burns more potently and brightly than most as a result.

Speaking personally for a moment, the first I heard of David Bowie's death was a text I received out of the blue from my niece, Tahlia. I still have it on my phone: "Have you heard? David Bowie died!" My initial response was, quite simply, disbelief. I texted her back with a message to the effect that it was almost certainly just a rumor—maybe a publicity/media beat-up timed to coincide with the release of *Blackstar*. The timing, coupled with a complete lack of prior news about any illness, made it very easy to disbelieve and dismiss like that. However, within minutes of Tahlia's text, I found myself fielding other calls, texts, and e-mails from friends, family, fellow fans, and media. A quick check on the Internet, and I quickly knew it was all too true. What a bombshell! The world I had lived in had always had David Bowie in it. But now it didn't.

Who and what was David Bowie? How did he become so good at what he did? What drove him continually to push himself and to change the nature of his work so often? Has anyone ever changed as much as David Bowie did? Who else could have come up with the sublime comedic novelty of "The Laughing Gnome" one minute, superbly summed up the Cold War space race the next with the saga of Major Tom, reinvented himself as the glittering alien androgyne Ziggy Stardust and conquered the United Kingdom in the process (the fake star becoming a real star and thereby providing us with the all-too-rare phenomenon of life following art), morphed into the best white Brit facsimile of a Philly Soul Man one could ever imagine when conquering the United States as a Young American, reemerging as the cool, distant, austere Thin White Duke, and then, just a year later, expressing every teenager's deepest and darkest alienation in the never-leave-your-room ambient electronic perfection of *Low*? And all this within the first decade of his career! Above all, how did David Bowie make such an enormous impact on so many people throughout the world and on the art forms in which he chose to work? Through the three sections of investigation presented in this book—"The Works," "The Man," and "The Legacy"—*David Bowie FAQ* seeks to address such questions.

I make no pretense at any stage during this book that I am anything other than an avid, dedicated fan. Some of my friends have used terms such as *fanatical* and *obsessed* with regard to my interest in and passion for David Bowie over the years. "You're writing about him *again*?," a couple of them said when I told them I was embarking on *David Bowie FAQ*. "Yes," I replied. By day, as mentioned above, I give lectures about all sorts of aspects of music in my job as an academic within a university performing arts school. But there is nothing academic about how I regard David Bowie. The term *academic* infers that one maintains a deliberate measure of distance from one's subject matter, that some kind of studied aloofness and/or lack of passion and emotion exists, that some kind of cool appraisal is in the offing. Such notions are about as far away as one could get from my actual true feelings toward David Bowie. Now sixty years old, I cannot imagine not having had David Bowie in my life ever since 1972, when I was age twelve. As a fan of forty-eight years, I don't pretend to have intimate biographical knowledge of every aspect of the man's life and work; nobody could. And it's a pity, perhaps, that he never felt motivated to write his autobiography. With all of this said, however, I do know a few people who would certainly do rather well on any David Bowie Mastermind-type quiz, and there are several biographies among the myriad books written about the artist that do an admirable job of presenting his life story. No single one of them tells the whole story in itself, but taken together, there is a wealth of information available about his personal and public lives to be devoured by the hungry.

While in no way a biographer, then, I do nevertheless consider myself to be one of David Bowie's most avid fans. I belong to that A-list category of fan who firmly believes that in David Bowie, we had one of those rare and infinitely valuable artists who changed peoples' lives for the better—who taught important lessons to those who needed them and imparted universal truths, ultimately helping many of us make sense of the troublesome and at times threatening world in which we lived. Discerning this impact is the primary focus of this book.

David Bowie wasn't just a "pop star" who made catchy music to hum or tap along to. Well, he was that as well, and if there are people for whom that is as far as it goes, then that's fine too. But his real point of difference was that he operated on multiple levels. His messages were layered, and fans could come in on any level and, a bit like in Monopoly, pass GO and then proceed more deeply into what he was all about and what he had to offer. At the deepest of levels, David Bowie provided a blueprint for self-betterment, for self-empowerment, for embracing change rather than fearing it, and—part and parcel of all of this—for never just settling for whatever life has handed to you. His message was that you could take control of your own life and destiny. Someone once said, if you doubt your powers, then you give power to your doubts. Throughout his career, David Bowie backed himself and dared to be different—at times *very* different. Seemingly unafraid of failure, he would try anything and everything and take the cumulative experience he gained into his next venture. Nothing was ever a waste of time. In this sense, then, David Bowie was as much a motivational teacher as a rock star. But yes, he created some catchy tunes, too, if you come to this book as just a casual fan. For those to whom David Bowie meant far more, however, I hope you find resonances with what is written here about numerous aspects of the man's life and career. My writing is not academic—it could never be so when the subject is someone that I owe so much to and, yes, in a sense, love. Enjoy.

Acknowledgments

Of course, at the very top of the list must be David Bowie. As he did for so many people, he had an enormous positive impact on my life, especially during my teenage years during the 1970s, when he provided a blueprint for the acceptance—even celebration—of difference. What a life-saver. And what a talent.

Much appreciation for helping me, in your various invaluable ways, to bring this book to fruition: Robin Lumley, Rob Burns, Robert Lecker, Della Vaché, Bernadette Malavarca, and Lisa Marr. Special thanks to Sue Videler and my kids, Ben, Mia, and Arlo, who always amaze me and keep me on my toes.

Part 1

The Works

1

David Bowie, Songwriter

Pinning Down the Artist's Approach

Despite all of his different performance personas and the purposeful qualities he would affect at times in his singing (the cockney twang of "The Laughing Gnome" or "Little Wonder" being fine examples), David Bowie nevertheless had a very distinctive voice, as all of the best rock performers do. It was a voice that stuck out from the pack and was instantly recognizable as his

Aladdin Sane, 1973   *Author's Collection*

and his alone. However, determining a distinctive songwriting style is a much more difficult task because of his deliberate and highly successful embracing of diversity and change. Putting aside for just a brief moment his collections of experimental and avant-garde compositions, such as *Low*, *Blackstar*, and so on, even when utilizing the long-established and standard songwriter's tool kit of melody, harmony, and rhythm, he was capable of great sophistication, complete simplicity, or absolutely anything in between. While well versed in how a song *should* go according to convention, he was far more inclined than most to go somewhere radically different simply to see what would happen if he did. Running the full gamut from the sheer audacious artistry of "Life on Mars" to the perfunctory perfection of "Rebel Rebel," then, with everything in between, no musical vibe, song form, or even mashup was considered off limits.

The Bowie-esque Twist That Comes from Left Field

When interviewed on the BBC documentary *Five Years* (2013), Rick Wakeman described Bowie's unique and brave compositional unpredictability. Having played the piano so memorably on the *Hunky Dory* album (1971), he used "Life on Mars" as his example and demonstrated Bowie's chord choices for the

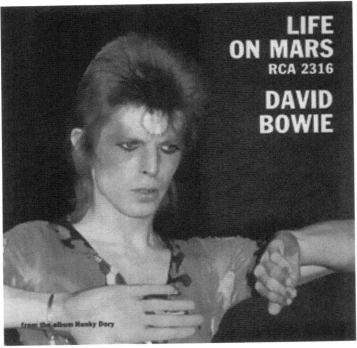

Cover of the 1973 UK single "Life on Mars"   *Author's Collection*

interviewer while sitting at the piano. He recalled, "It was a challenge in certain areas because of the chord structure.... He would lead you down the garden path with quite a bog-standard chord structure and then suddenly go awol. [demonstrates] ... He throws in a chord that you wouldn't expect. [demonstrates] ... Only David would do a thing like that!"

The Cut-Up Approach to Lyric Writing

One of Bowie's most effective points of difference in terms of his approach to his songwriting was his periodic employment of what is termed the cut-up technique. Attributed to beat poet William S. Burroughs and utilized famously in his groundbreaking novel *The Naked Lunch* (1959), the cut-up technique involves taking written sentences of prose and quite literally cutting them up and rearranging them in a new order—old-school cutting and pasting long before the home computer age. These newly separated excerpts of preexisting sentences can be rearranged as many times as desired until new meanings, to varying degrees of clarity or obfuscation, come through. Sometimes Bowie would use the rearranged words almost verbatim, sometimes he would tweak them, or sometimes he would not use the resultant wordings at all and would start over again. However, the very act of going through the exercise at times resulted in the stimulation of new ideas for him to work with. As he put it in the BBC documentary *Cracked Actor* (1975), directed by Alan Yentob, the technique was useful for "igniting anything that might be in my imagination."

The cut-up technique was one he would continue to utilize throughout his career. On the 1997 documentary *Inspirations*, directed by Michael Apted and filmed during the creation of the *1. Outside* album in 1995, Bowie can be seen at the keys of a Mac laptop using a digital version of the cut-up technique in an application called the Verbasizer, which he developed with technology guru Ty Roberts. As he explains to the camera, "It'll take the sentence, and I'll divide it up between the columns, and then when I've got, say, three or four or five—sometimes I'll go as much as twenty, twenty-five different sentences going across here, and then I'll set it to randomize. And it'll take those twenty sentences and cut in between them all the time, picking out, choosing different words from different columns and from different rows of sentences. So what you end up with is a real kaleidoscope of meanings and topic and nouns and verbs all sort of slamming into each other."

On *Earthling* (1997), Bowie's drum 'n' bass album, he was able to take the cut-up technique far beyond manipulating only the lyrics. Recording the entire album on digital technology instead of analog technology—a first for Bowie—meant that he could quite literally cut instrumental and vocal tracks at will in the recording studio and reposition them wherever and however he wished to create loops or even complete song structures. He both relished and utilized this freedom as the album's primary producer, alongside the like-minded Reeves Gabrels and Mark Plati, who were given coproduction credits.

The Geographical Approach

At times, geographical location would be a big player in Bowie's compositional palette. *Young Americans* is sublimely Philadelphia-infused, *Low* and *"Heroes"* do far more than tip their hat to Berlin, and *Reality* rings with multiple resonances of New York. In 2003, Bowie told Bill DeMain, in an article titled "The Sound and Vison of David Bowie" for *Performing Songwriter*, "Wherever I'm writing, that place tends to make itself very known, either in the atmosphere or sound.... I think the one thing that goes through *Reality* [2003] is the sense of New York. It feels very 'street.' There's a lot more about being a New Yorker, which indeed I am. The accent may not say that [laughs], but I am. I wrote the songs here, downtown where I live, and it does reflect that."

The Marshalling of the Forces

Bowie was a master at aligning his compositional and instrumental forces appropriately according to the requirement of individual songs, making the instrumentation a part of his thinking during the compositional process rather than an afterthought or something to be worked out after the pen was put down. For example, the beautiful jazz-inflected title track of the *Aladdin Sane* album became compositionally simplistic at the point where Mike Garson's piano solo began, thereby giving the piano maestro the most fundamental and unwavering of musical platforms on which he could improvise in as avant-garde a manner as he (or Bowie) wished. Because the rest of the instruments stayed put, the harmony simply sliding between G and A, and the rhythm remained unwavering, Garson had free rein to take all the musical risks in the world. It would never have worked if his solo had been required to occur over a complex, changing rhythmic and harmonic base.

Situating the Melody for Maximum Effect

How Bowie pitched his melodies was an important part of his songwriting bag of tricks. There is no better example than that of "Five Years," the opening track of *The Rise and Fall of Ziggy Stardust and the Spiders from Mars* (1972). At the beginning, he pitches his melody unchallengingly in the mid-range of his vocal register, but then as the action in the song progresses—as images are presented line after line of citizens panicking at the news of Earth's impending doom—he moves from being a casual observer looking on at the unfolding events to being swept up in the dire scene and as spooked as everyone else is around him. Accordingly, the melody lifts higher and higher as the song goes on, moving his vocal from the mid-range comfort where it began to the clearly, purposely strained absolute limits of his voice to saturate his lines with pure emotional angst. It is a masterful tactic that paints both the lyrics and the mood of a song and was a feature of Bowie's compositional style throughout his career. Such word painting abounds on the *Ziggy Stardust* album. Bowie admitted to borrowing a trick from the song "Somewhere over the Rainbow" from the movie *The Wizard of Oz* (1939), where a leap of a full octave occurs between the two syllables of "some-where," thus drawing the listener's attention skyward to "over the rainbow." Bowie uses this trick with equally great effect in "Starman." By setting the second syllable of the word an octave higher than the first, the listener is drawn literally skyward to where the starman is "waiting in the sky."

Consider too the cleverness of "Space Oddity," Bowie's career-launching epic tale of the unfortunate Major Tom. Aural painting begins the song, with the music ever so slowly drifting into the listener's consciousness from complete silence just as a spaceship might slip slowly and gracefully into view from out of the endless blackness of space. The transition in Bowie's voice from the calm euphoria that can be heard pre- and postlaunch at the beginning of the song to the panicked, danger-filled commentary at the point where things begin to go wrong is voice acting at its best. Similarly, the contrast between verse and chorus is highly effective in painting the action. The busy verses feature much variation in the melody and words set to faster note values, while the chords change with relative rapidity. At the chorus, however, which is literally launched into the heavens with the upward movement between the two words "for" and "here," the chord changes become sparse, the words are set to longer notes, and the comparative effect is one of floating. Major Tom is not in control; his spaceship is gracefully and slowly turning because control has been lost while Major Tom floats and drifts helplessly. Further, in a song full of drama and pathos, the crucial line "Tell my wife I love her very much" is made to stand out superbly with a complete change of voice timbre, becoming personal, regretful, and sad beyond words.

Eliminating Borders

There is one standout underlying principle that defines David Bowie's songwriting, and it is a distillation of his approach to his entire career. Simply, he loved to mix things up and avoid the restrictions of borders. As he put it to

Bill DeMain in 2003 in one of his most candid appraisals of his approach to composing, "I found that I couldn't easily adopt brand loyalty [laughs], or genre loyalty. I wasn't an R&B artist, and I was this artist or that kind of artist, and I didn't really see the point in trying to be that purist about it. What my true style was is that I loved the idea of putting Little Richard with Jacques Brel, and the Velvet Underground backing them—what would that sound like? [laughs] That for me was really interesting. It really seemed, for me, what I was good at doing. What I enjoyed was being able to hybridise these different kinds of music."

By avoiding blueprints, maps, and exemplars, David Bowie was able to free up his songwriting process enough to allow things to take unexpected twists and turns. His final word on this approach, also taken from the DeMain interview, is, "To allow the accidental to take place is often very good. So I trick myself into things like that. Maybe I'll write out five or six chords, then discipline myself to write something only with those five or six chords involved. So that particular dogma will dictate how the song is going to come out, not me and my sense of emotional self. Of course, I'll cheat as well. If I've got the basis of something really quite good coming out of those five or six chords, then I'll allow myself to restructure it a bit, if I think, well, that could be so much better if it went to F-sharp [laughs], or something like that. But to define the rules, then take it as far as you can go with that little rule, then break it, I find is really a way of breaking writer's blocks as well."

2

"My Brother's Back at Home with His Beatles and His Stones"

David Bowie Destroys the 1960s

Rock's Myth of Authenticity

In the 1960s, the overwhelming prevailing rock ideology was one of absolute, 100 percent authenticity. What a performer delivered to an audience either onstage or on vinyl was purported to be a seamless, truthful, absolutely faithful representation of what he or she truly believed and felt within. Simply, there was to be no division between the performer and the performance; it wasn't supposed to be an act. The notion that megastars such as Jimi Hendrix, Bob Dylan, Jim Morrison, Janis Joplin, the Beatles, the Rolling Stones, and others might incorporate into their work any kind of rock 'n' roll/showbiz/entertainment industry construction or artifice was the complete antithesis of what rock was supposed to be about. Rock was marketed as being the voice of the people, earthy, direct, unmitigated, and, above all, "real." Someone once termed this 1960s rock ideology the blue denim truth, and it's no coincidence that the clothing of the era consisted of natural fabrics: denim, muslin, and cotton, accompanied by long, flowing, unkempt hair that served as a virtual badge or beacon of its owner's apparent oneness with the unadorned, naturalistic world. The use of makeup was minimal and was strictly for women when used at all.

Of this time, Philip Auslander noted in his book *Liveness: Performance in a Mediatized Culture* (1999), "Rock ideology demand[ed] parity between the performer's stage and private personae." In his book *The Changing Room: Sex, Drag and Theatre* (2000), Laurence Senelick has further suggested of this façade of authenticity that "the performers are supposed to write their own material, direct their own shows and play 'themselves,' since it is usually self-defeating to differentiate their onstage personae from their offstage lives. For all the intercession of promoters, roadies and mammoth technological support such as the recording studio, an illusion is maintained that the musician is spinning it all from within."

When David Bowie, Alice Cooper, Marc Bolan, and other glam rockers entered the fray as the 1960s whimpered to a close and surrendered to the early 1970s, radical challenges to this prevailing but tired ideology of rock authenticity were about to occur. With their shiny man-made outfits of lurex, sequins, spandex, and polyester; their hair carefully coiffed; their faces masked in makeup; adopted names rather than real ones; and a plethora of stage poses, pouts, and theatricality, it's small wonder the hippies felt mortally threatened. Their ship was about to go down. Or, at least, it was about to list very heavily in the uncharted waters of the 1970s.

The Counterculture's Flagship Sinks

Rock music had been charged with a great responsibility as the flagship of the countercultural generation's hopes and dreams, supposedly epitomized by Woodstock's three days of peace, love, and music in 1969. As an agent for creating awareness of the world's injustices and abominations (for example, the Vietnam War), it had proven through the decade to be a fine rallying point for youth-oriented protest. But could the hugely revered musicians at the forefront of the counterculture actually deliver real change when they were, in reality, just human beings with flaws and defects like everybody else and even more susceptible to downfall because of the sex, drugs, and rock 'n' roll distractions and temptations put before them on a plate due to their cosseted status as icons? No. By the end of the decade, many of the idols had become fallen idols, and by the opening years of the 1970s, even the mighty Beatles had dissolved in acrimony. Brian Jones, Jimi Hendrix, Janis Joplin, and Jim Morrison were all dead. In the final countercultural event of the 1960s, no musician on the bill at the Altamont festival—not the least Mick Jagger—was able to stop the Hells Angels' violence toward the concertgoers that resulted in one death and numerous injuries. Hard on the heels of the Manson murders, things had gone sour indeed for the turn-on, tune-in, dropout generation. But with a new generation of rock fans waiting in the wings—the younger brothers and sisters of the countercultural generation—and a brace of talented new musicians with guitars in their hands and songs in their heads, things were about to be turned upside down.

David Bowie and the New Alternative

The highly intelligent Bowie, always a keen social and societal observer, set himself up in opposition to the prevailing rock ideology both knowingly and

Bowie's second album, 1969   *Author's Collection*

calculatedly. In Barney Hoskyns's book *Glam: Bowie, Bolan and the Glitter Rock Revolution* (1998), Bowie felt there was no "movement or any unified culture" in rock music of this time "because all that had fragmented by the time the seventies began." He also told *Uncut* magazine in 2003, "You have to try and kill your elders . . . we had to develop a completely new vocabulary . . . [take the] past and restructure it in a way that we felt we had authorship of . . . that was our world, not the bloody hippy thing." Further, Bowie confirmed the success of his strategy in Mark Paytress's book *The Rise and Fall of Ziggy Stardust and the Spiders from Mars* (1998), emphatically claiming, "I think I wiped out the sixties."

The extent to and manner in which Bowie lampooned the very industry he was working within in the early 1970s was highly offensive to rock purists. He further argued in Paytress's book, "The rock business has become so established, and so much like a society, that I have revolted against it . . . I won't take it seriously and I'll break its rules . . . that's why I felt naturally inclined to take the piss out of it." His method of doing so consisted of offering up the blatantly

ON STAGE
DAVID BOWIE
and
The Spiders from Mars

OPEN 8

SHOW 9

SANTA MONICA
CIVIC AUDITORIUM
FRI. OCT. 20th 1972

Ziggy Stardust 1972 US Tour Poster

Author's Collection

self-confessed manufactured star figure of Ziggy Stardust—alien, androgynous rock god—for the public scrutiny of the popular music audience and seeking to place his glorious caricature among the "genuine" established stars at the forefront of the popular music scene as if he, or at least Ziggy, were already one of them. Speaking to John Mendelsohn of *Rolling Stone* in April 1971, he famously declared that "rock music should not be questioned, analysed or taken so seriously. I think it should be tarted up, made into a prostitute, a parody of itself. It should be the clown, the Pierrot medium. The music is the mask the message wears—music is the Pierrot and I, the performer, am the message."

Traditionally, the sharpest arrow one could possibly fire at a performer was to accuse him or her of being a fake. What a fine neutralizing strategy, then, to put one's hands up and admit to being a fake—an actor—right from the very beginning. Prior to the full-blown artifice of the career-launching Ziggy Stardust concept and album, in the credits on the back cover of the *Hunky Dory* album (1971), Bowie referred to himself in his coproducer's role as "the actor," thereby showing his hand even before the rest of the world caught on to his revolutionary tactic. Later, at the time of the *Young Americans* album of 1975, he would refer to himself as "the Plastic Soul Man," once again deflecting the inevitable wave of accusations of fakery before they could even begin. Brilliant tactic though it was, some critics persisted, so affronted were they that the foundations of rock, such as traditionalists saw it, could be so decimated. In the United Kingdom's best-selling rock weekly, *New Musical Express*, in 1973, Nick Kent unleashed his venom thus: "David Bowie was last year's Ziggy Stardust, this year's Aladdin Sane and probably next year's Pinocchio. That's showbiz in the Twilight Zone ... the whole David Bowie mystique will soon be placed and solemnly laid to rest. And all the costume changes and mime poses in the world won't compensate for that, sweetheart."

The Construction of a Star

Bowie's dedication to parodying—and even exploiting—rock stardom is clearly evident in the groundbreaking marketing strategy employed for his 1972 U.S. Ziggy Stardust tour. Built on a foundation of calculated hype, the following excerpt concerning the strategy is taken from a management memo written by his manager Tony Defries and sent out to Bowie's entire entourage: "If we are to remain inaccessible then we must maintain a degree of privacy.... People should stay in the hotel provided for them and should be available at all times.... Please try and remember that I am feeding, clothing and paying everybody in a style to which they are not accustomed for the one specific purpose called SUCCESS!!! It is important that you pick the right kind of hotel. We prefer no Howard Johnson/Holiday Inn type. I feel a Royal Coach Inn where possible would be excellent. Something with charm."

This image-above-all strategy, an extremely radical one for the time, proved to be enormously successful. As David Douglas observed in *Presenting David Bowie* (1975), "The only other act to come over as a headliner from England was the Beatles; David Bowie's [tour] was second. By putting Bowie in such company ... he made Bowie look bigger than he was." Photographer Mick Rock, who accompanied Bowie on his British and American tours, recalled in the *Aladdin Sane* liner notes (rerelease, 2003) another ruse designed to make Bowie look larger than life: "The whole game was theatre. It was, like, David going to America with three bodyguards. When he got to America, yes, there was interest in certain areas, but if you went to the Midwest, you couldn't drag people off the streets to see him. It was part of the theatre to treat him like a star. And there I was; I came very cheap—in fact I came for nothing! DeFries could then start talking about David having an 'exclusive photographer.' People were saying, 'David Bowie's got an exclusive photographer. Who the fuck is David Bowie?' The people reasoned: 'If he's got an exclusive photographer and bodyguards, there must be something going on.' That was a piece of living theatre, if you like, part of the whole thing that Tony and David cooked up between them."

In his article "Space Oddities: Aliens, Futurism and Meaning in Popular Music" (2003), Ken McLeod has suggested that Bowie's "conscious construction of an alien rock star was designed to shed light on the artificiality of rock in general." Bowie highlighted what he saw as artificiality within popular music by presenting to the popular music audience an obviously artificial star figure, one that was so overtly fake that nobody could mistake it for being authentic. In *Strange Fascination* (1999), biographer David Buckley believes that through this strategy, "Bowie drew our attention to the fact that a person could play the part of a rock star before actually becoming one." This is certainly the case, and, as seen in Kevin Cann's *David Bowie: A Chronology* (1983), Bowie retrospectively stated of this scenario, "I wasn't at all surprised Ziggy Stardust made my career. I packaged a totally credible plastic rock star—much better than any sort of Monkees fabrication. My plastic rocker was much more plastic than anybody's." Nowhere was Bowie's playful raison d'être displayed better than in the lyrics of the song "Star" from the *Ziggy Stardust* album (1972) when he sang, "So inviting, so enticing to play the part—I could play the wild mutation as a rock 'n' roll star."

Here Bowie makes it clear that the role of a star is something to be played, much as an actor might play a role in a play. The star is not a real entity but is simply somebody, anybody, portraying that entity. Prerequisite talent aside, the idea that anybody could do this is strengthened as the singer relates how he could "play the wild mutation" or "make a transformation" to being a rock 'n' roll star and, in the process, leave behind the siblings and friends whom he names at the beginning of the song. If the ruse is carried off successfully, the rewards of fame and money await. This, in a nutshell, is how he destroyed the 1960s rock ideology.

Leaving the 1960s Behind

If the lyrics of "Star" make the tactic implicit, then the lyrics of "All the Young Dudes" most clearly lay out the difference between rock fans from the respective decades: "My brother's back at home with his Beatles and his Stones—We never got it off on that revolution stuff." Rather than presenting the by-now worn-out messages of countercultural unity—of the collective power of the people to make change—Bowie espoused the power of the individual to make change, starting with the remaking of oneself. David Bowie's revolution was new, daring, exciting, sexy, dangerous, confronting, and colorful.

3

"The Monster Was Me"

David Bowie's Outcasts, Aliens, Freaks, and Misfits

The magic of David Bowie for most of his fans was that he was able to harness their sense of being "different" and make it clear that such feelings were (1) normal and (2) a good thing instead of a bad thing. In a society where difference—psychological, physical, political, gender/sexual related, generational—was so frequently regarded with suspicion and derision, resulting in marginalization, alienation, and estrangement for those deemed to exist outside the boundaries of "normality," such a blueprint was both sorely needed and overdue. Bowie's message was that difference was exciting and sexy, positive qualities that were infinitely preferable to others that were more traditionally the lot of the freaks and outcasts of society: guilt for not being able to fit in, depression, at worst self-loathing, but often simply loneliness. Pop musicologist Simon Frith put it extremely well when he suggested, in his 1983 essay *Only Dancing: David Bowie Flirts with the Issues*, "Bowie's fans have always identified with him particularly intensely, because no one else has captured so well their sense of difference."

Bowie: The Personal Game Changer

During the early 1970s, when David Bowie came to prominence, he was *so* different from everything around him—even the other glam rockers with whom he was habitually lumped in—that he was impossible to ignore and was subsequently both loved and loathed in equal measure.

But it would never have been enough had he simply been outlandish/outrageous in his appearance only. That would have been superficial and fleeting—a flash in the pan, so to speak. For example, and with all due respect to the great glam bands such as Slade and Sweet, it is hard to imagine anyone ever arguing that these acts actually changed people's lives in any greatly significant way.

Diamond Dogs studio album cover, released May 1974   *Author's Collection*

They might well have given their fans a good, even great, time. They undeniably livened up a depressed and bleak Britain (and beyond) during their heyday. But they were never destined to be personal game changers for their fans in the way that David Bowie was. That was his shtick and his alone, with only perhaps Marc Bolan anywhere even remotely in the same league. He was the glam-rock artist with true depth, and this is the main reason he was able to continue on beyond the glam-rock era when almost all of the other big-name acts associated with the genre fell by the wayside, fatally typecast and ultimately buried in their platforms and sequins. Because he treated glam rock and rock music at large simply as a role to be played, in the guise of Ziggy Stardust he was able to abandon the role once he was done with it and move on to wherever his desire took him. The other glam rockers had no such distancing device, and once punk rock and new wave assumed the ascendency around 1975–1976, they quickly became irrelevant—last year's thing.

The Outcast

It's true that art is vital to humankind because it helps us make sense of the world in which we live. David Bowie's championing of the alienated is a superb example. All of the major characters that he invented and put on the rock stage and/or on vinyl were outcasts in some way: monsters, aliens, freaks, and misfits. *Space Oddity*'s Major Tom was cast off and alone in space, a complete misfit in his environment, estranged from his wife and the ones he loved, doomed through a misplaced trust in space-age technology to never return to them. Ziggy Stardust was an outcast, an androgynous extraterrestrial being that was alienated by gender and species right from the very start. Even the briefest of glances at the record cover confirms that he did not even remotely fit in to the surroundings in which he is pictured. This was a powerful rallying call to all those who felt similarly outcast. In David Bowie/Ziggy Stardust, there was someone who clearly understood what that felt like. On the *Ziggy Stardust* album, generational alienation was a central component, found, for example, in the lyrics of "Starman," "Let all the children boogie." This theme was established in the preceding *Hunky Dory* when, in "Oh! You Pretty Things," Bowie implored the parents, "Look out at your children—see their faces in golden rays. Don't kid yourself they belong to you—they're the start of a coming race." Such words were empowering to youth, a section of society who traditionally felt power*less*. Earlier still, in "The Width of a Circle" from *The Man Who Sold the World*, Bowie had sung a lyric destined to crop up again and again within Bowie studies: "Then I ran across a monster who was sleeping by a tree. And I looked and frowned and the monster was me." David Bowie was psychoanalyzing himself, expressing it through his art, and thereby providing a means by which other people with similar feelings of difference could begin to understand themselves and come to the realization that their fears and worries were not unique: they were part of a community.

Alienation: The Beginnings

That Bowie's critiquing and/or taking on the role of society's misfits was a feature of his work from the very start is clearly demonstrated when one ponders his very first album, the abject failure that was *David Bowie* (1967). In the song "Uncle Arthur," for example, Bowie presents a vignette of a highly dependent thirty-two-year-old man who finally moves out of his mother's house, against her wishes, after at long last meeting a girl. The experience proves to be more than he can cope with, however, and he retreats home to his mother. Similarly, the song "Little Bombardier" concerns an old, lonely career soldier who has trouble resuming normal life after his active service ends: "War made him a soldier … peace made him a loser." So once again Bowie is addressing a theme of estrangement from society, but the issue is not a topical one of teenagers against their parents or a "new breed" standing against authority. Indeed, the theme develops rather darkly to become one of suspected pedophilia. It's true to say that Bowie's outsiders at this nascent stage of his career were far harder to empathize with and lay a very long way from anything that would rally youth to him in the way that would happen so spectacularly just a handful of years later. Similarly obtuse, other lyrical themes on the debut album included the surreptitious observing of a grave-robbing gravedigger in "Please Mr. Gravedigger," a song sung from the perspective of a watching man who is the unapprehended murderer of a ten-year-old girl; a toymaker urging the children of rich parents to purchase his wares in "Come and Buy My Toys"; an appeal to a Tibetan child in "Silly Boy Blue"; and the travails of a cross-dressing soldier in "She's Got Medals." Endearing characters? No. Establishing a theme of exploring the lives of outsiders at the very earliest stage of his career? Yes.

Perfecting the Role

The powerful image on the album cover of *Aladdin Sane*, with its split-face depiction of schizophrenia, graphically continued the theme of alienation. After all, perhaps the most marginalized of all people in society are those deemed psychologically disturbed. Then, just a year later, he would offer on the cover of *Diamond Dogs* an image every bit as provocative. His anthropomorphized half-man, half-dog figure pictured lying before a billboard featuring two freak show performers (based on real-life Coney Island freak show performers Alzoria Lewis and Johanna Dickens) spread his net wider to include those alienated because of physical abnormality and disfigurement. He would emphatically ram home this trope in 1980–1981 during his surprise and much vaunted tenure on the Broadway stage playing the role of John Merrick in *The Elephant Man* (explored in more detail in chapter 15). On the *Diamond Dogs* album itself, is there a more graphic depiction anywhere in rock music of an alienated misfit than that described in the title track of Halloween Jack descending on a rope from a burned-out high-rise and running through the ruined streets of the Orwellian dystopian, postapocalyptic nightmare that was Hunger City?

Loneliness, Berlin Style

In 1977 came the magnificently bleak and stylistically groundbreaking ambient electronica of the *Low* album, in which rock music's most famous misfit was to be found cowering in the dark, gloomy depths of his room, unwilling and/or unable to venture beyond his door and out into the world.

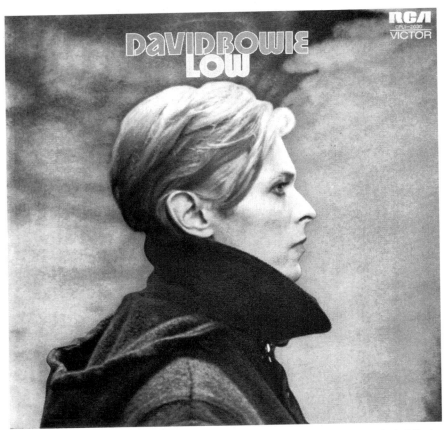

Low album, 1977

Author's Collection

In "What in the World," he captures the loneliness and despair of every person who has ever felt alienated for any number of innumerable reasons. The track—and *Low* in its entirety—is a universal testament to the lonely, and lonely teenagers, in particular, related to it in their droves. Finally, *someone* knew how they felt. With words a scarcity on the album—it is largely instrumental—Bowie communicated his feelings mainly through his music. Many teenagers—both then and now—are regarded as withdrawn and moody, uttering monosyllabic answers to the questions posed by their parents, teachers, and other authority figures. This, then, was music *made* for them.

Later that same year, *"Heroes"* was released, and, in addition to instrumental tracks that followed on in the vein of *Low*, Bowie here invoked the marginalization of Berlin's East/West divide. The image of young lovers kissing in the shadow of the Berlin Wall symbolizes imposed dispossession and estrangement, the Wall a quite literal symbol of separateness and division. The cover, meanwhile, with Bowie gesturing angularly with his arms and hands, was based on Erich Heckel's *Roquairol* (1917), in which Heckel sought to express inner turmoil or sickness through similar unnatural gestural twisting. Just six months earlier, Bowie's close friend Iggy Pop had released his album *The Idiot* (1977), which was cowritten and produced by Bowie, and the cover featured Pop pictured in almost identical Heckel-inspired fashion. In the time leading up to these releases, the two men had been together in Berlin, even living together for a time, and had a fondness for lengthy visits to the Brücke Museum, where many of Heckel's works were displayed.

By nature, a lodger (namesake of *Lodger* [1979], Bowie's thirteenth studio album) has no permanent home and is someone passing through a location without belonging.

In addition to the obvious transitory qualities of the disturbing album cover, a gatefold that finds the artist pictured on a postcard addressed to his record

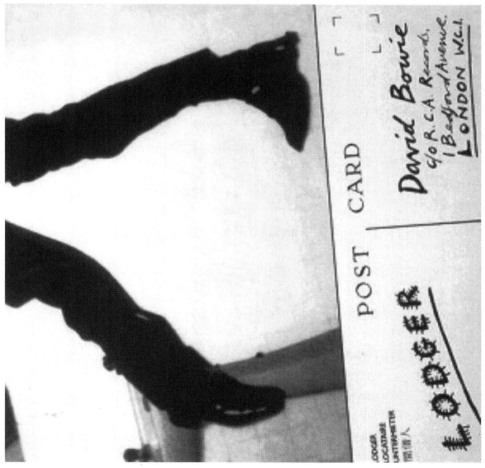

Lodger studio album cover, released May 1979   *Author's Collection*

company in London and seemingly a victim of some unidentified violent act committed in a public bathroom, the overall theme of the album is one of travel, set up emphatically by the first three tracks, "Fantastic Voyage," "African Night Flight," and "Move On." "Move On" makes things explicit, as Bowie sings, "Sometimes I feel that I need to move on, so I pack a bag and move on." Once again, he is an outsider, an alien, not fitting in. When describing *Lodger* at the time of its release, RCA spokesperson Mel Ilberman suggested, "It would be fair to call it Bowie's *Sergeant Pepper* . . . a concept album that portrays the Lodger as a homeless wanderer, shunned and victimized by life's pressures and technology." David Bowie is very firmly on the outside.

An Assemblage of Aliens

Scary Monsters (and Super Creeps) (1980) uniquely brought many of the artist's former performative selves together in one place. Visual recapitulations of *Aladdin Sane, Low,* "Heroes," and *Lodger* featured on the typically superb album cover. Once again formally locating himself outside mainstream society, as evidenced by his self-identification of former selves as scary monsters, to everyone's surprise he even brought back dear old Major Tom from 1969, now as estranged as ever not only by his abandonment in space but also by drug addiction. Bowie's outsider status and identification had never been so strongly expressed as it was on this album. As Debra Rae Cohen of *Rolling Stone* put it so superbly in her review at the time, "Slowly, brutally and with a savage, satisfying crunch, David Bowie eats his young."

The Drum 'n' Bass Outcast

The cover of *Earthling* (1997) found David Bowie as out of place as ever. While he swapped the drab urban environment of *The Rise and Fall of Ziggy Stardust and the Spiders from Mars* (1972) for a beautiful English pastoral scene and traded the glam-rock jumpsuit for a magnificent slashed and torn Union Jack–patterned greatcoat, the juxtaposition of subject and scene is as jarring and confrontational as ever. "Dead Man Walking" provides the bleakest of representations of alienation, as Bowie depicts "an alien nation in therapy" and nobody fits in. Is our existence, as he purports in the same song, "all just human disguise"? The closely allied notion of creating a false public face through lies and exaggeration—a coping tactic of the marginalized and estranged—comes through in the appropriately named "Telling Lies."

On the Outside to the Very Last

In the *Independent* of January 8, 2016, in his review of the artist's final album, *Blackstar*, Andy Gill summed up how David Bowie legitimized the experiences of legions of his fans. Bowie did so by wearing on his musical sleeve his own feelings of difference, his fears and vulnerabilities, from the beginnings of his career right until the end of his career. Gill observed, "For hundreds of thousands of heretofore ordinary, dead-end kids, art and literature and music were suddenly illuminated as ways of seeing and being, as worlds of personal possibility, in a way that school had rarely managed to reveal."

In Bowie's hands, popular music could be a real force for personal change and empowerment. Unlike punk, for example, and notwithstanding the magnificent expressions of rage and rightful disgruntledness that the best punk songs positively dripped with, David Bowie offered more than just a way to express one's feelings of group or personal alienation. In Bowie's hands, his art offered alternative models and tangible means of self-betterment by those prepared to follow his example. He made monsters, aliens, freaks, and misfits feel they were a *part* of society, not apart from society.

4

David Bowie and Art

A True Artist in Every Sense of the Word

The activities and achievements of most rock musicians are encapsulated very easily and neatly within that singularly simple and self-explanatory term *rock musician*. To describe an interdisciplinary artist like David Bowie as simply a rock musician is to collapse his activities into a wholly unsatisfactory straitjacket even if rock music was where he made both his name and his biggest splash. In the article "Only Dancing: David Bowie Flirts with the Issues"

Fan art by Tanja Stark   *Tanja Stark Collection*

(1988), Bowie contended to musicologist Simon Frith, "When you are an artist you can turn your hand to anything, in any style. Once you have the tools, then all art forms are the same in the end." This explanation provides an insight into the rationale behind Bowie's enormously expansive artistic palette. While everyone is aware of David Bowie's music and most people are aware of his acting prowess and his exploits onstage and in film, what is far less widely known is his involvement in the visual arts as both a highly respected advocate and a very active practitioner. In an interview in the *Telegraph* in 1996, he stated, "I do feel that there is a much more inclusive feeling among the arts communities in general—music, literature, the visual arts. And I'm determined that if I want to paint, do installations or design costumes, I'll do it. If I want to write about something, I'll write about it." Certainly, for David Bowie, rock music was just one of the tools of his trade, and while music afforded him his highest-profile achievements, he personally regarded it as no more worthy of reverence than any of the other art forms he was enthused about and involved himself in.

The Early Days

As a teenager, David Bowie (then David Jones) took art as one of his subjects at London's Bromley Technical High School, a school considered very liberal for its time. Indeed, art turned out to be the only O-level pass he would achieve in any subject before leaving school in 1963. Tutored there by the supportive, engaging, and enthusiastic Owen Frampton, father of another later-to-be-very-famous musician, guitarist, and vocalist, Peter Frampton, art was reportedly the only subject that the young Bowie took to with any relish, passion, or, indeed, success. After leaving Bromley Tech, he briefly studied at London's Croydon School of Art but quickly left, disillusioned, famously slagging off the entire suburb by using its name as an insult: "God, it's so fucking Croydon," he would say, adding that it "represented everything I didn't want in my life, everything I wanted to get away from." Such a damning put-down from one of the college's most famous ex-students did not deter the head of the school at the time of Bowie's death, Tim Strange, from describing Bowie in a tribute published in the *Independent* as "one of the few exceptionally creative artists that continually explored and pushed creativity and its possibilities. He is—and will continue to be—an inspiration for the students and staff at Croydon School of Art, where he is one of our illustrious alumni." Mr. Strange further added, "His talent was second to none and his constant impact on music, fashion, and art will be sorely missed. He was the exception to the rule as an artist and musician. South London should be very proud of the contribution Bowie has made to culture on a global scale, albeit on a very sad day for the Croydon School of Art community."

David Bowie Gets His Only Ever "Real" Job and Takes the Skills Away with Him

Beyond such schooling, Bowie briefly worked in advertising, taking up a job—his only-ever nine-to-five position—at the London office of a small Yorkshire-based agency, Nevin D. Hirst. Working as a runner, junior visualizer, and paste-up artist and carrying out duties that involved drawing sketches and coming up with ideas for potential advertising campaigns, he found this endeavor too to be anything but to his taste, and his stay was short lived. Nevertheless, the experience was to prove a valuable one for him, and fellow members of his early bands recall him designing advertising and publicity campaigns for their musical endeavors. As anyone who attended the *David Bowie Is* exhibition at the Victoria and Albert Museum in London in 2013 or at any of the subsequent locations the exhibition traveled to can attest, sketching out and bringing to life on paper his ideas for costumes, stage sets, album covers, and so on was an integral part of David Bowie's creative methodology. Sticking particularly in my memory is his storyboard for the "Ashes to Ashes" video and the set for *Diamond Dogs*' Hunger City, but there were many other examples to marvel at in the exhibition.

Mixing It Up

The list of media with which David Bowie engaged includes many kinds of mixed media: his own artworks, including sculptures (aluminum, chrome, plated bronze), paintings (on multiple surfaces), drawings (charcoal, pastel, pencil), pressed metal, lithography, serigraphy, gouache, woodcuts, linocuts, and more.

In short, there was simply nothing that he was not prepared to turn his hand to, whether to satisfy his own curiosity or to expand his artistic horizon and afford him brand-new ways to express himself and convey his message.

In 2017, Mick Brown of the *Telegraph* summed up David Bowie's interdisciplinary pursuits in a piece titled "I Have Done Just About Everything That It's Possible to Do": "You might describe him as all-purpose art-dilettante. He makes records; he acts . . . he collects paintings (German Expressionist and British contemporary) and paints himself; he designs wallpaper; he sits on the board of the art journal *Modern Painters*, for which he also writes art criticism."

Art at the High End

It's unlikely there has been any other rock star who has sat on the board of a highly prestigious art journal, but, as Brown points out, such was Bowie's expertise in matters of art that he was able to most successfully fill such a role on the

Amulet, aluminum sculpture made by David Bowie. One of 50 in the Remember series
Photograph by Michelle Chalklin-Sinclair, Ian Loughran Collection

board of *Modern Painters*, at times taking on editorial and interview duties and even writing features. The board of the quarterly journal, which originated in England but is now published in New York, welcomed Bowie in to their ranks in 1994, where he debuted with a 15,000-word piece, including an interview with Swiss painter Balthus. His writing is characterized not only by his clearly evident knowledge of art but also by his sheer unbridled passion for it. In another piece in *Modern Painters* written about one of his favorite artists Jean-Michel

Basquiat, Bowie enthused, "I feel the very moment of his brush or crayon touching the canvas. There is a burning immediacy to his ever evaporating decisions that fires the imagination ten or fifteen years on, as freshly molten as the day they were poured onto canvas. It comes as no surprise to learn that he had a not-so-hidden ambition to be a rock musician.... His work related to rock in ways that very few other visual artists get near."

David Bowie's Art Hoax

While on the board of *Modern Painters*, David Bowie met fellow board member William Boyd, the Scottish writer. Boyd is the man responsible—with Bowie's help—for one of the great practical jokes in the history of art. In 1998, Boyd published, through 21 Publishing (the publishing house that Bowie codirected with Karen Wright, who was at the time also editor of *Modern Painters*), a fictitious hoax biography titled *Nat Tate: An American Artist 1928–1960*. Cleverly combining the names of the two great London galleries, the National Gallery and the Tate Gallery, into the name of an artist who never existed, the ploy was designed to expose the snobbery and one-upmanship of the upper echelons of the New York art scene. An official launch was held in New York and hosted by David Bowie during which he read extracts from the book on the eve of April Fool's Day 1998. Often described by those who knew him well as a man with a great sense of humor, playing such a role with a straight face and appropriate gravitas must have appealed to him greatly, not to mention its appeal to his love of exposing pomposity. In addition, Picasso's biographer John Richardson was also in on the act (as was Gore Vidal, who wrote an endorsement on the book cover), speaking to the assembled glitterati of the nonexistent artist's close friendships with Braque and Picasso to solidify the hoax that some of those present—artists, dealers, collectors, writers, and critics—unwittingly bought into, much to the amusement of those who were in on the joke and those who had realized what was going on but played along regardless. It was a magnificent ruse and in a sense mirrored David Bowie's own send-up of rock stardom with his fictitious Ziggy Stardust character that had started it all off for him.

David Bowie: Art Collector

In addition to creating art himself, Bowie was an avid collector with the financial means to acquire high-quality works from some of the world's biggest names as well as to encourage unknown artists who took his eye by purchasing their work speculatively. As he explained to *New York Times* critic Michael

Kimmelman in 1998, "Art was, seriously, the only thing I'd ever wanted to own. It has always been for me a stable nourishment. I use it. It can change the way I feel in the mornings. The same work can change me in different ways, depending on what I'm going through."

And own art, he most certainly did. In November 2016, at the most famous auctioneer in the world, Sotheby's Auction House of London, an auction of Bowie's art collection titled "Bowie/Collector" was conducted on behalf of his estate, to which the money raised was returned. Over the course of two days, approximately 400 works, comprising about 65 percent of Bowie's total collection, raised £33 million ($45.7 million). This was far in excess of Sotheby's pre-auction estimate of £8 to £11 million. Bowie's estate did not offer the remaining 35 percent of his collection for sale, considering the works to be of what they termed "particular [private] significance." The works offered for sale included hotly sought-after pieces by the likes of Frank Auerbach, Jean-Michel Basquiat, Damien Hirst, David Bomberg, Henry Moore, Graham Sutherland, Eduardo Paolozzi, Patrick Caulfield, Leon Kossoff, and Marcel Duchamp. The most expensive pieces sold included Basquiat's *Air Power*, which went for £7.1 million, and Auerbach's *Head of Gerda Boehm*, which fetched £3.8 million.

The auction was a huge success, with packed attendances, hundreds of online bidders around the world, and unprecedented media attention underlining just what a fine and expansive collection Bowie had quietly accumulated over some considerable years. A *New York Times* article focusing on the auction of his collection and titled "David Bowie's Seal of Approval Bolsters Art at Auction" (2016) reflected the esteem in which Bowie was held as an art collector. As writer Scott Reyburn concluded in his critique of the event, "The allure of the David Bowie provenance pushed the values of Modern British art to a new level." Enthused about the collection's former owner, Christina Shearman, a British-born art adviser based in New York, concluded, "Bowie was a true collector. His acquisitions were not commercially motivated; he cared about the art, not the market. His was a deeply personal, eclectic collection, reflecting his British roots and his real passion for art."

The "Bowie/Collector" art auction was split into three parts by Sotheby's. The first—and biggest—part was titled "Modern and Contemporary Art." It was described in Sotheby's post-auction report as comprising pieces "led by Jean-Michel Basquiat's magnificent Air Power. At the heart of the auction is Bowie's collection of 20th-century British Art, which moves from Harold Gilman's Interior (Mrs Mounter), painted during the First World War, to works by Damien Hirst from the 1990s by way of David Bomberg, Henry Moore, Graham Sutherland, Eduardo Paolozzi, Patrick Caulfield, Frank Auerbach and Leon Kossoff. The selection is embellished by key works by Marcel Duchamp, who Bowie cited as a major influence, and Francis Picabia as well as a 16th-century Venetian altarpiece by Tintoretto."

The second part was also titled "Modern and Contemporary Art" and was described by Sotheby's as revealing "the full extent of David Bowie's eclectic and understated collection. Alongside paintings, drawings and sculptures by 20th-century British artists there are German Expressionist prints, Picasso ceramics, collections of Contemporary African and Outsider Art, and a Surrealist chess set by Man Ray, all of which provide a unique insight into Bowie's artistic vision and his passionate collecting journey."

The third part of "Bowie/Collector" was titled "Design: Ettore Sottsass and the Memphis Group." Sotheby's description detailed the collection: "Ettore Sottsass and the Milan-based Memphis group revolutionised design, introducing fun humour and strikingly bold colour combinations. This cutting-edge design with no limits, no boundaries was a fitting choice for one of the most radical musicians of his generation. 100 lots from David Bowie's design collection were offered in a dedicated sale, raising a total of £1.4 million. Highlights included David Bowie's record player, by Pier Giacomo and Achille Castiglioni, which fetched a record £257,000.... Also featured was a design classic, Bowie's lipstick red 'Valentine' typewriter by Sottsass, estimated at £300–500, sold for £47,500."

The Advantages of Artistic Interdisciplinarity

If the extent and quality of Bowie's art collection took many by surprise once it was brought out into the public eye at the auction, then it's a fair bet that many more people, beyond the hard-core David Bowie fan base, might be just as surprised to learn of his own extensive nonmusical artistic endeavors. It would be a mistake, however, and a very un-Bowie-like notion to see his musical and nonmusical endeavors as inherently unrelated. As he himself told the *New York Times* in 1998, "I'd find that if I had some creative obstacle in the music that I was working on, I would often revert to drawing it out or painting it out.... Somehow the act of trying to recreate the structure of the music in paint or in drawing would produce a breakthrough."

5

The Gnome Returns

Hauntings from the Past

In 1973, David Bowie was at the absolute peak of his game. The unchallenge-able coolest cat in town and glam-rock megastar, he'd become a rock 'n' roll sensation, a challenging, divisive, and magnificent youth idol, and a fashion icon, all in the wake of the release of *The Rise and Fall of Ziggy Stardust and the Spiders from Mars* (1972) and its attendant television appearances and sold-out tours. The media could not get enough of him, and legions of kids were to be seen clamoring and clawing for their new glitter-clad messiah in scenes reminis-cent of Beatlemania. David Bowie/Ziggy Stardust hairstyles were cut, platform shoes and boots were selling out all over town, boys were raiding their mum's and elder sister's makeup stashes, and dads all over the United Kingdom were in a cold sweat at the seemingly effeminate antics of their sons and heirs. Who would take over the butcher's shop, they wondered, and why had little Johnny stopped practicing his football and swapped his catapult for a hairbrush?

David Bowie, meantime, the absolute epitome of pop's cultural style guru and master manipulator of both image and media, basked in the attention and the glow of flashbulbs and spotlights. But then, something from his past returned unexpectedly—something about as cool as a pair of walking shorts worn with socks and sandals and about as embarrassing as a dodgy drunk uncle who'd turned up during the awkwardness of family Christmas and proceeded to thoroughly disgrace himself.

"The Laughing Gnome": A Fly in the Ointment of Cool

"The Laughing Gnome" is a comedic novelty song released as a single by David Bowie in 1967. The closest referent for it is most likely the song "The Witch-doctor," written and performed by Ross Bagdasarian and released under the name of David Seville and the Chipmunks in 1958 to great success, reaching number one in the United States and charting highly elsewhere in the world. Using the same sped-up-voice studio technique/trick, Bagdasarian's 1958 chip-munk became David Bowie's 1967 gnome. Painstakingly put together in the studio with the help of engineer Gus Dudgeon, who provided the gnome voices and special effects, "The Laughing Gnome" was an ambitious undertaking in a recording sense. While recorded during the sessions for the self-titled debut album *David Bowie*, it was not ultimately included in the track listing for the album and was treated as a separate undertaking. While many of the tracks recorded during these sessions were quirky and unconventional (to say the least), nothing else had the blatant comedic novelty quality of "The Laughing Gnome." Undergoing considerable reworking, Dudgeon and Bowie ended up spending almost two months working on the track, longer, in fact, than the entire debut album had taken to record. "The Laughing Gnome" was released as a precursor single on the Decca subsidiary label Deram ahead of the release of *David Bowie*. But it was all to no avail. At least, not then.

The story line of "The Laughing Gnome" concerns a man (David Bowie) who meets and befriends a gnome (Gus Dudgeon) with a constant penchant for laughing and humor and takes him home to his house. The Laughing Gnome's brother, Fred, also joins them, and, in an unexpected twist, it turns out that the two gnomes have quite a talent for writing music and "comedy prose for radio shows." The three become a team, and in return for making lots of money for their human benefactor, the two gnomes are allowed to happily live the good life up in the chimney of his house. The highlight and backbone of the song is a succession of puns on the word *gnome*—for example, "'Ere, 'aven't you got a gnome to go to?"—the result of numerous brainstorming sessions by Bowie and Gudgeon.

Even the most ardent detractors of "The Laughing Gnome" would be forced to admit that the song is extremely well written, with perfect rhymes and lyric lines that bounce along with a comedic pulse that is in perfect keeping with the jaunty rhythm that underpins the song. The lead instrument is the highly unfashionable (in a pop music sense) oboe, supported by a honking bassoon. Played straight in terms of vocal delivery for most of the song, albeit with a strong cockney accent, by the time the song's extended outro occurs, David Bowie is heard completely cracking up in the final utterances of the catch lines, "Ha ha ha—he he he. I'm the Laughing Gnome and you can't catch me." (This appears to be a none-too-subtle borrowing from the folk/jazz standard "Little Brown Jug," with its highly comparable line, "Ha ha ha, you and me. Little Brown Jug, don't I love thee.")

While the song was a complete flop on its original release in 1967 (as was the debut album that followed it and that was subsequently quickly shelved), once its architect had become a global superstar through the career-launching masterstroke that was *The Rise and Fall of Ziggy Stardust and the Spiders from Mars*, it was rereleased in 1973 by the canny record company Decca, which had taken a chance on the nascent talents of the young David Bowie by signing him to their Deram label but received no tangible reward. With

Decca seizing this opportunity to collect on a seemingly buried and forgotten back-catalog item and despite the fact that the song was as different as it could possibly be to the musical style (glam rock) that had taken David Bowie to the top of rock's hierarchy, "The Laughing Gnome," this time around, sold by the truckload to David Bowie's new legions of young fans. Frankly, at the time, they would in all likelihood have bought absolutely anything that carried the Bowie name on it, and as a result, his early bid for comedic greatness ultimately reached a lofty number six on the U.K. singles chart. Although yet to become a superstar of the same magnitude in the United States, during a year in which the singles "Life on Mars," "Drive In Saturday," and "Sorrow" all cruised effortlessly into the U.K. top ten (all reaching number three), to see "The Laughing Gnome" rubbing shoulders with such company is a wonderfully anachronistic footnote to the David Bowie story.

Although about as welcome as an embarrassing photo produced at a twenty-first-birthday party, David Bowie could do nothing to prevent Decca from rereleasing his failed Deram single from 1967, so he was forced to grin and bear it. Perhaps the income it generated was a partial salve, but certainly, if he could have prevented this seeming and risky blight on his ever-upward trajectory, then he would have done so. In an interview for *Musician* magazine in 1990, David Bowie offered the following appraisal of the Anthony Newley–influenced beginnings of his recording career, ruefully remarking, "Aaargh, that Tony Newley stuff, how cringey. No, I haven't much to say about that in its favor."

The Anthony Newley Factor

Back in 1967, while David Bowie was still shopping around for a stylistic hook to hang his hat on, as the strange mix of music hall and variety on his debut album clearly demonstrated, with just a couple of songs in the collection approaching anything like contemporaneity with the popular music scene of the day, one of his major influences was the novelty bent of Anthony Newley. Newley was an English actor, singer, and songwriter who found major success across a broad spectrum of performing arts endeavors. A star of hit musicals and films as actor, writer, and songwriter, moving with equal success into cabaret in his later career, he also found significant success on the pop music charts, with no fewer than twelve entries in the U.K. top forty over the four-year period from 1959 to 1962. He also cowrote songs and scores for others, two notable efforts being the now classic song "Feeling Good," cowritten with Leslie Bricusse and made popular the world over by Nina Simone, and the title track for the James Bond movie *Goldfinger* (1964), which was a major hit for Shirley Bassey and was written in partnership with Bricusse and John Barry. His success as a songwriter was recognized formally in 1989 when he was inducted into the Songwriter's

Hall of Fame. Aside from his admirable versatility, which was surely a major attraction for the artistically broad-minded young David Bowie, Newley's comic novelty songs, including "Pop Goes the Weasel" and "That Noise," seem to have influenced his young fan. (Note also the "Oompa Loompa" song from *Willy Wonka and the Chocolate Factory* [1971], the film score for which Newley and songwriting partner Leslie Bricusse received an Academy Award nomination.)

The 1970s: When Novelty Reigned

While seemingly an anachronism for David Bowie, "The Laughing Gnome" was not noticeably out of place in the charts because novelty songs continued to thrive during the 1970s almost as much as they had done during the 1950s and 1960s. In the United Kingdom, the decade was ushered in with shameless catchiness by the Pipkins' "Gimmee Dat Ding." In 1972, the year before David Bowie's eyebrow-raising effort, the uber-quirky "Mouldy Old Dough," a piano-led instrumental with occasional growled utterances of the song's title, hit the number one spot for Lieutenant Pigeon, while in 1976, the Wurzel's "Combine Harvester" (a parody of Melanie Safka's "Brand New Key") made farmers and townies alike chuckle into their breakfast cereals. Across the Atlantic, Chuck Berry's "My Ding-a-Ling" hit the number one spot in the United States in 1972, and Ray Stevens did likewise two years later in 1974 with "The Streak." Truckers had their moment in the spotlight when C. W. McCall's "Convoy" lumbered its unlikely way to the supreme position in 1976, a feat matched later that same year by Rick Dees and his Cast of Idiots' "Disco Duck." Not hitting the top of the charts but seemingly ever present in the top forty were the inimitable Cheech and Chong with efforts such as "Sister Mary Elephant," "Earache My Eye," "Santa Claus and His Old Lady," and the superbly titled "Basketball Jones Featuring Tyrone Shoelaces."

The Comedic Backlash

Always seen as an embarrassment for David Bowie, a comedic Achilles' heel little mentioned by the man himself or by his hard-core fans, its presence in his back catalogue delighted Bowie detractors and mischief makers. When David Bowie announced in 1990 that the set list for his forthcoming Sound + Vision tour would be determined by a telephone voting system whereby fans could phone in their favorite songs, *New Musical Express* magazine attempted to rig the vote with a campaign asking fans to call in and "Just Say Gnome," and they even printed and circulated T-shirts carrying the slogan. Ultimately, the experiment was abandoned when Bowie discovered the ruse. More amused than angry, he told rival music weekly *Melody Maker*, "I'll tell you what... I was thinking of doing 'Laughing Gnome' and was wondering how to do it, maybe in the style of the Velvets or something, until I found out that all the voting had been a scam or something, perpetrated by another music paper. I mean, that was an end to it. I can't pander to the press, now can I?" Nevertheless, the devilish attempt to force the artist to perform on the world stage what was seen as his most publicly embarrassing song garnered quite some attention and a great degree of mirth.

For many people, "The Laughing Gnome" remains a Bowie classic and, at the very least, further proof—if it were needed—of the artist's extraordinary versatility and limitless give-anything-a-go attitude to his art.

6

Pinups

A Reappraisal of David Bowie's Surprise Covers Album

Never one to pretend that he'd plucked ideas out of thin air or been the recipient of a Nietzschean-style thunderbolt of enlightenment from above, David Bowie was always extremely up front and forthcoming about acknowledging his influences. This candid tipping of his hat to the music and musicians that had inspired him was nowhere better expressed than in 1973, when he released his one and only album solely dedicated to cover versions, *Pinups*.

Pinups album, 1973

Author's Collection

A work that was comparatively poorly received by critics compared to the reception given to his other albums of the era—though the same did not hold true for fans, who bought it and enjoyed it by the truckload, taking it all the way to number one on the U.K. album chart—it deserved a better appraisal both then and now. Not only was the music of a typically high standard, but the song choices and the iconic album cover art spoke volumes about an artist who was at the peak of his game at the time and who was, as always, saying something important through his work.

David Bowie the Mod

In a sense an autobiographical snapshot of Bowie's musical tastes around 1964–1967, given the fact that he was releasing his cover versions just five to eight years after the originals had been on the charts themselves, their influence on him must surely have been fresh and keenly felt. At the time of release, following straight after the exceptional trio of career-making original albums *Hunky Dory*, *The Rise and Fall of Ziggy Stardust and the Spiders from Mars*, and *Aladdin Sane*, the album was largely maligned by critics. Some saw it as mere marking time, others as a contractual obligation, and still others as a cynical cashing in on his then current wave of popularity; very few regarded it with anything like genuine enthusiasm. Reviewer Greg Shaw of *Rolling Stone* concluded, "Although many of the tracks are excellent, none stands up to the originals.... The songs were originally conceived as trashy, instant pop fodder.... Bowie's vocals float carelessly above the music, and his excessively mannered voice is a ridiculously weak mismatch for the material." Ouch.

He fared no better elsewhere. *New Musical Express* reviewer Ian MacDonald was even more damning in his appraisal, stating that Bowie had "failed to live up to the essence of those times [1964–1967] convincingly.... *Pin-Ups* slowly, but surely, dies a death ... [it] fails to live up to its promise."

Covers album releases weren't uncommon at the time. The Band, John Lennon, Bryan Ferry (indeed, Ferry's *These Foolish Things* was released on the same day as *Pinups*, reaching a highly creditable number five placing on the U.K. album chart), and the Isley Brothers, to name just four others, all released covers albums during the early to mid-1970s.

But the narrow focus of Bowie's album—all stylistically aligned songs by mod bands occurring within a four-year time span—rendered his rather different and more meaningful. His handwritten message on the back cover confirmed that all of the tracks were personal favorites, and this spoke volumes about his high regard for the material he'd chosen. It was clear that all of the cover versions on the album were intended as bona fide tributes and not some mere shallow dalliance or throwaway stocking filler. Backing up this

BRYAN
FERRY

These Foolish Things album by Bryan Ferry, 1973   *Author's Collection*

interpretation, in *Sounds* magazine in August 1973, Bowie told Martin Hayman, "These are all songs which really meant a lot to me then—they're all very dear to me. These are all bands which I used to go and hear play down The Marquee between 1964 and 1967. Each one meant something to me at the time. It's my London of the time."

While reviews at the time of release, with a few notable exceptions, might have suggested that David Bowie's versions paled in comparison to the originals, the songs on *Pinups* actually were recorded in a style remarkably close to those originals in terms of arrangement, instrumentation, and production. As Steve Bailey noted in his article "Faithful or Foolish: The Emergence of the 'Ironic Cover Album' and Rock Culture" (2003) in the academic musical journal *Popular Music and Society*, all of the *Pinups* songs were presented in "a reverent and reasonably straight-forward manner. There are few, if any, drastic alterations to the material, and the performances suggest aesthetic validation . . . rather than critique." As had been the case with the original renditions, Bowie's versions are full of punch, depth, and edge, lacking absolutely nothing in terms of energy, vitality, and zing. For many Bowie fans (myself included) who missed the songs the first time around and who discovered them through their purchase of the *Pinups* album, the Bowie versions remain the definitive ones to this day. Because he used the Spiders from Mars to back him in the recording studio (with the exception of drummer Woody Woodmansey, who was replaced by Aynsley Dunbar), the sonic continuity with his immediately preceding studio albums was very strong. The signature sounds of guitarist Mick Ronson, bassist Trevor Bolder, and de facto Spider pianist Mike Garson flowed effortlessly from the original studio albums into *Pinups*, and this ensured a familiar glam sound for Bowie fans that, at the same time, lifted the 1960s songs into the 1970s, breathing new life into them for the new audience and linking together seamlessly the music of two generations like nobody else ever did or could have done.

The Personal Touch

The fact that Bowie handwrote the song titles on the back cover along with an explanation for his choices can be seen as a kind of de facto ownership: he might not have written these works, but he claimed nevertheless a significant personal connection with them. Handwriting rather than typography is considered to be a "stand-in" that gets one closer to the real person—it is why autographs of famous people, signed photographs, and so on have always been and remain so sought after by fans and collectors. In the same way that he handwrote the liner notes on the back cover of *Hunky Dory* two years earlier, Bowie's handwriting personalizes *Pinups* considerably. Even mistakes are allowed to stand. For example, he mistakenly lists track 3 on side 2 as "Shapes of Things," crossing out the "3" and inserting "4" next to it before scrawling the title of the actual third track, "Don't Bring Me Down," above. He does likewise with track 5. Once again, as on *Hunky Dory*, the impression given is one of somebody informally writing on a napkin or pad or such rather than on a formal album cover. It provides a close personal connection between the artist, his fans, and his message. Confirming this as an intimate, firsthand message from Bowie himself, he then signs off with the concluding line, "Love-on ya!," a highly informal and familiar sentiment such as one might use to a close friend, family member, or lover. As an emphatic stamp of authorship, he then signs his work with a heavily stylized but easily legible "Bowie," underlined and with a heart shape instead of a dot above the "i." It is an intensely personal statement.

In selecting songs geographically located in London, identifying performance venues in his back-cover message to underline the point (the Ricky Tick Club, Eel Pie Island, and the Marquee Club), and providing strict parameters in terms of a short and specific time frame, Bowie creates a context for his work in much the same way that he did so visually with his drab urban

London scene on the cover of *The Rise and Fall of Ziggy Stardust and the Spiders from Mars*. Creating a cameo of the London scene of 1964–1967—the very height of "Swinging London"—on *Pinups*, he re-presented the sense of excitement, danger, and youth euphoria synonymous with that scene. While that era had clearly passed—comparatively recently, certainly, but also most emphatically—Bowie nevertheless repackaged aspects of the era for his new glam-rock audience of the early 1970s. This repackaging included the importance of image, as the bands that Bowie referenced on the album—Pretty Things, Them, Pink Floyd, the Kinks, the Easybeats, the Who, the Yardbirds, the Mojos, and the Merseys—were, in their own time, renown for being immaculately costumed. Looking sharp was an important aspect of mod culture, and the bands attracted audiences because, like Bowie himself, they were something to be seen as well as to be heard. Thus, the album title, *Pinups*, drawing attention to the visual aspects of the art, is apt.

Introducing . . . Twiggy!

The cover of *Pinups* is one of Bowie's most striking and enduring, a work of art in its own right and worthy of more attention than has been afforded it. It's also remarkable in being the only time on any of Bowie's album covers that he shared the limelight with anyone else. Although the juxtaposition of Bowie and top 1960s fashion model Twiggy being pictured together was new, each was already an established identity in their own right and the subject of numerous pinups due to their respective statuses as music and fashion icons. At the time and previously, individual images of the two stars were widely available to their fans in the form of posters, magazine centerfolds, and other ephemera. To see them described as pinups on the album cover, therefore, was not in any way inaccurate.

Clearly, Twiggy's appearance imbued the cover with a sense of nostalgia for the popular culture of London in the 1960s. Because of the nature of her celebrity, however, it was a generalized nostalgia that went far beyond her primary role as a top fashion model to evoke certainly a strong revisitation of the music but also the wider cultural climate of the era. Mod culture encompassed both music and fashion. Several aspects of Twiggy's approach to her career and the widespread attraction she garnered with the public bear direct comparison to Bowie's approach and appeal, and therefore there is more to Twiggy's presence on the cover of *Pinups* than just an evocation of nostalgia. As a model, Twiggy had an androgynous image. Her body was thin and boyish, her hair was frequently cut short and styled with a parting (much like a man's), and she would at times wear clothing, including business suits, that had masculine associations. A headline from *Look* magazine (1967) encapsulates this quality: "Is it a girl? Is it a boy? No, it's Twiggy!" Having firmly established androgyny as a central part of his own style, Bowie would have valued the same clearly evident quality in Twiggy. The image is one of androgynous chic that effortlessly spans both mod and glam eras.

Similarly, and in keeping once again with Bowie's own ideas on the malleability and constructedness of stardom and celebrity—notions firmly established on the albums that preceded *Pinups*—Twiggy was widely seen as a constructed identity, an everyday girl playing the role of a fashion model celebrity. As described in an article titled "Twiggy: Click! Click!" in *Newsweek* (1967), "She is a magic child of the media. Where there are no cameras, she ceases to exist." The links to Bowie here and what he was doing with his Ziggy Stardust character with regard to critiquing the very notion of celebrity and stardom as a construction are very strong.

Twiggy's real name was Lesley Hornby, a cockney born in a poor area of North London who had a working-class upbringing. Much credit for Twiggy's success is attributed to her boyfriend, mentor, and photographer, Justin de Villeneuve, who shot the *Pinups* cover photograph. Villeneuve was the invented alter ego of Nigel Davies, also a cockney, who assumed several different names during his career. As Dominic Lutyens noted in the *Independent* (2002), "[Davies] was one of the many cocky, cockney, working class characters who helped erode Britain's rigid class system in the still stuffy early Sixties. Ironically, he did so by assuming new personae, each with a pseudo-aristo name." As was the case with Twiggy and Bowie/Ziggy, acknowledgment of the construction of one's identity was a hallmark of Davies's approach to his career. Twiggy frequently credited Davies for her reinvention and elevation to the status of a supermodel, asserting in her wonderfully titled autobiography, *Twiggy: How I Probably Just Came Along on a White Rabbit at the Right Time, and Met the Smile on the Face of the Tiger* (1968), "Twiggy isn't just me, it's me and Justin. Honestly, sometimes I think Justin invented me." Such critiques on the nature of stardom would clearly have resonated with Bowie. Twiggy is, in a sense, a female version of Bowie's performance persona: androgynous, constructed, supremely image-conscious, and media-savvy. It is clear, then, that Twiggy's presence on the cover of *Pinups* incorporates significant, layered meaning. The two of them together are a perfect visual representation of the spirit of glam rock. It is the conscious reinvention of the self as espoused by David Bowie and others, the notion that one doesn't have to settle for whatever life hands to you. Instead, you can forge a new "you" in your own self-made and idealized image. Along with *Aladdin Sane*, *Pinups* is one of David Bowie's most iconic album covers—and for good reason.

One of the most overlooked Bowie works, *Pinups* deserves to be more highly regarded than it has been. Dismissed as lightweight in comparison to the original studio albums that preceded and succeeded it, the album can be seen in retrospect as a link between the mod 1960s that inspired him and the glam 1970s that he dominated. Only David Bowie could have managed such a feat. To those fans who might have it languishing at the back of their record collection, get it out and give it another spin and gaze at that iconic cover for a while. In its own very different way, multilayered and unexpected as it was, it's as good as anything Bowie ever did, and despite being a bunch of covers, it is unquestionably him—as Ziggy—in full flight. (And it's a pity Iggy Pop couldn't have joined Bowie and Twiggy in the album cover shoot. A Ziggy, Twiggy, Iggy triumvirate would have been a fine thing.)

7

Taking On *Sgt. Pepper*

How the Beatles Demolished Bowie's Debut Album

The Big Day Arrives

On June 1, 1967 (the official release date, although some copies were rush-released earlier in the United Kingdom, on May 26), the mighty Beatles released their eighth studio album, *Sgt. Pepper's Lonely Hearts Club Band*. The band of the decade, the band that changed the face of popular music, the most famous band in the world, the release of *Sgt. Pepper* was a monumental occasion the whole world over. It had been a year since the release of *Revolver*, and the Beatles had given up touring and live shows. To a world that hung on every action and utterance from Liverpool's famous mop-tops, the new album was feverishly awaited by all.

Long lines of Beatles fans stood impatiently clutching their precious copies of the hot-off-the-press record, awaiting their turn at the counter so they could then race home to put needle to vinyl. As they stood there amid the excited hum of voices, they eagerly perused its now equally famous cover, designed by Peter Blake and Jann Haworth, that showed the Beatles in brightly colored faux military attire standing amid many colorful cutouts of famous people and, next to them, four waxworks from Madame Tussauds depicting themselves in their earlier Beatlemania incarnation. Over record shop speakers all over the country, songs rang out that are now part and parcel of the 1960s soundscape; songs such as the fanfare-like title track, "When I'm Sixty-Four," "Lucy in the Sky with Diamonds," and "With a Little Help from My Friends." The initially tall stacks of *Sgt. Pepper's Lonely Hearts Club Band* quickly went down as stocks dwindled and more were ordered in. While Capitol Record company executives smiled broadly, there wasn't a music fan anywhere who didn't know it was *Sgt. Pepper* day.

Also newly sitting on shelves in record shops that day was a debut record titled *David Bowie*, from the rather less fashionable Deram label, a subsidiary of Decca and then home to a young Cat Stevens.

Bowie's first album, 1967   *Author's Collection*

David's parents, John and Peggy Jones, must have been very proud of their son. The cover showed a close-up portrait of David as an unsmiling, earnest-looking young mod. The high-neck garment he wore, with gold button visible carrying the crown insignia, was also reminiscent of a military tunic. But that is where any comparison to the fun, color fiesta of the Beatles cover began and ended. David Bowie, unknown artist, had assembled a very odd bunch of songs for his debut. Just like "For the Benefit of Mr. Kite!" and "When I'm Sixty-Four" on *Sgt. Pepper's Lonely Hearts Club Band*, there were songs on Bowie's record done in a music hall style. There were a couple more mainstream pop-like offerings, some very odd brass band and orchestral efforts, and even a spoken radio drama ("Please Mr. Gravedigger"). But almost nobody took a copy down off the shelf to listen to or to buy. This was a Beatles day, and the hard-earned money clutched in the hot hands of music fans was not to be gambled with. The Beatles *always* delivered. No one was going to take a chance on an unheralded newbie.

Sgt. Pepper's Lonely Hearts Club Band would go on to spend an incredible twenty-seven weeks at the top of the U.K. album chart and fifteen weeks at the top of the U.S. Billboard album chart. In addition, it would win four Grammy awards in 1968, including the Grammy for Best Album. When "best-ever-album" polls are run in magazines, on radio stations, and other such formats, *Sgt. Pepper's Lonely Hearts Club Band* is a frequent winner. The 2012 *Rolling Stone* readers' poll is just one of numerous examples. At the end of the poll, they say in summary, "Sgt. Pepper is the Number One album of the RS 500 not just because of its firsts—it is simply the best of everything the Beatles ever did as musicians, pioneers and pop stars, all in one place."

Partial Late Redemption Courtesy of Ziggy Stardust

As for *David Bowie*, the album would end up selling reasonable numbers retrospectively once its architect had become a global superstar through *The Rise and Fall of Ziggy Stardust and the Spiders from Mars* and, beyond, through reissues demanded by curious David Bowie fans keen to collect everything he'd ever done. However, such late interest could not change the nature of the recording, and biographer David Buckley has suggested that the album was "as un-rock 'n' roll as one could imagine." Another noted rock writer, Mark Paytress, concluded that the work was "idiosyncratic to the point of self-immolation. The album . . . wasn't consistent enough to tap into any established market." While never making a habit of discussing his debut and frequently overlooking it altogether, in 1990, Bowie did give his own long-after-the-fact appraisal in *Mojo* magazine, concluding that "lyrically I guess it was striving to be something, the short story teller. Musically it's quite bizarre. I don't know where I was at. It seemed to have its roots all over the place, in rock and vaudeville and music hall and I don't know what. I didn't know if I was Max Miller or Elvis Presley."

In stark contrast to Bowie's considerably less-than-glowing appraisal of his own album, Beatles drummer Ringo Starr proudly proclaimed in the autobiography *The Beatles Anthology* (2000) that "Sgt. Pepper was our grandest endeavor."

Although David Bowie would go on to become as big, as successful, and as famous as Liverpool's finest quartet, when they met on this midsummer's day in 1967, there was only one horse in the race. And it wasn't David Bowie, left languishing in the stalls as the mop-tops crossed the finish line.

Other Notable Album Releases in June 1967

It wasn't just the Beatles that David Bowie was up against in June 1967, of course. Other releases that jangled the tills that month included *Double Trouble* (a sound track) by Elvis Presley, *From the Beginning* (a compilation) by the Small Faces, *Moby Grape* by Moby Grape, *Small Faces* by the Small Faces, *Flowers* (a compilation) by the Rolling Stones, *Evolution* by the Hollies, *The Fastest Guitar Alive* (a sound track) by Roy Orbison, *James Brown Plays the Real Thing* by James Brown, *Ray Charles Invites You to Listen* by Ray Charles, and *Tom Jones Live!* by Tom Jones. Even if one were able to take *Sgt. Pepper's Lonely Hearts Club Band* by the Beatles out of the equation, June 1967 would have remained a particularly hard month for a debut album by an unknown act. For the young and undoubtedly hugely excited David Bowie, success was still years away.

8

"Space Oddity"

The Story behind Bowie's First Taste of Success

David Bowie began his performing career in 1962 at the age of fifteen with the Konrads and released his first recording, "Liza Jane," in 1964 with the King Bees. By June 1969—a full seven years later—he'd had many other single releases with his various early bands plus further singles and two full albums released under his own name. Despite all of this and the countless gigs performed along the way, he was still not a well-known performer outside of his own environs. Plenty of people had him marked down as someone to watch, and many a bandmate had been consumed with jealousy because of the way that Bowie would be singled out for special attention in any group setting, leaving the rest of the band in the shadows. In addition, despite there being no hint of commercial success anywhere in his track record, a succession of record companies had continued to sign him, only to release him again after their faith and investment brought no reward. For all of this promise and recognition of his talent, there had been little tangible reward for anyone, David Bowie included. Thankfully, all that was to change in the unlikely form of "Space Oddity."

Something New

In December 1968, David Bowie and his manager Kenneth Pitt assembled a series of promotional videos into a single film titled *Love You till Tuesday* with the intention of using it as a promotional tool with which to advertise Bowie's multifaceted skills to television and film companies and producers.

With all of the compiled songs drawn from Bowie's highly eclectic back catalog, Pitt asked his charge for one more song to add to the mix—something new. Bowie duly agreed, and with the help of his friend and fellow musician John Hutchinson, who provided some interesting chord variations to replace those originally suggested by the less guitar-savvy Bowie, a most unusual song,

FOR THE FIRST TIME ON DVD
VIDEO
• 'THE LOOKING GLASS MURDERS'
• 5.1 SURROUND SOUND
• EXTENSIVE PHOTO GALLERY
0602498233603

David
Love You Till Tuesday
BOWIE

Love You Till Tuesday DVD (2004). This 1969 promotional film was designed to showcase
Bowie's talents.   *Author's Collection*

quite unlike anything Bowie had written before, quickly took shape. Recorded
for the *Love You till Tuesday* project in the first week of February 1969 and
with a low-budget video being shot just days afterward, the highly promising,
career-launching "Space Oddity" took its first-ever demo-quality form.

Original sheet music for "Space Oddity," 1969   *Author's Collection*

Just months earlier, Bowie had seen Stanley Kubrick's blockbuster movie *2001: A Space Odyssey* (1968) and been mightily impressed by it. The debt that Bowie and "Space Oddity" owe to the movie is blatant and unapologetic, going well beyond the movie's barely altered title that Bowie adopted for his song. Based on the book by Arthur C. Clarke, *2001: A Space Odyssey* was released at a time when the space race, as it was popularly termed, between the United States and the Soviet Union was at its peak. Worldwide public interest in space exploration was at its height, with the first successful moon landing occurring in July 1969, just a year after the film's release. Space travel and science fiction were both fashionable and marketable. Bowie borrowed from the movie the idea of an astronaut becoming stranded in space, thereby exploiting humankind's universal recognition of the real-life astronauts' vulnerability and alienation. When everyone was looking upward to the heavens and wondering, "What would it be like to be up there?," David Bowie provided them with a canvas on which those fears and imaginings could be painted. A masterstroke of timing coupled with pinpoint recognition of mass societal excitement and unease, "Space Oddity" was the perfect song to accompany the successful Apollo 11 moon mission. As stated in the opening moments of every single episode of the now iconic U.S. sci-fi series *Star Trek*, "Space [is] the final frontier." But with Apollo 11 and a man now on the moon, science fiction was fast becoming science nonfiction, or, better, science fact. The unattainable, impossible dream held by centuries of humankind to visit the moon had now become both attainable and possible. Imagined danger was now real danger because these were not actors—these were real flesh-and-blood people up there in that hostile environment so completely foreign to human survival. This was a quantum shift in thinking, and small wonder that the world was held in thrall at the events of the Apollo mission. Effectively, what David Bowie did was to write a sound track to accompany this momentous occasion. In response to an interview question regarding the origins of "Space Oddity," reprinted in the publication *David Bowie Black Book* (1980) by Barry Miles and Chris Charlesworth, he explained that "the publicity image of a spaceman at work is an automaton rather than a human being and my Major Tom is nothing if not a human being. It comes from a feeling of sadness about this aspect of the space thing. It has been dehumanised so I wrote a song-farce about it to try and relate science and human emotion. I suppose it's an antidote to space-fever, really."

In Kubrick's film, there is a poignant scene where the doomed astronaut Frank Poole receives on his birthday a prerecorded transmission from his parents back on Earth, their images flickering on the small screen on the far wall as Frank lies on his bed in the sterile and lonely confines of his cabin. On this ostensibly happy occasion as his parents sit at their kitchen table back on Earth with Frank's birthday cake before them, candles alight and making small talk for the camera, sad, mournful strings undermine the forced joviality of their voices, and the scene's celebratory premise is destroyed, serving only to underline the astronaut's estrangement and vast distance from home. This same helplessness is present in Major Tom's communication with Ground Control and especially in his fateful and despairing line "Tell my wife I love her very much," where all of the technological achievements of the space race are reduced to naught because, at the end of the day, what is really important is not the ability to travel into space but human love and relationships.

The relationship between movie, moon landing, and song was much commented on at the time and indeed almost worked against the song's success. Many commentators viewed it as a one-off novelty song, and statements along the lines of the following from Bowie biographers Henry Edwards and Tony Zanetta were frequent: "His record had received airplay only as a novelty accompanying a one-shot public event. When the event was over the record died."

The uneasy relationship between technology and humanity that Kubrick problematizes superbly in *2001: A Space Odyssey* is also brought to the fore by Bowie in "Space Oddity." At its worst, the notion of technology ruling over humans—so often the subject of science fiction—threatened the ultimate destruction of humankind, with people held at the mercy of their own creations. Hal, the onboard computer of the *Discovery One* spaceship, coldly and calculatedly kills the astronauts that accompany him into space. In "Space Oddity," the technology that bore Major Tom into space just as easily abandons him, as related in the line "And I think my spaceship knows which way to go," sung as Major Tom and his ship drift apart, condemning Bowie's creation to a cold and lonely death.

Tony Visconti Says, "No Thanks"

Producer Tony Visconti, who was recording Bowie's second album at the time, famously refused to record the single version of the song that met with such success, instead handing over the role to a delighted Gus Dudgeon. In 1993, Dudgeon told Elizabeth Thompson and David Gutman, editors of *The Bowie Companion*, "I listened to the demo and thought it was incredible. I couldn't believe that Tony didn't want to do it ... I don't think it was like anything he'd ever done before. I guess in a way it wasn't like anything *anybody* had done before and that's why, today, the record is still a classic. I'm very proud to have been associated with it."

In contrast and with the wonderful benefit of hindsight, to the *New York Times* in March 2013, Visconti ruefully recalled, "I thought it was a desperate cash-in because Bowie was a kid, who, like everyone else I worked with, needed a hit. I said, 'Why are you doing this when you've got these other great songs?' On reflection, none of those other great songs were a hit—he was writing great album cuts. I have kicked myself many, many times since then, because I was completely and utterly wrong."

In his autobiography published in 2007, Visconti elucidated further on one of the worst decisions of his professional life: "I thought the song was a cheap shot to capitalize on the first moon landing. I also thought it was too vocally derivative of John Lennon and Simon and Garfunkel.... My mistake was seeing what was wrong externally with this song—the subtle rip-offs. What I didn't realize at the time was that the music was just window dressing for a subtler subject—alienation—and the setting was outer space."

As is often the case in the murky world of popular music, that "Space Oddity" became a hit was due to more than just fortunate timing and a good song. Despite the failure of a halfhearted attempt by Kenneth Pitt to rig the song's chart impact—he paid a chart rigger £140 to get the song into *Record Retailer*—on its initial release, sales were disappointing and slowed quickly. However, and highly serendipitously, Bowie's new record company, Philips/Mercury, had a severe lack of new material from their stable of acts to push during August and September, so all staff were instructed to put their efforts into resurrecting the fortunes of Bowie's unusual offering. It was to be a highly effective campaign, and, sure enough, "Space Oddity" went on to reach number five on the U.K. singles chart in September 1969, just two months after the moon landing. Finally, David Bowie was getting a taste of the success his talent had always suggested would one day come.

The song is extraordinarily filmic in the way it is written, with the emotive and highly descriptive lyrics working in conjunction with the instrumentation to build images in the listener's mind. You can actually *see* Major Tom "stepping through the door" of his "tin can" and out into the vast, cold expanses of space. The swirling mellotron; the floating, unfinished effect of the major-seventh chords; and the extra resonances of the twelve-string acoustic guitar—all such touches combine to bring to life the narrative. The production—painstakingly worked out between Bowie and Dudgeon—is superb.

The Extraordinary Rise of the Stylophone

Adding much to the novelty song quality was the unexpected star instrument of the track, the humble Stylophone, appearing in its most-famous-ever role. The Stylophone is a small, metallic analog keyboard that the player holds in the palm of the hand. Marketed as "the original pocket organ," it has two settings—"normal" and "vibrato"—and is operated with a small stylus held between thumb and forefinger. It is to the keyboard group of instruments what the kazoo is to woodwind insofar as being taken seriously goes. Operated by Bowie himself on "Space Oddity," this rather budget and decidedly non–rock instrument played a starring role with its semitonal movements suggesting the most endearingly tacky science-fiction allusions. The Stylophone manufacturers were, of course, delighted to see their product in the limelight at the top of the charts, even more delighted to hear that it was on the Stylophone that David

Bowie had begun writing the song, and were quick to sign him as an endorsee to join their previous top draw card, Rolf Harris, in the marketing of the instrument. Sales soared as a result.

Industry Recognition

On May 10, 1970, Bowie received an Ivor Novello award for originality for "Space Oddity." This awards ceremony, known in entertainment circles as "the Ivors," has run since 1955 and honors exceptional songwriting and composing as voted by the British Academy of Songwriters, Composers and Authors. "Space Oddity," then, had brought David Bowie not only his first taste of commercial success but also the regard of his peers. (The award of the Ivor Novello prize to David Bowie is addressed in more detail in chapter 37.)

While further commercial success at such a level would be relatively slow in coming, when it did come in 1972 with the launch of Ziggy Stardust and the success of the "Starman" single, the groundwork that had been provided by "Space Oddity" ensured continuity of the already established science-fiction theme. David Bowie was confirmed as rock music's most futuristic, science-fiction–themed star, an entirely appropriate perception that would be sustained throughout his career. From the time of its release until the end of his life, "Space Oddity" remained one of the most requested—and most frequently rerecorded—of Bowie's songs, and today there are many versions to be found. It also has something of a life of its own, appearing in numerous space-related documentaries and thematically aligned presentations in other media.

The Extraordinary "Space Oddity" Postscript

"Space Oddity" would notch up another incredible achievement very late in David Bowie's career, and it was one that is said to have thrilled the song's architect to the very core. Real-life astronaut Commander Chris Hadfield, a musician with more than twenty-five years of experience fronting bands back home in Houston, recorded a cover version of the most famous space-related song in popular music history while serving on the International Space Station in May 2013. Hadfield announced the release on his Twitter feed: "With deference to the genius of David Bowie, here's Space Oddity, recorded on Station. A last glimpse of the World." The video—the first music video ever to be recorded in space—immediately went viral and received rave reviews from numerous quarters. A delighted David Bowie, who wittily prefaced his tweet back to Hadfield with "Hallo Spaceboy" (a song title from his 1995 album 1. Outside), himself enthused on his Facebook page that it was "possibly the most poignant version of the song ever created." After surviving a couple of publishing rights challenges (traditional publishing rights agreements do not cover works created in—and posted from—space!) and with the songwriter's full support that it be permanently and freely available for viewing, at the time of this book going to print, the clip has now racked up almost 45 million views. Hadfield's version of the song was recorded while orbiting Earth at a distance of approximately 400 kilometers (248 miles). "Planet Earth is blue," David Bowie had sung back in 1969, and in Hadfield's video, that is exactly how our planet looks from the windows of the International Space Station, clearly visible behind the astronaut as he looks straight at the camera and sings his unique and heartfelt tribute. Intended simply as a fun project, in conjunction with his son and a couple of musician friends, and designed to pass some onboard downtime, Hadfield never imagined the impact his initiative would have. A beautiful melding of art and science, it is no wonder David Bowie approved, and the fact that Hadfield took the liberty of updating some of the lyrics to make it more pertinent to his situation also met with the songwriter's full approval. In Hadfield's hands, Major Tom no longer meets disaster in space but instead returns to Earth, his mission complete.

In interviews, Chris Hadfield talked of how impressed he was with how accurately David Bowie had imagined the sense of isolation and loneliness would be when one is so far removed from Earth and how skillfully he had captured such feelings and emotions both in his lyrics and in the overall vibe of that original 1969 version of "Space Oddity." Hadfield was completely delighted with David Bowie's approval, telling *Lateline*, an Australian Broadcasting Corporation program, "I think, for him, he knew he was ill—it was getting to the end of his life. He wrote that song at the beginning, when he was still 19 or 20, before we had even walked on the moon. He had always fantasised about flying in space—Starman, and Mars, and all that other stuff, and I think for him it was just like a gift, to have that song updated with the lyrics, performed actually in space, just a couple of years before he was taken. To me that might be the best part: that he got delight out of my particular version of the song."

9

Toy Story

The Lost Album

Of considerable intrigue to David Bowie's avid fans—and highly worthy of "check it out" status for any newcomers to the artist's recorded legacy—is the lost 1960s-themed album *Toy*, recorded in 2000 and scheduled for a release in 2001 that never eventuated. David Bowie himself described the album in the lead-up to the recording sessions as "not so much *Pinups II* as an *Update I*." (*Pinups* was his album of 1960s cover versions released almost three decades earlier in 1973.) He also promised fans that "some of the songs from the sixties were never recorded, let alone released, so will be as new to you as any of the new ones that I've written."

When Things Began to Go Wrong for *Toy*

Alarm bells began ringing about the album's uncertain future on Monday, June 4, 2001, in an online chat session on bowiewonderworld.com. David Bowie candidly answered a question regarding the album's release thus: "I'm finding EMI/Virgin seem to have a lot of scheduling conflicts this year, which has put an awful lot on the back burner. *Toy* is finished and ready to go, and I will make an announcement as soon as I get a very real date. Meantime, I'm already started writing and recording for another album (untitled at the moment). So far I have to say it's back to experimental. But knowing me, it doesn't mean that's how it'll turn out. I shall be writing and recording throughout the summer, but daddyfying is really my priority at the moment."

With the birth of Alexandria, his daughter, to Iman on August 15, 2000, *Toy* possibly became a quickly decreasing priority, as he alludes to in this answer. In addition, the other album he mentioned, one that would end up as *Heathen* (2002), increasingly pushed *Toy* into the background. In his biography, Tony Visconti (who would produce much of *Heathen*) suggested of *Toy*, "It was a great idea to give those old songs a fresh reading in the twenty-first century." But then he added, "But there wasn't enough material, even though David had hundreds of his own compositions he could re-record, it was these particular songs he wanted to sing." Regardless of this caveat, the problems Bowie was having with Virgin/EMI proved the biggest hurdle to *Toy* being released, and ultimately the decision was taken, largely by the record company and reportedly to Bowie's displeasure, to shelve the project entirely. In Bowie's own diplomatic and carefully chosen words in October 2001, as *Toy*'s release faded further into uncertainty, "Virgin/EMI have had scheduling problems and are now going for an album of 'new' material over the *Toy* album. Fine by me. I'm extremely happy with the new stuff. I love *Toy* as well and won't let that material fade away. If you've been following the newspapers, you'll have seen that EMI/Virgin are having major problems themselves. This has not helped. But all things pass."

The conflict had a more lasting effect than just this one issue over the release of *Toy*, however. It was to mark the end of David Bowie's relationship with his record company. Subsequently, when *Heathen* (and the albums beyond) did come out, it was released through Bowie's own label, ISO, in conjunction with Columbia Records. EMI/Virgin was out of the picture.

What Was *Toy* Like?

Produced by Mark Plati, who had coproduced *Earthling* and *"Hours..."* with Bowie, *Toy* features a veritable who's who of Bowie collaborators, with credits including his highly regarded then current touring band of Earl Slick (guitar), Gail Ann Dorsey (bass), Mark Plati (bass, guitars), Sterling Campbell (drums), Lisa Germano (violin), Holly Palmer (backing vocals), Emm Gryner (backing vocals), Gerry Leonard (guitars), and Mike Garson (piano). In addition, there were arrangements by Tony Visconti, brought back into the fold after a lengthy hiatus and particularly notable given that he had produced the earliest of the tracks being revisited for the album, including "Conversation Piece" and "Let Me Sleep Beside You."

While *Toy* never saw an official release, two of its tracks, "Uncle Floyd" and "Afraid," were reworked for *Heathen* (the former retitled as "Slip Away"), while three others, "Baby Loves That Way," "Shadow Man," and "You've Got a Habit of Leaving," were released as B-sides for *Heathen*'s singles.

Track Listing

Uncle Floyd	Let Me Sleep Beside You
Afraid	Toy (Your Turn to Drive)
Baby Loves That Way	Hole in the Ground
I Dig Everything	Shadow Man
Conversation Piece	In the Heat of the Morning

You've Got a Habit of Leaving   Liza Jane
Silly Boy Blue   The London Boys

The Unexpected Twist in the Tail of the *Toy* Story

With its non-release such a momentous disappointment for fans who, with considerable difficulty, had to swallow the fact that an entire album of material by their hero would remain forever locked away unheard, a twist was yet to come in the saga of *Toy*. This unexpected and sensational twist would see *all* of *Toy*'s sought-after tracks enter the public domain for all and sundry to acquire. More than this, they were all *free*!

Much intrigue and speculation circulated for many years about the album that never was until, a whole decade later and as reported in *Rolling Stone* on March 22, 2011, under the news-flash–style headline "Unreleased David Bowie LP *Toy* Leaks Online," the entire fourteen-track collection of new, rerecorded, and original tracks was mysteriously leaked to the Internet and made available for free downloading through BitTorrent. While the Bowie camp remained mostly tight-lipped about the leak—aside from reports that the man himself was furious at the breach—Bowie fans around the world reacted with delight at receiving such unexpected pennies from heaven. According to torrentfreak .com, the album was initially available for a full hour in 256 kbps quality MP3. From that point onward, its spread was understandably rapid and unstoppable. As torrentfreak.com put it in its closing summation, "*Toy* is out of the box now, and it's never going back."

Various theories exist as to how the album came to be leaked. A Bowie fan named Brigstow, from Bristol, United Kingdom, is often cited as the uploader, with suggestions (which he denies) that he bought a bootleg of the album on eBay and uploaded it to stop others profiting unfairly from selling it illegally. Other theories exist—even one conspiracy theory that has Bowie himself as the uploader. While the latter seems unlikely in the extreme, in truth it matters little how the leak occurred. The fact is that Bowie's long-lost album of new, reworked, and original recordings was in the public domain for anyone who wanted to avail themselves of it—lost/embargoed/buried no more.

Musical Beginnings

The Early Bands

David Bowie found fame and fortune in 1972 with the launch of his Ziggy Stardust persona and accompanying album, *The Rise and Fall of Ziggy Stardust and the Spiders from Mars*. Backed in this groundbreaking initiative by the inimitable Spiders from Mars—Mick Ronson on guitar, Woody Woodmansey on drums, and Trevor Bolder on bass—Bowie's band career had actually started in a far more modest fashion a full ten years earlier in 1962. Over the course of the next four and a half years, he would go through five bands during the process of refining his goals, developing his performance style, and perfecting his songwriting skills. Although many of the musicians Bowie encountered and left behind during this formative period of his career saw him as ruthless at worst and supremely driven at best, each of these bands now occupies a small place in popular music history, thanks to their small but important contribution to the development of the one outstanding musician with whom they all once shared a stage.

The Konrads—aka the Kon-rads (Bowie's tenure, mid-1962 to mid-1963)

A semiprofessional show band modeled on the Shadows with its often identically dressed members ranging between four and eight in number during the time that Bowie (then David Jones) performed with them, the Bromley-based Konrads focused on presenting to their audiences a "best of" selection of the pop hits of the day. These songs came complete with Shadows-esque choreographed dance steps in their gigs at church halls, clubs, weddings, dances, and other community social events. Along with Bowie's lifelong friend George Underwood on vocals and guitar, other members included Dave Crook, Neville Wills, Dave Hadfield, Roger Ferris, Christine Patton, Stella Patton, and Alan Dodds. Joining initially as the band's saxophonist in its original four-piece format, in this, his first proper band, David Bowie unexpectedly and prophetically stepped up to the role of lead vocalist one night when then lead singer Ferris stepped on broken glass immediately prior to a performance in a South London pub, the Green Man, in Blackheath. As Ferris was rushed to hospital with his foot badly cut and heavily bleeding, this was the moment David Bowie experienced the front-man spotlight for the first time in his career. "I was a better singer," said Ferris in an interview with the *Telegraph* newspaper in 2016, "but I had nowhere near his personality or charisma on stage." Ultimately unhappy with the band's direction and its preference for pop over rhythm and blues, Bowie—who was by now temporarily experimenting with a new stage name, "Dave Jay"—would leave the Konrads in late 1963. Much later, drummer Hadfield noted to biographer Peter Doggett of his famous ex-bandmate, "He could see real potential in what we were doing, but he was young and impatient. . . . He started to push for a break-through, and when it didn't come, he decided to leave." Nevertheless, the Konrads continued on in Bowie's absence for a time, with their most notable achievement coming in 1965, when they were selected as one of the support bands on a fourteen-date Rolling Stones tour through the United Kingdom, a lineup of acts that also included the Hollies.

The King Bees (Bowie's tenure, mid-1963 to late 1964)

Teaming up once again with George Underwood in what was initially a short-lived blues trio called the Hooker Brothers—the third member being drummer Viv Andrews—after just a handful of gigs, this lineup quickly morphed into five-piece blues band the King Bees, named after the Slim Harpo song "I'm a King Bee." With Andrews now gone, the other three members of Bowie's second band were Roger Bluck, Dave Howard, and Bobby Allen. With a repertoire much more stylistically aligned to Bowie's tastes, the band's fortunes looked promising when they quickly secured a record deal with the Decca label's bottom-rung subsidiary, Vocalion Records. The resultant single "Liza Jane" was a reworking of an old standard, although its writing was credited to talent scout and band manager Leslie Conn, who had arranged the recording deal for the band. Despite the group being featured on influential television pop shows *Juke Box Jury*, *The Beat Room*, and *Ready Steady Go!*, the song failed to trouble the charts. Notable, however, was the alteration to the band's name by this point to Davie Jones & the King Bees, the lead singer thus being singled out from the pack for extra attention. In the meantime and even while the single release was occurring, the ever-forward-looking Bowie had been rehearsing with another band, the Rolling Stones–influenced Manish Boys, so named after a Muddy Waters song.

The Manish Boys (Bowie's tenure, mid-1964 to mid-1965)

Playing for a short period of time with both the King Bees and the Manish Boys, Bowie took the decision to leave the former in order to concentrate on his newest act, to whom he'd been introduced by Leslie Conn. A band already in existence before Bowie's inclusion, the other members were Johnny Flux, Bob Solly, John Watson, Paul Rodriguez, Woolf Byrne, and Mike White. The Manish Boys was a hardworking and established band that also had seemingly bright prospects, which included securing a spot on a national tour with Gene Pitney, the Kinks, and Marianne Faithful during December 1964. The band's billing immediately became an issue, however, with the group reluctantly changing its name to Davie Jones and the Manish Boys to accommodate its new lead singer. Such tension continued, and when the band's debut single, "I Pity the Fool," a cover of a Bobby Bland song, was released under the band name alone as the Manish Boys due to pressure from his bandmates, the by-now fiercely ambitious Bowie once again became quickly disillusioned. With the failure of the single, he was ready to move on again. Said Solly decades later to Mark Paytress in *Record Collector* magazine in May 2000, "He was probably aiming higher than the rest of us. He was more ruthless. At the time his departure seemed bloody-minded and disloyal. But I think he was a nice fellow who sometimes had to be nasty in order to get on. He had no other thought in his head than success. He was absolutely positive that he would succeed."

Of particular note with regard to the Manish Boys' failed single, however, was the fact that the B-side, "Take My Tip," marked David Bowie's debut song-writing credit, surely a pivotal moment in the development of his growing confidence and an effective foil to the lack of success of the successive singles.

The Lower Third (Bowie's tenure, mid-1965 to February 1966)

Originally a semiprofessional five-piece band from the coastal resort town of Margate in Kent, three of the members of the Lower Third relocated to London—then often referred to as Swinging London and seen as the epicenter of the pop music scene—seeking to become a fully professional act. Denis Taylor, Les Mighall, and Graham Rivens quickly set about finding a lead singer, the role for which David Bowie auditioned and quickly was taken on. With seemingly little opposition, the new recruit quickly became the bandleader of this Who-inspired ensemble, and a single, the ironically titled "You've Got a Habit of Leaving" (ironic given the rapidity with which Bowie was changing bands), was released in August 1965 under the name of Davy Jones and the Lower Third. The songwriting credits for both the A-side and the B-side ("Baby Loves That Way") of the record were attributed to the lead singer alone, another significant step forward for the artist. This single too once again failed to make any mark on the charts, and another was released in January 1966. It was at this point that Davie—or Davy—Jones began calling himself David Bowie, and thus the release of "Can't Help Thinking About Me" (with another of his compositions, "And I Say to Myself," on the B-side) marks the moment in rock history when the name of David Bowie (albeit on this occasion followed by "and the Lower Third") made its official debut in the popular music industry.

Tensions within the band, financial pressure, the failure of the second single, and manager Ralph Horton's increasing lack of interest in anyone in the band other than Bowie—reportedly tantamount to outright possessiveness—all contributed to the demise of the Lower Third, and by February 1966, it was all over. Another band had failed to hold David Bowie.

The Buzz (Bowie's tenure, February 1966 to December 1966)

By now it was clear that in any group containing David Bowie, the other members could be backing musicians only, supporters and contributors certainly, but not equals. There could only be one star. The Buzz was therefore the first band formed with this understanding made clear right from the outset; the first band assembled primarily as a vehicle for showcasing the talents of the primary performer—David Bowie.

On the demise of the Lower Third, manager Ralph Horton organized auditions for the instrumental roles in the Buzz. Pye Records, which had released Bowie's efforts with the Lower Third, retained its interest and belief in the artist, and once the lineup of John Hutchinson, Derek Fearnley, John Eager, and Derrick Boyes was confirmed, the band was ushered quickly into the studio to record their first single, "Do Anything You Say." Backed by "Good Morning Girl" on the B-side, both tracks were written by Bowie, but the familiar and disappointing pattern of releases not reaching the charts continued. A management change from Ralph Horton to Kenneth Pitt occurred in April, and subsequently the band returned once again to the studio to record "I Dig Everything." On the advice of producer Tony Hatch, who was singularly unimpressed with the backing musicians in the Buzz, the recording was scrapped, however, and the song was recorded once again using studio musicians instead, along with a B-side titled "I'm Not Losing Sleep." Unsuccessful yet again in terms of chart success, this release nevertheless occupies an important place in Bowie history because it was released solely under the name of David Bowie, with no mention of the Buzz or any other backing musicians.

This was the end of the road for the recording deal with Pye, however, and Pitt instead negotiated a new deal with Decca Records on the strength of three demo recordings made with the Buzz: "The London Boys," "Rubber Band," and "Please Mr. Gravedigger." More than just being the end of the road for Pye, this signing—reportedly for a £100 advance—also spelled the end for the Buzz, who had served their purpose and were summarily dispensed with as Bowie's backing band at this point.

While David Bowie and the Buzz had ostensibly parted company by the end of 1966, the members of the band still contributed to the recording of his 1967 self-titled debut solo album, their names listed among the many others who helped with Bowie's biggest and most ambitious project to date.

Going It Alone

And so it was that David Bowie, solo artist destined for greatness, was born. Many lessons had been well learned through the passage of negotiating the Konrads, the King Bees, the Manish Boys, the Lower Third, and the Buzz. His talent had transcended—at times fractiously—all of the groups that he had attempted to be a part of while he found his feet. In rock 'n' roll, not everyone was born equal, and this by now had become more than evident. Many, many years later, when the demands and expectations of post–*Let's Dance* (1983) superstardom became too much for Bowie to bear, he would eschew solo artist status and once again seek the relative anonymity of being "just" another member of a band in Tin Machine. But for now, he was on his own (although with a devoted and canny ally in his manager Pitt, a point not to be underestimated), and while still relatively unknown and with a string of failed singles behind him—each of which just seemed to spur him on with more determination instead of disillusioning him—he possessed undented, even enhanced, confidence that he would succeed. The world was at David Bowie's feet.

11

Rock, Theater, and Mime

The Uniqueness of David Bowie's Artistic Palette

M any people noted from the very earliest days of Bowie's performing career that he possessed a theatricality when both onstage and offstage that was unique among rock performers, a quality brought to its logical conclusion through the invention of characters to carry his messages. Indeed, this inherent theatricality was one of the qualities that set him well apart from his

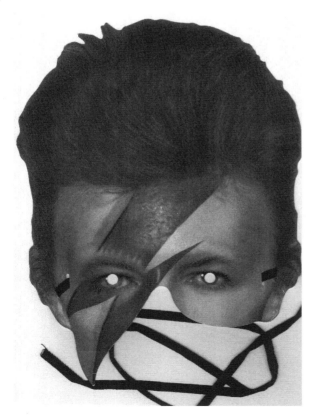

Aladdin Sane paper mask
Author's Collection

peers because it meant he communicated with his audiences through his body every bit as much as his voice, far more than was the norm for rock performers. Of course, an artist like Mick Jagger also used his body to great effect when performing, but there was never any suggestion that he was portraying anything other than himself; his movements were largely to embody his songs with qualities such as sexuality and aggression, not to tell stories in a theatrical sense. In the case of David Bowie, he could, at will, become something "other"—most famously of all, a genderless alien being called Ziggy Stardust. For David Bowie, the act of singing involved the whole body, the sound produced by the throat being just one part of the equation. The gestures and movements he employed onstage, in his videos, and even in interviews and other public appearances were not accidental, off-the-cuff, or ad hoc. They were calculated, selected, and carefully used to convey meaning just like his words were.

Origins: The Essential Lindsay Kemp Factor

Notwithstanding a considerable degree of natural talent, additional credit for this performative expertise can be laid largely at the feet of Lindsay Kemp, the leading British proponent of an avant-garde, or "alternative," theater that mixed elements of mime, burlesque, ballet, music hall, cabaret, improvisation, and Japanese Noh and Kabuki theater styles. Bowie and Kemp met in the summer of 1966–1967 after Bowie's then manager, Kenneth Pitt, supported by the enthusiastic urging of his assistant (and Bowie's girlfriend), Jan, sent a copy of his self-titled debut album to Kemp, who responded positively and invited the young artist to attend a performance shortly afterward. As David Bowie himself told it in the book he cowrote with Mick Rock, *Moonage Daydream* (2005), "A major influence and mentor during my 'cultural gestation' was the fantastical Lindsay Kemp. In 1967, a girlfriend of mine, Jan, the secretary-cum-receptionist for my then manager, Ken Pitt, had been raving to me about Kemp for some time. She knew my liking for both the theatre and the unusual and had prodded me for weeks to go with her and see this mime. A mime, what could be less interesting? Then she told me that he was using my one album (an early Decca/Deram release) as his interval music. A mime, how interesting." The two men instantly recognized themselves as kindred spirits and admirers of each other's work, leading to Bowie joining Kemp's mime company and coming under the tutelage of Kemp himself, who taught his young charge the rudiments of mime and dance and gestural and nonverbal communication. While Kemp was intrigued by Bowie's songs, he was even more impressed with his attitude, the master's appraisal at this time being that "he wasn't a very good mover, but he was equipped with the essential thing: a desire to move. And I taught him to exteriorize, to reveal his soul. And he had all this inside him, anyway."

During performances with the troupe, Bowie would sometimes perform in heavy theatrical makeup and costuming, giving him additional experience of the magic, power, and potential of theatrical transformation and role playing. In addition, he was given the opportunity to perform his original songs as a part of the productions, ensuring that right from this early stage of his career, his music and his other onstage performance activities were not separate, stand-alone entities but were instead fully merged components of an overall interdisciplinary amalgam. It was the crucial foundational beginnings of an artist who could and would never be "just a singer." David Bowie would always be a performer in the most well-rounded and all-encompassing definition of the term.

For a short time, Bowie's relationship with Kemp went beyond master and pupil when they became lovers. In Kemp's words when interviewed in the *Guardian* in 2016, "Yes, he was one of my great loves. There haven't been many. I counted up the other day and I think there were five. So I think it was a great love, though I think a great love would last a bit longer. I got over it!"

Marc Bolan (of T Rex), Bowie's friend and rival throughout the late 1960s and early to mid-1970s, was certainly one who regarded Bowie's skills highly, employing him as a support act as a solo mime for his 1969 U.K. tour. At this point, Bolan, while not yet the global superstar he would become in the early 1970s, was still considerably farther up the British who's-who-in-entertainment ranks than was Bowie. Reviews and reports from the day suggest that Bowie was not at all well received by audiences in this support guise, but this may be attributed more to the fact that the piece Bolan insisted Bowie perform was a contentious routine depicting China's invasion of Tibet than to any lack of performance skill. On many of the tour dates, Bowie's set was "ruined by heckles of left-wing students and hippies irate over his damning portrayal of China's Red Guard," suggests writer Simon Goddard in his *Ziggyology: A Brief History of Ziggy Stardust*.

Just as Bowie was always very generous in his praise of Kemp, so too the mime master reflects positively on his most famous charge. As he told Tim Lewis in *The Guardian* on April 24, 2016, "Ziggy Stardust put glam rock, gay rock, theatre rock on the map.... It was the first time we saw this marriage between theatre and rock 'n' roll, particularly my kind of avant-garde theatre."

Kemp is featured performing in the official video for the release of Bowie's single "John, I'm Only Dancing" (1972). Meanwhile Bowie, performing as Cloud, can be seen in the Scottish Television production of Kemp's pantomime *Pierrot in Turquoise/The Looking Glass Murders* (1970). Bowie's prowess as a mime can be seen in the short piece titled "The Mask," which was included in the promotional film *Love You till Tuesday* (1969), which was an attempt by manager Kenneth Pitt to bring Bowie's multiple talents to the attention of a wider audience. Tellingly, the Bowie-written piece tells the story of a young man who discovers a mask and achieves increasing tiers of fame and fortune through wearing it. Tragically, however, he dies at the end after a performance at the London Palladium when the mask strangles him, the moral of the story being that the lines between the performer and the role being performed had become so entwined as to be fatally indiscernible. Just a few years later, Bowie would make similar claims when retiring his career-launching and most-successful-ever performance persona, Ziggy Stardust: "It was quite easy to become obsessed night and day with the character. I became Ziggy Stardust. David Bowie went totally out the window. Everybody was convincing me that I was a Messiah . . . I got totally lost in the fantasy."

Body Mastery on and beyond the Rock Stage

Bowie performed mime during his Ziggy Stardust concerts. An excellent example of this can be seen during the song "The Width of a Circle" in D. A. Pennebaker's film *Ziggy Stardust and the Spiders from Mars* (1973), which documents the now famous concert at London's Hammersmith Odeon on July 3, 1973, when Bowie unexpectedly announced, live and onstage, his retirement of Ziggy, to the incredulity of audience, critics, and bandmates alike.

Bowie's mastery over his body was never better exhibited than when he played the role of John Merrick in the Broadway production of *The Elephant Man* at the Booth Theatre in 1980–1981. Without the aid of prosthetics, Bowie's portrayal of the severely facially and bodily deformed former freak show exhibit was a revelation, completely silencing critics who'd scoffed at the notion of a rock star playing such a role in serious theater and engendering rave reviews across all media. (See chapter 15 for a more in-depth critique of *The Elephant Man*.)

Similarly, the transferable skills learned through his mime training—Bowie's awareness that every gesture and bodily movement he made was loaded with nuance and meaning—are what helped him become a fine, sought-after movie actor able to play a plethora of different roles and bring them to convincing life.

Other notable performers to have benefited from Lindsay Kemp's training include Peter Gabriel, Mia Farrow, and Kate Bush. The song "Moving," from Bush's hit debut album, *The Kick Inside* (1978), is written about and in gratitude to Kemp.

In his autobiography *Bowie, Bolan and the Brooklyn Boy*, career-long collaborator and friend Tony Visconti recalls watching Bowie practice his newfound skills. He writes, "I would watch him execute the ordinary task of walking to the fridge to get a pint of milk, but on the way there he would be working out in his head how he could do it gracefully and artistically as Kemp might do; he would make a little movement that would send a wave-like ripple through his body. Other times he would go to a mirror just to check a head angle, or he would brush his hair back in a particular way. At the time I thought that he was just being incredibly vain; later I realized that he was always working on himself, constantly honing his stage persona."

There is no doubt that Lindsay Kemp played a vital role in the development of David Bowie's inimitable performance style. The mime-derived lessons in body language and nonverbal communication were well absorbed, internalized, and fully utilized throughout Bowie's career, giving him an edge over the communicative talents of almost all of his creative peers.

The Importance of Feathers

Mention must also be made of another important formative cog in David Bowie's theatrical development: Feathers. A short-lived three-person performing arts group that he formed with his girlfriend Hermione Farthingale and close friend John (Hutch) Hutchinson (initially, the third member was guitarist/vocalist Tony Hill, but he was swiftly replaced by Hutch), the trio was originally called Turquoise, a hangover from the Lindsay Kemp production *Pierrot in Turquoise*. David Bowie would later claim that he formed the troupe largely to spend more time with Farthingale. Nevertheless, it afforded him a valuable opportunity to try out his original music with support from Hutchinson on bass and Farthingale on acoustic guitar. In addition, they performed works by Leonard Cohen, Jacques Brel, the Byrds, and others. More than being solely about the music, however, the group also performed short mime routines and Roger McGough–style poetry in an eclectic and very arty mix.

While Feathers lasted for less than six months and by the end had been reduced to an all-male duo with Farthingale and Bowie's romance having ended, the experiment served an important embryonic role in David Bowie's development. In addition to the live-performance experience it afforded the emergent artist, it also provided opportunities for others to see David Bowie in action due to some of the high-profile gigs and venues in which Feathers appeared. In early 1969, they even played in support of the mighty Who. After watching a performance at the Roundhouse in London, two such audience members would prove very valuable to him in the near future: Angela (Angie) Barnett, who would soon become his lover, wife, and, for a crucial formative time, his biggest and most passionate champion, and Calvin Mark Lee, who, on joining the staff of Mercury Records, would enthusiastically endorse the man and his music.

Feathers can be seen in action today immortalized in the short film titled *Love You till Tuesday* (1969), put together by David Bowie's then manager, Kenneth Pitt, as a promotional tool for his then largely unknown young charge. Check out the song "Ching-a-Ling."

The Beckenham Arts Lab

Also highly important to David Bowie's gestation period was an experimental arts project he started in Beckenham with his then landlady and lover, Mary Finnigan. Called the Beckenham Arts Lab, it was held in the local Three Tuns Pub on Sunday evenings. Interviewed on the subject by Chris Welch of *Melody Maker* in September 1969, Bowie enthused, "I run an arts lab which is my chief occupation. It's in Beckenham and I think it's the best in the country. There isn't one pseud involved. All the people are real—like labourers or bank clerks. It started out as a folk club; arts labs generally have such a bad reputation as pseud places.... We started our lab a few months ago with poets and artists who just came along. It's got bigger and bigger and now we have our own light show and sculptures, et cetera. And I never knew there were so many sitar players in Beckenham." The eclectic and highly varied nature of the lab's performances is confirmed by one of the other regular performers at the events, guitarist Keith Christmas, who recalled in Christopher Sandford's biography *Bowie: Loving the Alien* (1996) that the musical acts performed by the likes of himself and David Bowie would be surrounded by mime, art, poetry, Buddhist chanting, tie-dying classes, and even free-form jazz. Clearly demonstrating David Bowie's love for multiple artistic disciplines in the Arts Lab's welcoming and expansive performative palette, the forum crucially offered its instigator the ideal chance to test-run his new songs in public before a sympathetic and encouraging audience and the opportunity to work on his stage presence.

Theater and Rock 'n' Roll? No, Thanks!: David Bowie's Detractors

David Bowie's introduction of overt theatricality to rock music did not find favor with everybody. In an essay titled "Music as Film" (1995), Mark Sinker suggested that "actually Bowie is a belated Tommy Steele, an all-singing, all-dancing light entertainer ... a part of the vaudeville tradition ... you'd feel he'd do a tap if his agent advised him to." Although Sinker's comments are almost certainly meant in a derogatory manner, he is correct up to a point, as Bowie is, in one sense—as is arguably Alice Cooper given that both use the same interdisciplinarity (singing, acting, dancing) employed by vaudevillians—indeed part a transplanted vaudeville tradition. But to dismiss these artists as "light entertainer(s)" is clearly ludicrous. Other critics had similarly themed axes to grind. The (in)famous rock writer Nick Kent, in a piece for *New Musical Express* titled "David Bowie: Not Just a Pretty Face?" (1972), offered the following damning appraisal, maintaining that Bowie's "act draws from over-diverse sources. From Lou Reed to Jacques Brel, to mime and then to a blast of good old rock 'n' roll transsexual outrage is just too much ground to cover for anyone. His shows always go on for too long and are never tangible enough to be rock 'n' roll, nor worked out quite well enough to be theatre.... Bowie falls into a limbo." Lisa Robinson, also writing in *New Musical Express* two years later, in a piece appropriately titled "David Bowie Has Left the Theatre" (1974), suggested that "his greatest dilemma is that he wants so very much to create 'theatre,' but his real talent lies in rock 'n' roll."

The mistake made by all of these writers (and many others) was to treat all of the disciplines and influences brought together by David Bowie as different and incompatible entities. Rock and theater need not exist in silos. David Bowie's talent (and, again, Alice Cooper's—notwithstanding their highly different approaches) was precisely *not* to treat artistic disciplines in this outmoded, separatist, puritanical 1960s rock ethos way.

The Biggest Stage of All: Living One's Life as Theater

During his Ziggy Stardust/glam-rock era especially, when the boundaries between his onstage and offstage personas became extremely blurred, David Bowie, very much in the manner of one of his major influences, Andy Warhol, lived as if his very life itself was a stage. "In the future, everybody will be famous for fifteen minutes," Warhol claimed, his own "theater" displayed continuously both onstage and offstage. Immortalized in Bowie's song of homage, the transparently titled "Andy Warhol" from the *Hunky Dory* album (1971), clever lines, such as "Can't tell them apart at all," critiqued the notion that artifice and authenticity were qualities that at times were impossible to tell apart. Although singing about Warhol, David Bowie might just as well have been putting the lens on himself. As quoted in the book of quotations compiled by Miles, *Bowie in His Own Words* (1980), he made a conscious decision to blur these lines: "I thought I might as well take Ziggy out to interviews as well. Why leave him on the stage? Why not complete the canvas?"

In *Popular Culture: The Metropolitan Experience*, Iain Chambers, when examining the underlying ethos of 1960s pop art, suggested, "The individual constructs her- or himself as the object of street art, as a public icon: the body becomes the canvas of changing urban signs. Contemporary art slides into the art of contemporary life, where, in the words of that master of metamorphosis, David Bowie, we can all be 'heroes just for one day.' ... We find ourselves selecting and putting together signs of a public identity from the circulating collage of everyday commerce and culture."

David Bowie, then, more than any other popular music icon in history, was theatrical through and through, from his training and background, through to his performance methodology, and even into how he lived his life both onstage and offstage; theatricality was his very raison d'être. In his own words in 1987, as cited in David Buckley's biography *Strange Fascination: David Bowie, the Definitive Story*, the artist clarified his approach: "It's a very hard thing to convince people that you can be quite different off stage in rock 'n' roll than you are on stage. One of the principles in rock is that it's the person himself expressing what he really and truly feels—and that applies to a lot of artists. But to me it doesn't. It never did. I always saw it as a theatrical experience."

Ziggy Stardust cutout book   *Amanda Mills collection*

12

Hidden Gems

Lesser-Known David Bowie Songs That Seriously Rock

Everyone knows "Space Oddity," "Rebel Rebel," "Starman," "Life on Mars," "Golden Years," "Ashes to Ashes," "Let's Dance," "Blue Jean," "Where Are We Now?," and all of the other global Bowie hits that remain a staple on classic hit–format radio stations the world over and probably will do so forever. True Bowie aficionados also know of a treasure trove of other wonderful songs hidden away as album cuts, failed singles, B-sides, demos, outtakes, and so on. In this chapter, we explore a selection of superb album tracks, one song chosen from each and every one of his studio albums. Of course, all of David Bowie's albums contain hidden gems such as these, so my selection is admittedly quite subjective. Nevertheless, I consider them to be "must-listens" for anyone looking to spread their David Bowie wings.

David Bowie (the Debut Album)

From Bowie's debut album, *David Bowie* (1967), an eclectic mishmash that completely and unceremoniously bombed and owed more to music hall than rock 'n' roll, one song that deserved a much better fate is the rather wonderful "Love You till Tuesday." Rerecorded in a different version as a single release—which failed just as miserably as the album that spawned it—it is nevertheless the one song (maybe "Join the Gang" can be excepted too) on the collection that was entirely consistent with the music scene of Swinging London in the late 1960s. Its jaunty pop melody, frothy vibe, and cheeky subject matter combine to create an endearing snapshot of the era that can hold its own against any top-line competition from back in the day. In contrast to the oddly square instrumentation that dominates elsewhere on the album (brass band, orchestra, and so on), here standard pop instruments seize their moment to take center stage, and the strings, for example, while still present, simply support things instead of being afforded the spotlight. Bowie's throwaway comedic line of "Well I might stretch it to Wednesday" that is delivered at the very end as things fade out—one can easily imagine him delivering it with a nod and a wink—is sheer smile-inducing gold. It's a glimpse of Bowie as a cheeky, cockney lad-about-town despite the fact, of course, that he was never a cockney.

David Bowie/Space Oddity

From his second album (1969), also titled *David Bowie* (later rereleased and better known as *Space Oddity*), "Wild Eyed Boy from Freecloud" is a tour de force of the artist's budding songwriting prowess and a clear indication of his growing disillusionment with and estrangement from the 1960s counterculture. With lyrics that strike at the heart of all that the hippies held dear and sacred set to a sophisticated, lushly orchestrated, and complex musical platform, this is pure musical theater and provides a great foretaste of what was to come.

The Man Who Sold the World

"All the Madmen" from Bowie's third album, *The Man Who Sold the World* (released in the United States in 1970 and in the United Kingdom in 1971), is another look-what-he's-capable-of moment. Critiquing society's madness-ver-sus-sanity conundrum and the alienation of those whom it judges to fall on the wrong side of that equation, Bowie throws everything, including the kitchen sink, at this dense, ever-evolving showcase. "All the Madmen" is experimental, deep, and poignant, and when the song really starts to rock out at the three-min-ute, five-second, mark, it's a moment of pure foot-stomping adrenalin that is enough to get any headbanger's head banging.

Hunky Dory

In my opinion, the fourth studio album, *Hunky Dory*, is David Bowie's song-writing Shangri-La, such is the consistency of sheer quality across the two sides of vinyl. As well as containing three timeless Bowie favorites in "Life on Mars," "Changes," and "Oh! You Pretty Things," there are so many other fine songs to choose from that it seems almost sacrilege to do so. Nevertheless, track 5, "Kooks," still manages to stand out. Ostensibly a children's song—written for David and then wife Angie's newborn son Zowie (who would later change his name to Duncan)—the combination of innocent and naive melody, harmony, and rhythm, coupled with playful but empowering words of advice to his tiny offspring, results in an irresistible anti-bullying/power-of-difference statement that resonates just as powerfully today, nearly fifty years later. It should be required listening in any parenting class.

The Rise and Fall of Ziggy Stardust and the Spiders from Mars

Choosing a hidden gem from the career-launching *The Rise and Fall of Ziggy Stardust and the Spiders from Mars* album presents almost as much of a challenge as with the preceding *Hunky Dory*. Beyond the songs that sit so prominently in Bowie history—titles such as "Starman," "Ziggy Stardust," "Suffragette City," and the like—there remains almost nothing that could be classed as filler—with the possible exception, that is, of the album's surprising inclusion and only cover version, "It Ain't Easy," by Ron Davies. However, the second song of the album, "Soul Love," provides a memorable lesson in how to utilize dynamics to their full potential in a pop song. Beautifully crafted, the verses are laid back and relaxed with their bongo drum and acoustic guitar vibe. In the choruses, though, rock instrumentation kicks in with sudden aggression, and the song sits up and barks gloriously as Bowie takes apart, in his carefully crafted lyrics, humankind's traditional faith and belief systems of religion, politics, and love. An upward key change before the last verse paints beautifully the search for deliverance and enlightenment sentiment, and in all ways, "Soul Love" is a cleverly written, arranged, and recorded piece of lesser-known David Bowie magic.

Aladdin Sane

Bowie's sixth studio album, *Aladdin Sane*, spawned one of his mightiest glam-era hits with "The Jean Genie." But perhaps the masterstroke of this collection of Ziggy-goes-to-America songs lies in Bowie's decision to introduce U.S. pianist Mike Garson to his lineup of instrumental accomplices. Avant-garde jazz pianist Garson brought to the album a decadence reminiscent of Weimar-era cabaret—exactly what Bowie hoped he would do—and the result added a new dimension to rock music. Nowhere is this exemplified better than in the under-rated, gorgeous title track, where Garson was instructed by Bowie to abandon all restrictions and conventions and just improvise wildly. In perhaps the most exciting and unrepeatable recorded piano performance in rock music history (Bowie tribute bands and cover bands understandably tend to avoid this song at all costs), this highly gifted performer covers more ground in his mid-song extended solo over a simple two-chord harmonic platform than most pianists would manage in a year of performing. Accordingly, the title track of *Aladdin Sane* is an absolute must-hear.

Pinups

Although *Pinups* is regarded by some as being something of a filler album, sitting between the two classics that are *Aladdin Sane* and *Diamond Dogs*, Bowie's only covers album deserves better. Aside from spawning an enormous worldwide hit with his version of the McCoys' song "Sorrow," this collection of his favorite songs spanning the years 1964–1967 is an important document in Bowie history that shows and acknowledges his roots and influences. More than this though, the record finds both Bowie and his Spiders from Mars (albeit with Aynsley Dunbar replacing Woody Woodmansey on drums) at the top of their game, and able to do more than simply pay homage to Bowie's selections. Rather, they bring them into a new era—glam rock—and accordingly give them a new edge, a new audience, and a whole new lease on life. "Friday on My Mind" is a great case in point, with the energy and excitement of the original version by the Easybeats preserved but the glam sparkle and Bowie's affected vocal style brilliantly re-presenting it for the glam-era audience. When *Pinups* was released in 1973, many a young Bowie fan had missed these songs the first time around, and here in the hands of their hero Ziggy Stardust/David Bowie, these versions of the songs, "Friday on My Mind" and all of the rest, remain the definitive ones despite the howls of protest from their older brothers and sisters.

Diamond Dogs

And so to *Diamond Dogs*, a favorite album of mine and reportedly a huge influence on a very young Marilyn Manson back in 1974. In an interview with *Rolling Stone* on David Bowie's death, Manson recalled his introduction to the artist: "I went for a dizzying car ride through the Hollywood Hills and listened to *Diamond Dogs*. All of my nostalgia, instantly turned to awe. I was hearing him sing about fiction as a mask to show his naked soul. This changed my life forever. Every song of his was a way for me to communicate to others. It was a sedative. An arousal. A love letter I could never have written. It has become and remains a soundtrack to a movie he painted with his voice and guitar." Amid this filmic apocalyptic soundscape sits the trilogy "Sweet Thing/Candidate/Sweet Thing (reprise)." These nine minutes of Bowie magic take the listener on a journey from yearning sweetness and aching beauty to raw ugly emotion, aggression, and degradation and then back again. "Rebel Rebel" might have been the deserved hit single from Bowie's last glam-rock album, but the quality of the songs on the rest of the album is right up there too and deserves much repeat listening.

Young Americans

In a huge stylistic swerve from the-man-who-was-once-Ziggy, 1975 ushered in the self-proclaimed Plastic Soul Man of *Young Americans*. While the massively danceable "Fame" packed dance floors and shot to the upper echelons of charts around the world, the ultracool and sophisticated "Somebody Up There Likes Me" embodies the spirit of the album every bit as well with its cool saxophone, its gospel hand claps, and stylistically perfect "woo hoos" from the backing vocalists. Perfect in the songwriting, performance, and production stakes, "Somebody Up There Likes Me" demonstrates emphatically the quality of Bowie's transformative powers. Of the mascara-clad glam rocker, nothing remains.

Station to Station

Nineteen seventy-six—another year, another album, and another stylistic shift. On *Station to Station*, Bowie assembled the smallest-ever number of songs on one of his albums, presenting his ever-growing fan base with just six. With that said, the total length of the album, at just under thirty-eight minutes, was only half a minute shorter than the running time of *The Rise and Fall of Ziggy Stardust and the Spiders from Mars* with its eleven songs. On *Station to Station*, the six tracks average six and a half minutes, with the opening title track sitting at over ten. While the second song, "Golden Years," was the hit single, it is that gargantuan opener that anybody who is just beginning their journey into David Bowie's recorded legacy and going beyond the greatest-hits packages must hear. It's a full three minutes and seventeen seconds before his voice even enters the track, constituting an introduction lasting longer than the entire span of most pop songs of the day. And if the song itself is all about a journey, then that is exactly what the listener experiences when listening to it. Changes in dynamics, rhythmic changes, melodic shifts, mood swings, emotional fluidity—it's all there to experience.

Low

Low, that most divisive and confounding of albums when released in 1977, is chock-full of hidden gems. "Sound and Vision" might well have secured the limelight, but the true extent of Bowie's risk-taking innovations exists on side 2, where vocals take a backseat and allow the ambient electronic world to lay waste to rock music convention. A filmic picture of bleak alienation, "Subterraneans" closes the album and lingers in the listener's head long afterward. This lengthy, unhurried, and meandering jazz-tinged tribute to East Berliners trapped behind the Berlin Wall eschews traditional popular music description and is simply, by equal measures, haunting and beautiful. Toe-tapping it isn't. Brain engaging it is.

"Heroes"

Exceeding the album-every-year pace, 1977 also saw the release of *"Heroes,"* widely regarded as the second album of the oft-called "Berlin trilogy" of Bowie albums. The supremacy of the title track aside, other gems abound for the serious and the curious. Slightly more accessible in conventional terms than its predecessor, the Bowie/Eno collaborations on side 2 nevertheless bring more timeless soundscape experimentation, and "Moss Garden" in particular is outstanding. Fronted by the gentle fragility of the koto, the five minutes of the track—it's hard to call it a song—are like a meditation. True to its title, listening to "Moss Garden" is like taking a little time out from the frantic pace of modern life to sit within the walls of a secret Japanese grotto with its flowing water and lush greenery. Inducing a natural calm if listened to while reclining with eyes closed, this piece is pure Bowie therapy.

Lodger

After a much-needed gap year, Bowie returned in 1979 with *Lodger*. Aside from the hits, "DJ" and "Boy's Keep Swinging," the songs on his final album of the decade are a highly eclectic stylistic mashup. Always taking his fans to new places, the second song of side 1 takes the listener into the world of dysfunctional freelance bush pilots in "African Night Flight." The effect is one of a postcard brought to life as the aural imagery of Swahili lyrics and chant mixes with jungle noises and African instruments. Heavily rhythmic, it's another example of Bowie visiting a foreign land and bringing its musical essence to a new context, into the popular music mainstream, à la "Moss Garden."

Scary Monsters (and Super Creeps)

The dawn of the new decade saw a new album from David Bowie, and *Scary Monsters (and Super Creeps)* would turn out to be one of his most acclaimed and best loved. No one expected that in 1980, Major Tom would resurface from his tragic eleven-year estrangement in space, let alone as a tragic junkie "strung out in heavens high." "Ashes to Ashes" and "Fashion" hit heights in the singles charts, delighting fans, while the title track rocked as hard, frenetically, and disturbingly as anything he had ever done. It is on another album cut, however, that we gain clear insight into Bowie's thoughts on his career and the music industry at large. "Teenage Wildlife" is a cynical, reflective, even funny critique of the faddishness of the pop music industry—the current flavor of the month, new wave—and can be regarded as a companion piece to the far better-known "Fashion." With a similar pace and vibe to "Heroes" achieving a pleasant familiarity through the verses and a wonderful pop hook hallmarking the choruses, this is one of the artist's best songs, and the fact that it is not better known is something of a travesty. However, that makes it an absolute boon of a find for anyone delving deeper into David Bowie for the first time.

Let's Dance

A three-year gap later, and David Bowie hits the commercial stratosphere in 1983 with the *Let's Dance* album. It spawns hits galore, including the title track "China Girl," "Modern Love," and, in some surprising locales such as New Zealand, Norway, and Sweden, "Cat People (Putting Out Fire)." However, the hits aside, finding a hidden gem is not so easy, with an uncharacteristic number of less inspiring songs included on the album. Perhaps the most promising of these fillers is the unusual choice of a little-known cover—an obscure 1977 song by Metro titled "Criminal World," in which the bisexual undertones of the lyrics hark back to glam rock's androgynous heart.

Tonight

The following album, *Tonight* (1984), is one of David Bowie's least loved despite the mastery and success of "Loving the Alien" and "Blue Jean." These two excellent songs aside, all of the other songs on the nine-song album are either collaborations or cover versions. The Bowie brand and trademark is thereby considerably diluted, and as a result—as was the case with *Let's Dance*—it is hard to regard any of them as hidden gems. If pushed, perhaps the cover version of Jerry Lieber and Mike Stoller's "I Keep Forgetting" is worth a listen just for curiosity's sake, but this is hardly a ringing endorsement.

Never Let Me Down

Another three-year wait, and it was on to the equally much-maligned *Never Let Me Down* (1987). Three rather modestly (by Bowie standards) successful singles ensued—"Day In Day Out," "Time Will Crawl," and the hauntingly beautiful title track—but again, the rest of the album disappoints, and it is hard to uncover a diamond in the rough. "Zeroes" is interesting, and one wonders how it might have sounded if afforded a different, far less cluttered arrangement.

Tin Machine (I and II)

The years 1989 and 1991 saw Bowie's two-album withdrawal from being a solo artist, as he attempted to retreat into the lessened spotlight of being "just another band member" in Tin Machine. Sick of the huge pressures of superstardom and dismayed at his falling stocks in terms of critical acclaim, it was a tactic designed to take the heat off himself. While it confused and disappointed many, it worked well for him in that regard. On both Tin Machine studio albums, there are gems for the inquisitive. From the first, *Tin Machine* (1989), "Heaven's in Here" is a killer of a track and an emphatic opener. From the second and last album, *Tin Machine II*, again the opener, "Baby Universal," is a classic cut well worthy of being checked out. While both of my suggestions for the Tin Machine novice are, quite by chance, opening tracks, exploring the whole of both albums is a rewarding experience, and other gems abound that lay waste to the clinically produced, slick pop sounds of *Let's Dance*, *Tonight*, and *Never Let Me Down* and instead offer grungy sandpaper roughness. In Tin Machine, David Bowie recovered his edge and his outsider status. No longer on the inside looking out, he was again on the outside looking in, which is exactly where his lifelong fans wanted him to be.

Black Tie White Noise

The *Black Tie White Noise* album (1993) was the long-awaited solo comeback album, and it was a ripper, going straight to the number one position in the United Kingdom, though faring poorly in the United States by comparison, reaching only thirty-nine. Short on hits but with moderate success for the songs "Jump They Say" and "Miracle Goodnight," there is a plethora of other material to explore here. To pick out just one track, one should listen to the highly autobiographical second song, "You've Been Around." Featuring trumpeter Lester Bowie, who shines here and elsewhere on the record, Bowie outlines his journey as a loner and his salvation in the arms of a lover—touchingly referencing his recent marriage to Iman Abdulmajid. In a moment of amusing self-referencing, he acknowledges to Iman, "But you've changed me, ch ch ch ch ch ch changed me." With all of this set to an infectious jazz/funk/hip-hop beat, it's wonderful stuff.

The Buddha of Suburbia

Frequently overlooked as a bona fide David Bowie studio album is *The Buddha of Suburbia* (1993). Wrongly discounted because of its links to the BBC television dramatization of Hanif Kureishi's 1990 novel of the same name—people assumed it was simply a TV sound track and not a stand-alone album—*The Buddha of Suburbia* actually contained much fine work, not the least of which is the pairing once again of David Bowie with pianist Mike Garson. Sounding like the love child of *Aladdin Sane* and *Black Tie White Noise* is the superb "South Horizon," reason enough alone to purchase this largely lost and misunderstood work.

1. Outside

Another frequently underrated album followed two years later, in 1995. *1. Outside* is one of the artist's most disturbing works, unrelentingly dark with its serial-killer concept, commercially bereft, daring, and yet magnificent. Described by its creator as "a nonlinear Gothic drama hyper-cycle" and containing no fewer than eighteen tracks, one of the most interesting is "Hallo Spaceboy," in which 1970s Ziggy is brought into the present as a far more world-savvy character, supported by techno/industrial/jungle beats that are aggressive and unrelenting. As was the case with *Space Oddity*'s Major Tom when he returned many years later in "Ashes to Ashes," when David Bowie brings a persona back to life, it is usually subverted and somehow twisted in the process.

Earthling

The 1990s truly were a creative boom time for David Bowie, being a decade during which he clawed his way back to considerable critical acclaim even as his sales spectacularly failed to match the heady 1980s pop days of *Let's Dance*. Another excellent and groundbreaking album appeared in 1997 in *Earthling*. Often referred to as his drum 'n' bass record, it's a fair enough moniker, and for the first time, an entire David Bowie album was recorded using only digital technology—no analog. This allowed him to cut and paste vocal and instrumental tracks with ease, something he fully embraced. With only the excellent "I'm Afraid of Americans" seeing any chart action, there are nevertheless plenty of hidden gems on *Earthling*. "Seven Years in Tibet" gets my vote, a song that, although based on the simplest of drum loops, manages to pack massive dynamic shifts and textural gymnastics into its dramatic musical narrative. The violence of the chorus juxtaposed against the tranquillity of the verses is a masterstroke.

"Hours . . ."

"Hours…" followed in 1999 and was a fine way to end the twentieth century for one of the most impactful and important artists in popular music history. Also a favorite of many hard-core Bowie fans, the gentler texture and vibe of the work has drawn comparisons to the early *Hunky Dory*. While that may be going a little too far, the hard edge of his most recent albums was certainly absent here, and the beautiful simplicity of a great songwriter's skill was left to permeate the album. A standout instrumental is "Brilliant Adventure," which unexpectedly welcomes back the Japanese koto of Bowie's Berlin period, a welcome return in a beautiful and atmospheric track.

Heathen

And a new century dawns. If ever there was a twentieth-century rock star who was equipped to excel in the twenty-first century as much as he had in the preceding one, then it was ever-futuristic, hammock-avoiding changeling David Bowie. And so it was that in 2002 he produced his twenty-third studio album, the provocatively titled *Heathen*, delivered in the shadow of 9/11 and with its shadow cast over several tracks. Devoid of hits, it is nevertheless a fine album and particularly notable for Bowie's reunion with producer Tony Visconti, doyen of his 1970s successes. Putting to one side the (very) modestly achieving single "Slow Burn" that featured Pete Townshend of the Who, if there is a better David Bowie track anywhere than "Slip Away," then I'd like to enter that argument. A wistful appeal for better and simpler times, the passing of youth, and the truism of aging, all delivered imaginatively through the eyes of two puppets who used to appear in the TV program *The Uncle Floyd Show*, this is a monster of a song, a template for writing about the human condition.

Reality

Just one year later, and the second Bowie album of the new millennium arrives to the immense pleasure of fans reinvigorated by *Heathen*. Accompanied by a massive global tour of the same name, *Reality* was the ironically named (for an artist who had invested so much in purposeful artifice) twenty-fourth work of Bowie's career, and such was the critical acclaim that it put him right back at the top of the rock hierarchy, an elder statesman with his own teeth—and very sharp ones they were at that. Like its predecessor, *Reality* went top ten all over the world even without the propulsion of a hit single, with the exception of the

United States, where it reached only number twenty-nine on the Billboard chart. A very strong album throughout, there can nevertheless be only one choice for *Reality's* hidden gem. The final track is "Bring Me the Disco King," and it is possibly the most beautiful and haunting piece of music ever composed by Brixton's most famous son. Almost eight minutes long, it is an autobiographical confessional piece delivered over brush-on-snare with wonderful jazz flavorings. Pondering both the past and the future, it is David Bowie's pièce de résistance and an absolute must-listen, no question.

The Next Day

And then—silence. Where had David Bowie gone? This was the question on the minds of fans all over the world for a decade. And the very understandable consensus among us all was that he had retired without (typically, for the master of surprises) telling anyone about it. It seemed to be a tasteful withdrawal from the music industry rat race by an artist for whom "cool" and "decorum" were intrinsic qualities. But no. We were all proven wrong when, on January 8, 2013—Bowie's sixty-sixth birthday—a surprise new album, *The Next Day*, was announced. Everyone pondered, how could such a secret have been kept in the digital age? It was a masterstroke. And the world—not just rabid David Bowie fans—was delighted and eagerly awaited the release date two months later. The delight was tinged with a degree of nervousness, however, because, well, what if it was a disappointment? There had been many occasions in rock history where old rockers hadn't known when to hang up their guitar or microphone and gracefully withdraw from what was increasingly becoming a young person's game. But such worries proved unfounded, as *The Next Day* topped charts all over the world and critical acclaim came thick and fast from all directions. The single "Where Are We Now?" also achieved high chart placements the world over, and sure enough, David Bowie was well and truly back. Andy Gill in the *Independent* described it as "the greatest comeback album in rock 'n' roll history," and his was not a lone sentiment. Littered with references to the past but still looking to the future, high points abound throughout the work. Bowie really showcases his voice on *The Next Day*, and it's a fine reminder not only that this artist is a fine songwriter, social commentator, and artistic conduit but also that he possesses a remarkable voice. In terms of this, just listen to the range and emotion in "You Feel So Lonely You Could Die." It is Bowie at his vocal best. And as the song fades out with a recapitulation of the drum pattern from "Five Years" from the *Ziggy Stardust* album of 1972 and as a listener and lifelong Bowie fan, it's hard not to get a little emotional and nostalgic.

Blackstar

Only one album remains in the Bowie catalog of studio releases. *Blackstar* was released once again on Bowie's birthday, January 8, 2016. Just two days after turning sixty-nine, he passed away. His liver cancer had been a well-kept secret and took the world by surprise. The outpouring of grief and respect was unprecedented for a rock musician, testament to the millions he had touched through his work. *Blackstar* itself is a dense, complex, but magnificent work, a telling monument to a great artist who remained vital and relevant right to the end of his life. *Every* track on *Blackstar* is a hidden gem. Producer Tony Visconti confirmed that he and David Bowie sought to create anti–rock 'n' roll, and the jazz-inflected amalgam of musical styles and juxtapositions is not always an easy listen. It demands much of its audience. Above all, David Bowie required his fans to think. In opposition to the one-hidden-gem-named-per-album approach of this chapter, then, any and every track on *Blackstar* should be regarded in that way. One can take one's pick.

13

"Sound and Vision"

A Lesson from Mr. Bowie in Matching Cover Art to Music

One of the most remarkable features of David Bowie's work was the way in which he merged the aural and visual components of his art, in his own words (and the title of his 1977 hit), the "Sound and Vision." In this chapter, I focus on his first six album covers in order to show how quickly in his career he mastered this feature, something that would become a cornerstone of his work.

Breaking the Album Cover's Promise

An album cover is supposed to not only package and keep safe the vinyl recording it houses but also convey to a potential purchaser some sort of visual representation of what's inside: the kind of music a band or artist plays and the topics or themes addressed in the lyrics of the songs. Throughout the golden age of the 33-rpm vinyl record during which David Bowie came to prominence, album covers were hugely important as advertising and marketing tools. Effectively, they "spoke" for both the artist and the music. While David Bowie would become a master of synergy between his album cover art and the music that it both promoted and protected—to the point where his example was emulated by numerous other artists—it was not always so, and this quality was something he appeared to learn quickly as his career developed.

There's a vast difference in the coherence between sound and vision of his earliest albums and those that would follow. In fact, on his debut album, *David Bowie* (1967), the image and the music are in total opposition to each other. And for an artist making his first-ever foray into the popular music marketplace—the name David Bowie was almost completely unknown at this time—it was a fatal flaw. Here on his self-titled debut, his portrait on the front cover screamed mod, and his look was totally in keeping with other mod musicians in Swinging London at the time. However, the musical content contained in the grooves of the record was about as far away from the Who, the Kinks, the Small Faces, and so on as it was possible to be. Further aligning him with the prevailing mod culture was the psychedelic-styled lettering used to write his name. A biography printed on the back cover by manager Kenneth Pitt fully backed up the promise of the front-cover image, seemingly announcing an album full of rhythm and blues. Further, because his clothing hinted at being militaristic, a link was promised in the biography to other major acts of the day who at times wore such costuming, including the Beatles and the Rolling Stones: "David is very much a product of the fast moving era in which he has spent his teens. An early desire to create took him to art school, but Little Richard discs turned him on to music as a more satisfying art form. At 13 he was playing good enough saxophone to be a credit to his teacher, Ronnie Ross. He formed one or two of Britain's early R&B groups. Then somebody gave him a shove and he was out front singing. He was immediately impatient with the songs they were to sing and began to write his own. Songs he believed in, songs that were part of him, songs he could sing with feeling. They spilled out all over the place in rapid labour. He moved so fast that everything he did was two years too soon. Why, he was even photographed in 1964 wearing a military jacket!"

Mark Paytress has commented on this stylistic distance between Bowie's work and the popular music of the day, comparing the contents of this first album to the established styles of acid rock, blues rock, and, at the other end of the spectrum, the bubblegum style of the Monkees and Tremeloes. Finding no common ground, in his "Classic Album" book on *Ziggy Stardust* released in 1998, he suggested that Bowie's work was "idiosyncratic to the point of self-immolation. The album ... wasn't consistent enough to tap into any established market."

Given such deviation from the popular music mainstream, then, does the music contained on *David Bowie* have a stylistic home? In his 1999 biography, David Buckley sums up the early stages of Bowie's career, including this first album, thus: "His early work, influenced by Anthony Newley, had little in common with the dominant rock styles of the day and he was largely overlooked." Indeed, several critics have commented that this album was more aligned to musical theater than to rock 'n' roll, including Jerry Hopkins, who suggested in his simply titled book *Bowie* (1995), "The songs were a strange lot ... [they] almost certainly did come as a result of David's fascination at the time with Lionel Bart type musicals. In fact, nearly all fourteen songs which eventually appeared on the album fit that description." This is perhaps not surprising in light of the fact that David Bowie had previously been involved in writing a musical based on Bart's *Oliver*, titled *Kids on the Roof*, with his previous manager Tony Hatch. Regarding this venture, Kevin Cann, author of *David Bowie: A Chronology* (1983), believes that "the musical became the spine of material included on his first LP." But this stylistic anomaly did not serve Bowie well. Finally, in *The Complete David Bowie* (2002), Nicholas Pegg, who contends that the album is the least well regarded of all Bowie's work, suggests that it was "mercilessly mocked as music-hall piffle, derived from a passing Anthony Newley fad."

Certainly, then, allusions to mod begin and end with the album's cover. Despite the style allegiance promised, neither the music nor the thematic alliances of the lyrics allow for anywhere near such a hip categorization. Biographers Peter and Leni Gillman reflect on the problems presented by the work, suggesting that "perhaps the most noticeable was the difficulty in categorizing it at all." Paytress, meanwhile, ruminated more generally on the difficulty that Bowie's succession of different record labels experienced in marketing him in these early years of his music career for this very same reason, stating, "Neither Decca nor Philips/Mercury... understood how to market a singer with no obvious commercial, or even subcultural, home." So disparate are the myriad influences evident on the album that biographer Buckley goes so far as to describe it as "the vinyl equivalent of the madwoman in the attic."

Improving the Synergy

Remarkably, following the yawning gap between sound and vision of the debut album, things improved markedly on the second album. Released by Philips in the United Kingdom, it too was titled *David Bowie*, and this repetition of title has led to considerable confusion over time. In the United States, the work was released by Mercury Records as the less problematic *Man of Words/Man of Music*. Even more confusing, however, is the fact that this second album was subsequently reissued by RCA Records in 1972 under the title *Space Oddity*, a title that has been retained for all subsequent rereleases and the one by which this album is now most commonly known.

The overarching theme of this second album is one of technological alienation, of human anxiety and concern about the rapid advancement of technology across a range of fronts. It is a theme drawn largely from the Cold War and especially pertaining to the space race between the United States and the Soviet Union. This anxiety was represented within the arts at large at the time in a variety of ways, and Bowie's album cover draws heavily on a particular technique called Op Art (optical art), which was highly popular at the time within the visual arts. Op Art creates an illusion of movement with its relentless repetition of shapes and on a deeper level represents the triumph of mechanization over humanity. Based on the work of Victor Vasarely but here created by Vernon Dewhurst, the purple and blue dots that dominate Bowie's album cover win the battle for supremacy because they continue across the photograph of his face at the picture's center. Because they lighten as they near the middle, they don't fully obscure his face, but the implication of dominance—of humankind's ultimate subservience—is clear. From the album's now famous opener, "Space Oddity," the message of the cover rings true as Major Tom epitomizes the folly of humankind's poorly founded trust in space technology. Like the astronauts in Stanley Kubrick's *2001: A Space Odyssey* who are consigned to a cold, distant death by HAL, the murderous computer, Major Tom too falls foul of technological failure and ends the song drifting doomed into endless space while imploring Ground Control to tell his wife "I love her very much." On the Op Art–inspired cover, Bowie's face too is cut off and drifting from the foreground amid the mechanized relentlessness of the dominating dots. Other songs on the album address the same human-versus-technology theme. Through the course of the song "Saviour Machine," for example, a fictitious "President Joe" rises to power, promising to save the world. Ultimately, however, he lets the populace down, handing power over to a supposed utopian supercomputer that then proceeds to turn on its human creators. In "The Cygnet Committee," Bowie paints a frightening view of a technologically driven conflict in the future where technology-gone-wrong decimates the human population: "The silent guns of love will blast the sky ... I see a child slain on the ground as a love machine lumbers through desolation rows ploughing down man, woman." In "God Knows I'm Good," a woman shoplifter is apprehended while "the cash machines were shrieking on the counter." And aliens enter the fray in the album's closing track, "Memory of a Free Festival," with images painted in the listener's mind of "machines of every shape and size" and "tall Venusians passing through." While some critics criticized the album's musical style as derivative of artists such as Bob Dylan and Donovan, the alignment between the themes of many of the songs contained on the album and the front-cover image show significant development between the first album and the second.

The cover of the U.K. release of Bowie's third studio album, *The Man Who Sold the World*, features the infamous and much-commented-on image of the artist wearing a dress and reclining on a couch or chaise longue. The image is a parody re-creation of the Pre-Raphaelite femme fatale archetype as portrayed by artists such as Gabriel Rossetti, and Bowie readily acknowledged as much in media interviews at the time. While there is no single Rossetti painting that can be convincingly matched to Bowie's parody—*Lady Lilith* and *Regina Cordium/ The Queen of Hearts* appear to be the closest referents—his poem "The Card Dealer" would appear to be the actual, much-overlooked inspiration and shows a quite literal translation in Bowie's hands. An examination of the lyrics of *The Man Who Sold the World* adds support to the gender play of the cover. The most obvious line is in "All the Madmen" when Bowie sings, "My libido's split on me." Elsewhere, especially in "The Width of a Circle," the theme of homosexuality is plainly evident, and the gender-play element inherent to this cover is the first clear visual depiction of what would go on to become a Bowie hallmark. There are, however, further art-historical inferences to be discerned in the Pre-Raphaelite femme fatale parody. One of the inherent features of such figures was the quality of emotional removal and psychological masking. Such figures always beg the question in the viewer's mind, what *is* she thinking? Elements such as the absentminded touching of the hair and the unreadable, unfocused gaze on something beyond what can be seen in the picture show a theatrical duplicity that was inherent to the style of the Pre-Raphaelites. Highly affected, it displays a heavy investment in artifice over authenticity. The cover of *The Man Who Sold the World* is, therefore, Bowie's first important role play even if present more in the image than in the music at this point.

Hunky Dory, the fourth studio album, continues along the same lines even if it is a very different composition to its predecessor.

Immediately evident to the viewer is the fact that Bowie retains the element of gender play that dominated the previous image by presenting himself again

Hunky Dory album, 1971   *Author's Collection*

as highly feminized. In addition, he once again locates his performance within a specific borrowed context, a context that is preloaded with meanings and associations, including alienation and gender ambiguity, that he recontextualizes for his own ends. On this occasion, he parodies the stereotypical image of female "silver screen" film icons of the first three decades of the twentieth century. Lyrics support the historical allusion, with references to the "silver screen" and to the "cinema," both of these appearing in the song "Andy Warhol." There is no doubt about the influence of film on Bowie, a point that several critics and biographers have made in regard to *Hunky Dory*. Nicholas Pegg regards the cover as Bowie "reflecting the album's preoccupation with the silver screen ... a close-up of Bowie living out his Bacall/Garbo fantasies, gazing wistfully into space as he pushes the flowing locks back from his forehead." Philip Cato, author of the breezily written personal reminiscence of the glam-rock era titled *Crash Course for the Ravers: A Glam Odyssey*, believes that "on the cover he came over like a low rent Lauren Bacall," while Bowie's biographers Peter and Leni Gillman suggest that "the photograph ... showed David staring wistfully into space and looking for all the world like Greta Garbo." Indeed, in the song "Quicksand," Bowie directly name-drops Garbo and asserts that he is "living in a silent film." With regard to this, however, David Bowie has also said that it was meant as a reference to Juan Pujol, the British double agent in World War II. Perhaps it conveniently has two meanings.

As was the case with the femme fatale parody of *The Man Who Sold the World*, the silver screen stars that Bowie mimics here were considered aloof, untouchable, highly affected, and archetypal, with an air of androgyny thrown into the mix. Bowie's gaze is once again fixed on higher, unseen things denied to the viewer of the picture, his hand again touching his hair in an act of contemplation and emotional removal from the physical environs. Bowie is once more adopting a mask and asking viewers to make of it what they will. On *Hunky Dory*, Bowie asks all of the big philosophical questions, addressing light and dark, good and evil, religious faith and secularism, reality and fiction, gender ambiguity, technology and humanity, and so on. In the cover image, we see the artist in exactly the same search-for-enlightenment pose—the subject's mind above and beyond the earthly travails—that one might expect of a Byronic hero: a societal outsider whose burden it is to find the truth in all things. In short, Bowie's iconography, as evidenced by this album cover, is now reflecting his work with ever-increasing effectiveness. His growing propensity toward using his image to draw on preexisting symbolism and archetypes from the arts to further his own thematic agendas is laid out nowhere more clearly than on the back cover, where, amid the album credits, he refers to himself in his coproducer role as "the actor." Bowie is now taking rock music somewhere that it has not been before.

Getting It Right

The fifth studio album, *The Rise and Fall of Ziggy Stardust and the Spiders from Mars*, is the one, of course, that sent Bowie's career skyrocketing.

The album cover brilliantly casts him as a frontier hero, alone and dwarfed by the bleak cityscape that surrounds him, a strange figure completely out of place and alienated by his foreboding surroundings. The electric guitar casually slung at his side is akin to a military hero's sword or gun, and with one leg forward of the other, he mirrors statues of military heroes and adventurers the world over who are cast poised to step into the unknown on a heroic quest of some kind (or "K. West" as the sign above fortuitously suggests). Facing the viewer front on, the pose is one of confident defiance; he is ready to take on whatever challenges await him. And, of course, the challenges for David Bowie as Ziggy Stardust are laid out right from the first moments of the album when, in the opening song, "Five Years," we learn of Earth's imminent destruction by

The Rise and Fall of Ziggy Stardust and the Spiders from Mars album, 1972   *Author's Collection*

an unnamed forthcoming cataclysmic event. Ultimately, through the course of the album, our hero becomes an antihero as he succumbs to the sex, drugs, and rock 'n' roll dangers and delights of rock stardom, winding up in the final track, "Rock 'n' Roll Suicide," a mere husk of his former self, staggering home at dawn washed up and beaten and fully cohering to the "Rise and Fall" bookend promise of the album's title. While the art-historical borrowing is not as blatant as on the previous two album covers with their Pre-Raphaelite and silver screen parodies, the triumph of the cover here is that for the first time the role being played is one totally of Bowie's own making: Ziggy Stardust—an androgynous, extraterrestrial rock god who has come to save us all. While he's by no means Bowie's first character (Major Tom, in particular, can claim that honor and prior to that the fleeting eccentric figures of the doomed debut album), it is the first time a character of his own invention has been fleshed out and put on display for the world to see, visually and physically brought to life on the album cover and on the concert stage. On *The Rise and Fall of Ziggy Stardust and the Spiders from Mars*, sound and vision synergize like never before. And unlike the (albeit endearing) stylistic mashup of the preceding *Hunky Dory*, the songs and instrumentation here are honed and consistent and tie in perfectly with the electric rock promise of Bowie's jumpsuited, purple-booted appearance.

Bowie produced so many superb album covers that it seems unfair to single just one out, and it's undoubtedly cheeky of me to suggest that the one I have selected is his finest. Indeed, the way that he so seamlessly and convincingly transferred his primary themes from an aural medium to a visual one and vice versa is part of his legend. Nevertheless, in order to show the depth of thought and thematic communication he was capable of—a talent frequently brought to bear throughout his career—the cover of *Aladdin Sane* serves as a sublime example.

Released in April 1973 following the commercial and critical successes of *The Rise and Fall of Ziggy Stardust and the Spiders from Mars* (1972) and the resurgent *Hunky Dory*—originally released in December 1971 but achieving its peak chart position in the wake of the *Ziggy Stardust* album's career-launching popularity—Bowie's sixth studio album, *Aladdin Sane*, gave him his first number one chart placing. Notably, it was his first release written from the perspective of actually being a star as opposed to his previous works where he was still an aspirant. Reaching the top position on the U.K. album chart and fueled by more than 100,000 advance orders, *Aladdin Sane* also marked a surge in popularity for the artist in the United States, the market that had always proven to be significantly more difficult for him to this point, with the album entering the top twenty and eventually peaking at number seventeen. While he would far surpass this mark in the future, this was an important declamatory statement.

Bowie regarded *Aladdin Sane* as a schizophrenic album. Described by the artist himself as being the story of Ziggy Stardust in America, the album was written while he was on tour in the United States in 1972, with lyrics scribbled on a notepad balanced on his lap or his tray table while peering through the window of a train or a Greyhound bus as he traversed the vast expanses and viewed myriad foreign sights for the first time. In interviews, he described this as a schizoid experience: of being a part of proceedings and yet removed from them at the same time. This wasn't *his* world—it was a far cry from his familiar London environs—and yet here he was smack-dab in the middle of it. Parts of the experience were dangerous and exciting, and parts were dull and monotonous. And at the same time, the division between David Bowie and Ziggy Stardust was blurring as his success in the guise of his alien alter ego burgeoned and he became lost somewhere in the middle. As he told Cameron Crowe in a *Rolling Stone* interview in 1976, "I fell for Ziggy too. It was quite easy to become obsessed night and day with the character. I became Ziggy Stardust. David Bowie went totally out the window. Everybody was convincing me that I was a Messiah ... I got totally lost in the fantasy." Originally penned as *A Lad Insane*, division and the dark tension of opposing forces, both physical and psychological, became the underlying theme of the self-knowing and wittily titled *Aladdin Sane*. In a sense, David Bowie felt he was indeed going insane, and as the best artists do, he channeled that highly fertile material into his work.

The cover of *Aladdin Sane* is by equal amounts striking and disturbing and a firm favorite of many Bowie fans for its blatant "otherness." No one but David Bowie could ever have come up with such a concept in 1973; he was already established as a style icon as well as a rock star. On the album's release, *New Musical Express* writer Charles Shaar Murray began his review with the following comment on the record's packaging, "Firstly, the cover, which will be a definite asset to any chic home. You'll see it strewn on Axminster carpets in expensive colour supplement stereo ads, and carried with token attempts at unobtrusiveness under the arms of the fashionable." More recently, the *Guardian*'s Mick McCann has described it as "the Mona Lisa of album covers." Reproduced on innumerable items of clothing and other merchandise over the years, the cover of *Aladdin Sane* has become one of rock's most endearing and potent images and perhaps the most instantly recognizable of all Bowie's works.

The cover image is a heavily manipulated photographic portrait shot by the late Brian Duffy (1933–2010) that is bordered only by the physical edge of the cover itself and results in Bowie having a kind of floating vibe. A glam-rock image shot through with artifice, he is pictured with long orange hair, red lipstick on his slightly parted lips, red eye shadow, no eyebrows, and long black eyelashes. Dominating and splitting his face from top left to lower right is a red, black, and blue lightning flash symbol that mirrors the backdrop used in his Ziggy Stardust shows and carries long-established connotations of danger that range from Nazi Storm Trooper insignias to the warnings on electrical fuse boxes. Many later acts would use similar iconography, Black Sabbath and KISS to name just two. A further and even more potent connotation of the lightning bolt insignia is the inference of mental imbalance, of schizophrenia, which will be discussed in more depth shortly. Bowie's face is unnaturally pink, and his high cheekbones are heavily accentuated. Contrasted against these bright colors is the metallic gray of his upper shoulders and neck that then blends to an overexposed, brilliant white for the remainder of his visible torso, a hue that closely mirrors the background that surrounds him. Bowie casts no shadow, which imbues the image with a lack of context. It is as if he is floating in nothingness, a vacuum. With his eyes fully closed and therefore eliminating any possibility of direct communication with the viewer, there is a neutrality of expression. Inexplicably, a pool of liquid lies collected at his left collarbone, following the contours of his body yet defying gravity and contributing much to the overall unreal quality of the image.

If the eyes are the oft-held window to the soul, then here Bowie is at his most secretive. On the covers of the earlier *The Man Who Sold the World* and *Hunky Dory* albums, the viewer was charged with wondering what the artist was thinking in those pictures, as the Pre-Raphaelite and silver screen goddess parodies carried with them purposeful inherent qualities of emotional removal and psychological absence from the subject's immediate environs. On those covers, Bowie was pictured gazing up and outward, pondering matters beyond those the viewer could see. On *Aladdin Sane*, however, he goes a step further by having his eyes completely closed, something that introduces a range of possibilities. He could be fully awake and inwardly ruminating, or he could be asleep. He could even be dead. Certainly, the whiteness of his skin does nothing to suggest that blood flows through his veins and that life exists within. And if it does exist, then he must be more alien than human.

Adding to the sense of unreality of the image, the space surrounding Bowie is both featureless and borderless, effectively creating a visual portrayal of nothingness that simply fades away and does not contextualize him in any way. There is nothing in the background at all to aid the viewer in locating the image, being plain, unbroken white, and although Bowie's vividly colored head and hair stand out in stark contrast, at the point where his torso meets the bottom of the cover, the white background bleeds into his body.

One of Bowie's finest talents beyond his unmatchable performance skill set was the ability to tap into existing art and even well back into art history in order to borrow symbolism to recontextualize for his own ends. He did it with the Pre-Raphaelite parody on *The Man Who Sold the World*, the silver screen goddess parody on the cover of *Hunky Dory*, the Erich Heckel–inspired pose on *"Heroes,"* and elsewhere. On *Aladdin Sane*, he borrows once again from existing iconography to depict insanity in the form of schizophrenia—and with great effect. Many examples of split-face symbolism exist that predate *Aladdin Sane*. In the art of Paul Klee (1879–1940), for example, similarities to Bowie's

Aladdin Sane image can be seen, especially in the divided faces of *Physiognomic Flash* (1927) and *The Clown* (1929). As Bowie was an enormous enthusiast for the visual arts, the awareness of such paintings surely lurked in his mind. Klee's art, in particular, was frequently concerned with expressing mental illness, especially the paranoid-schizoid condition. Klee's splitting of the face in both *Physiognomic Flash* and *The Clown* was based on the beliefs of Swiss poet, writer, philosopher, physiognomist, and theologian Johann Kaspar Lavater, who believed that dualities, even the fine line between madness and genius, could be physiognomically detectable in human faces. Bowie's *Aladdin Sane* image, with the album title playfully backing it up, clearly mirrors this notion.

Even in the far less arty field of medicine, the symbolism of the split face was established to convey the schizophrenic condition. Two psychology textbooks from the 1970s display this and are in a comparable vein to Bowie/Duffy's work: *Soul Murder: Persecution in the Family* (1973) by Morton Schatzman and *Schizophrenia: An Introduction to Research and Theory* (1978) by Glenn Shean.

Bowie's interest in mental illness and psychological disturbance existed well before 1973 and indeed was a cornerstone of his work that lasted throughout his career. Most critics rightly attribute this interest largely to his childhood experiences with his psychologically troubled half brother Terry Burns, his mother's son and his father's stepson, ten years David's senior. Various biographers have painstakingly pieced together the relationship between David and Terry. The consensus is that in David's early to preteen years, they were very close indeed, with the young David rather idolizing Terry, who, among other things, introduced him to literature, including the work of the beat poets, and music, particularly jazz and rhythm and blues. With a deteriorating relationship in the family home between Terry and his mother and stepfather, who seemingly resented his wife's firstborn son, Terry finally moved out when called on to do National Service, and the two siblings parted ways, from then on seeing each other only periodically. From 1969 on, afflicted by increasingly frequent incapacitating panic attacks, Terry began to be hospitalized regularly at London's Cane Hill Hospital—also called Cane Hill Asylum. Eventually, in the late morning of January 16, 1985, the then forty-seven-year-old Terry, by now diagnosed as suffering from severe schizophrenia, slipped out of Cane Hill and made his way to the nearby South Coulsdon train station, where he stood waiting on the platform. Just after midday, as the Littlehampton-to-London express approached the station, he stepped down from the platform and lay down across the tracks, facing away from the train, with his neck on the rail. The driver saw him but had no chance of stopping in time, and Terry was killed instantly.

Terry was not the only example of psychological disturbance in Bowie's childhood; indeed, such diagnoses were not at all uncommon in Bowie's family. Terry and David's mother, Peggy, had three sisters who were affected. Her sister Vivienne was diagnosed with schizophrenia; a second sister, Una, was treated with electroshock therapy for depression and schizophrenia; and a third sister, Nora, had a lobotomy in order to cure what was described as "bad nerves." As for Terry, a few years before his death, he had tried to end his life by jumping out of a window at Cane Hill, fracturing his arm and leg in the process in an act that would later inspire the song "Jump They Say" on his famous half brother's album *Black Tie White Noise* (1993). And just three weeks before his successful suicide, he had gone to the same train station with the same intention but had changed his mind at the last minute, climbing back onto the platform as a train approached.

In an interview in U.S. rock magazine *Creem*, at the time of the release of *The Man Who Sold the World*, interviewer Patrick Salvo commented on the apparent personality disorders evident in the songs, to which Bowie replied, "You're right. It happened to my brother ... I mean, there's a schizoid streak within my family, so I dare say I'm affected by that." Five years later in an interview with *Playboy* magazine in 1976, he was asked, "Does the fact that there is insanity in your family frighten you?" Bowie replied, "My brother Terry's in an asylum right now. I'd like to believe that the insanity is because our family is all genius, but I'm afraid that's not true ... I'm quite fond of the insanity, actually. It's a nice thing to throw out at parties, don't you think? Everybody finds empathy in a nutty family. Everybody says, 'Oh, yes, my family is quite mad.' Mine really is. No fucking about. . . . Most of them are nutty; in, just out of, or going into, an institution. Or dead."

Bowie's critiquing of his direct experiences with mental illness was seldom overtly expressed—the above-mentioned "Jump They Say" and "All the Madmen" from *The Man Who Sold the World* being two notable exceptions. Rather, he tended to write more expansively in ways that encompassed multiple alienations: psychological, gender-based, physical (*Diamond Dogs*), and generational. Nevertheless, it is on the cover of *Aladdin Sane* that he gives his most potent visual realization of alienation due to psychological disorder.

From this point on, every David Bowie album cover would offer a carefully considered and highly effective visual gateway to the music inside regardless of whatever musical style he was visiting at any given time. It had been a very short journey from the total disparity between the two elements of the debut album, *David Bowie*, to the seamless synergy of *The Rise and Fall of Ziggy Stardust and the Spiders from Mars* and the timeless depiction of one of his primary thematic concerns—psychological disturbance and alienation—of his pìece de résistance, *Aladdin Sane*, a rock 'n' roll marketing lesson well (and quickly) learned.

14

"Hooked to the Silver Screen"

David Bowie the Movie and TV Actor

It has often been noted that David Bowie adopted an actor's approach to his career as a musician, playing a succession of roles and changing image and/or musical style much like an actor might pick up different roles in an ongoing succession of plays or movies. Rather than suggesting he was a musician who behaved *like* an actor, perhaps it's more accurate to regard him as an actor first and foremost, whose role-playing talents and other allied theatrical skills were clearly evident and at the foundation of whatever medium he undertook to express himself through, music or otherwise. Certainly, this is the view he had of himself, in interviews often referring to his trade as acting rather than music and as early as 1971 crediting himself on the back cover of the *Hunky Dory* album as "the actor." One thing is certain: his skills as an actor were of the highest quality, as his on-screen track record examined in this chapter demonstrates.

Just after David Bowie died, on January 10, 2016, Anthony Lane wrote the following tribute in the *New Yorker*: "Bowie, who died on Sunday, at the age of sixty-nine, was a man of the movies ... his career, so conscientiously self-wrought, was more akin to that of a movie star than to that of a rocker, and it also suggested that he grasped the force of the moving image, and its fragile half-life, more acutely than many of those who bestride the dramatic profession. 'What do you think I'm like?,' he asked Dick Cavett, who was interviewing him in 1974. 'A working actor,' Cavett said. 'That's very good,' his guest, who had yet to appear in a feature film, replied."

Those who have not followed David Bowie's screen career may well be surprised at the number of appearances he has made. (He also appeared with great success on the Broadway stage in *The Elephant Man*, a feat explored in chapter 15.)

Promotional poster

The Big Movie Roles

The Man Who Fell to Earth (1976)

When David Bowie made his movie-acting debut in a leading role, it was appropriately as an alien in the highly regarded, now cult status Nicolas Roeg movie *The Man Who Fell to Earth* (1976). As Thomas Jerome Newton, Bowie's character had come to Earth from his dying, dehydrating home planet to seek water, but once there, through a complex series of events, he finds himself unable to return. Becoming addicted to the earthly delights of alcohol, television, and sex and exposed as an alien, he ends the film washed up and impotent in a manner not dissimilar to the end that befell Ziggy Stardust four years earlier on Bowie's career kick-starting album *The Rise and Fall of Ziggy Stardust and the Spiders from Mars* (1972). Bowie is cast superbly in this fine movie. He was handpicked for the role by Roeg, who saw a natural quality of alienation in him that Roeg was convinced would transfer well to film despite Bowie's lack of film credits up to that point. Roeg had seen footage of his chosen leading man in Alan Lentob's BBC documentary *Cracked Actor* (1975), and this was the moment he became convinced that David Bowie was to be his man. The specific scene that attracted Roeg occurs at around five minutes into *Cracked Actor*, when an unhealthily stick-thin and pale David Bowie is seen sitting in the back of a limousine traveling through the desert, as cocooned and as out of place with the environment through which he is traveling as it is possible to be. Drinking milk from a carton, he compares the alienation that he felt as an Englishman transplanted to the United States to that of a fly in his milk—the fate of a foreign object. Weird, experimental, daring, and, at times, quaintly dated, *The Man Who Fell to Earth* is essential viewing for Bowie fans as well as being deservedly considered a groundbreaking milestone in science-fiction filmmaking.

Just a Gigolo (1978)

Bowie is cast once again as an outsider in this (mostly deservedly) much-maligned and unlikely black comedy directed by David Hemmings. He plays the role of Paul Ambrosius von Przygodski, an unemployed soldier who has returned home to Berlin after World War I and finds the world that he had once known changed forever. Unable to find work, Bowie's character becomes entangled in the Berlin underworld and takes employment as a gigolo at a local brothel run by Baroness von Semering, played by Marlene Dietrich in her last-ever feature film. In a street brawl between the Nazis and Communists, he is killed by a stray bullet, leaving both sides squabbling over his body. Ultimately, the Nazis win the battle, and he ends up buried as a martyr by the perpetrators of a cause he never supported. Bowie agreed to do the movie because of his interest in gigolos and in Berlin and because of Marlene Dietrich's involvement. Regrettably, Dietrich's scenes were shot in Paris while the rest of the movie was shot in Germany, and the two never met. The end result was a film that Bowie was not proud of, quipping in an interview with *New Musical Express* in 1980, "Everybody who was involved in that film—when they meet each other now, they look away.... Listen, you were disappointed, and you weren't even in it. Imagine how we felt.... It was my 32 Elvis Presley movies rolled into one." *Just a Gigolo* is most decidedly nonessential viewing.

The Hunger (1983)

In this mostly well-regarded cult classic that is, unsurprisingly given the subject matter, particularly popular with goths, David Bowie plays the role of an eighteenth-century cellist and music teacher named John Blaylock, who also happens to be a vampire living in modern-day New York. Bowie was reportedly delighted to be in a movie directed by Tony Scott. Bowie's character and Miriam, his 6,000-year-old lover played by Catherine Deneuve, have a penchant for prowling Manhattan's discos in search of prey, but things go wrong when he begins aging fast despite his blood intake. In desperation, he attacks, kills, and drinks the blood of one of the couple's music students, but it is to no avail. After he collapses, Miriam places him in a coffin, where he is destined to suffer eternal damnation, and begins an affair with a doctor played by Susan Sarandon. From there, the events remain as messy as the preceding scenes have been, and the plot reaches a suitably tragic end. *The Hunger* has been criticized for being heavy on atmosphere but less so on action, while other critics have regarded it as a case of style over substance. Nevertheless, *The Hunger* does have its share of fans and is well worth viewing for those who would wish to make up their own minds about it. Of particular note to Bowie fans is the rather wonderful trivia fact that, according to scriptwriter Michael Thomas, rather than have a professional cellist perform in the scene that required Blaylock to actually play the instrument, David Bowie went above and beyond the expectations of an actor by learning how to play it himself to the standard required of the scene.

Merry Christmas, Mr. Lawrence (1983)

The highly regarded Japanese director Nagisa Oshima had David Bowie in his sights for the leading role as far back as 1980 after seeing him perform in *The Elephant Man* on Broadway. Set in a Japanese prisoner-of-war camp during World War II, Bowie plays the role of Major Jack Celliers, a captured New Zealand soldier. The plot of the film centers on the relationships and power struggles that exist between Celliers and three fellow captives, including the film's titular character Lieutenant Colonel John (Mr.) Lawrence (played by Tom Conti), and their Japanese captors. Remarkably, while Oshima directed other actors with considerable detailed instruction, he requested of Bowie that he largely ad-lib his role, something he relished doing, and Bowie reportedly delved deeply into himself in order to do so. Celliers's treatment of his family before he went away to war—especially his failure to protect his handicapped brother from bullying and other harm—is the guilty secret that he admits to Lawrence in the camp, and as he admitted in interviews at the time of the film's release, this plot twist forced Bowie to consider his actions toward his own family, especially his half brother Terry, who suffered decades of psychological instability and incarceration in mental institutions. (Terry would go on to commit suicide in 1985.) For the sheer quality of the acting and the superb direction alone, *Merry Christmas, Mr. Lawrence* is one of the most successful and highly respected of David Bowie's movies and is definitely a must-watch.

Absolute Beginners (1986)

The considerable contribution of his music aside—especially the hit theme song that bears the movie's name—in *Absolute Beginners*, David Bowie features for only about twenty minutes in the entire film. Nevertheless, his character is a strong and memorable one, and the movie is much the better for his inclusion. Set in the tumult of a hot London summer in 1958 against the Notting Hill race riots and underlying and ongoing postwar tensions, the plot is a kind of coming-of-age for England's capital as it enters the jazz and early rock 'n' roll era. Disaffected youth search for meaning and belonging within a rapidly changing and increasingly consumer- and advertising-driven cultural milieu. Admitting that he drew on his experiences during a brief tenure in an advertising agency after leaving school, Bowie excels as the somewhat loathsome advertising executive Vendice Partners, who speaks in advertising slogans and epitomizes hype and the shallowness and cynicism of the new way. Director Julien Temple said of Bowie's acting, "The character he plays really represents the whole change of Britain in the fifties—the frozen food, the cars with fins. David knew just how to get the right mid-Atlantic accent for an adman trying to be so slick and American but every so often slipping back into cockney." While *Absolute Beginners* received a very mixed reaction from critics, anyone interested in watching the full gamut of David Bowie's acting prowess should definitely watch this contentious film.

Labyrinth (1986)

Surprisingly a significant underachiever at the box office on its release in spite of the extremely high pedigree of those creating it, David Bowie's well-known and much-loved kids' movie has over time become a staple in the fantasy musical genre, with an appeal far more widespread than the cult status achieved by many of his works. Post-theater releases on video and DVD have been consistently high sellers, and the movie today can be considered something of a longer-term success story for all those involved. Involving heavyweights Jim Henson of *Muppets* fame and George Lucas of *Star Wars* fame, with Brian Froud as conceptual designer and Terry Jones of *Monty Python* as one of the notable screenwriters, *Labyrinth* was intended to be a lighter-weight development of an earlier movie that Henson and Froud had worked on together, *The Dark Crystal* (1982).

In *Labyrinth*, David Bowie plays the leading role of Jareth the Goblin King, who steals the young brother, Toby, of the movie's other main protagonist, Sarah Williams, played by Jennifer Connelly. In order to rescue Toby—or otherwise lose him forever—Sarah is given thirteen hours to solve Jareth's labyrinth. The movie follows her journey as she battles Jareth to save Toby, both aided and hindered by a host of typically weird and wonderful Henson puppets. Bowie's character is funny, sexy, charming, and hugely endearing; a villain that one cannot help but love regardless of one's age. In terms of Jareth's appearance, his swashbuckling, flamboyant, hands-on-hips image bears some resemblance to Bowie's early 1970s glam-era persona Ziggy Stardust. In addition to acting in his lead role, Bowie wrote and recorded five songs for the movie, singing four of them as Jareth. The most popular and enduring of these was the up-tempo dance number "Magic Dance," which was also released as a single.

It is *Labyrinth* that boasts the mantle of David Bowie's most loved and probably best movie, perhaps being shadowed to the finish line by the (albeit very different) work that is *The Man Who Fell to Earth*. A perennial children's favorite, *Labyrinth* has also been highly effective in keeping the David Bowie name alive from decade to decade and introducing a host of new fans to his wider work. As David Bowie told interviewer Virginia Campbell for Movieline in 1992, "Every Christmas a new flock of children comes up to me and says, 'Oh! You're the one who's in *Labyrinth*!'" For numerous reasons, *Labyrinth* is an absolute must-see.

Basquiat (1996)

Jean-Michel Basquiat was a graffiti artist who briefly became the toast of the New York art scene prior to his drug-related death in 1988. As a fan of Basquiat's mentor and friend Andy Warhol, David Bowie seemed a natural fit for the role of Warhol in the film. He had met the famous artist in person and had admitted that Warhol was a significant influence on his own work. He was also a genuine fan of Basquiat's work. Highly fictionalized, the movie is a critical commentary on the uber-fickle cliques of trendy art movements and scenes, and this was one of the most attractive aspects of the work for Bowie, who was extremely enthusiastic about the project throughout. Many commentators believe that Bowie steals the show in *Basquiat*, portraying Warhol as funny and tragically flawed, a genius and speculator. Certainly, Bowie is at the very top of his acting game, showing genuine understanding and fondness for the role he is playing. While far more arty than any household-name commercial blockbuster, the critically acclaimed *Basquiat* is not one of Bowie's better-known films, but it is certainly one of his better ones. His portrayal of Andy Warhol is eerily superb; he looks extremely like his subject—something aided by his wearing of Warhol's actual clothing and wig—and his mannerisms and speech are faultless. *Basquiat* is a David Bowie gem.

More Minor Movie Roles

The Virgin Soldiers (1969)

David Bowie's first role in a feature film lasted literally just a couple of seconds. Set in Singapore in 1950 during the Malayan Emergency, *The Virgin Soldiers* is a forgettable film in which soldiers stationed in the outpost dream of winning the love of their sergeant major's daughter. Bowie appears very briefly in a non-speaking role in a bar scene, being bodily propelled toward the door by another soldier—presumably being evicted for disorderly behavior.

Christiane F.: Wir Kinder vom Bahnhof Zoo (1981)

For the first time playing himself in a movie, this bleak, hard-hitting, but moving story directed by Ulrich Edel remains a cult classic. Marketed as a real-life biopic, the film portrays a young teenage girl's ruination in a seedy underworld of drugs, exploitation, and prostitution. Bowie's performance consists of giving a concert early in the film that is attended by the movie's antihero star, Christiane, who is a big fan. In addition to his on-screen appearance as himself, music from his *Low* and *"Heroes"* albums makes up the bulk of the sound track. While *Christiane F.* is at times difficult viewing, it is also essential viewing.

Yellowbeard (1983)

Probably appreciated more today than it was at the time of release, *Yellowbeard* should have been better given its very strong cast of well-known comedians, especially the *Monty Python* crew. David Bowie appears in a brief cameo as a character named Shark, complete with a fin protruding from his back.

Into the Night (1985)

This John Landis–directed comedy-thriller features David Bowie as a British hit man. A complex tale of international jewel smuggling, the film was notable for the large number of cameo appearances by big-name directors and filmmakers, leading *Time Out* to comment in its review, "The casting of innumerable major film-makers in small roles seems an unnecessary bit of elbow-jogging, but David Bowie makes an excellent contribution as an English hit man."

The Last Temptation of Christ (1988)

Long a fan of Martin Scorsese, Bowie was very pleased to take on the cameo role of Pontius Pilate in this contentious dramatization of Jesus' life. With a plot based around critiquing how Jesus coped with various temptations—the most controversial and polarizing scenes being the depictions of him imagining being involved in sexual activity—Bowie's interrogation of Jesus is excellent, portraying Pilate as cold, clinical, aloof, and cynical.

The Linguini Incident (1991)

One of the most maligned of Bowie's movies, this comedy set in New York finds him cast as a British bartender who is desperate to marry an American woman in order to get a green card to allow him to stay in the United States. He pursues his fellow worker Lucy (Rosanna Arquette), who is a would-be Houdini-style escape artist, leading to a teaser written on the promotional poster that promised, "He wants to be tied down. She wants to be tied up. It's not what you think." Reviews were mostly negative on release, and the movie hasn't fared much better with time, Charlie Lyne of the *Guardian* titling his 2016 review of the movie's reissue "The Linguini Incident: A Bowie Rerelease Nobody Needs to See."

Twin Peaks: Fire Walk with Me (1992)

Also a big fan of *Eraserhead* director David Lynch, in *Twin Peaks: Fire Walk with Me*, prequel to the television series, Bowie plays a short and extremely weird scene as a flamboyant FBI agent named Phillip Jeffries. The plot concerns the investigations into the murder of a girl named Teresa Banks and the last week of life of another girl, Laura Palmer, in the fictional town of Twin Peaks. Bowie, as Jeffries, mysteriously reappears after being missing for two years, and while it is uncertain if he is alive or dead—his appearance is completely otherworldly—he is undeniably stylish. Described in *Rolling Stone* as a "nattily attired prophet of doom," he warns of a mystery woman named Judy before ranting on further in an over-the-top U.S. southern accent. David Bowie's appearance in *Twin Peaks: Fire Walk with Me* is impossible to fathom but highly impactful.

Gunslinger's Revenge (1998)

Widely regarded as one of Bowie's worst movies, receiving mostly terrible reviews on release and since, this Italian spaghetti western, directed by Giovanni Veronesi and set in 1860, has little obvious merit beyond being a curiosity. In it, a notorious killer, Jack Sikora (played by Bowie), provokes a gunslinging legend, Johnny Lowen (Harvey Keitel), who comes out of retirement to settle the score. Bowie's performance is nevertheless interesting in that it shows him in an uncharacteristically nasty and villainous role, raping and murdering and being generally obnoxious. As noted by many critics, while his acting is good, his accent compromises his believability. Aside from some admittedly fine visual moments, the movie's most redeeming feature is perhaps the unexpected twist at the end, where Jack is killed—not in his long-sought-after duel with Johnny but instead in an accidental fire caused by the village idiot.

Everybody Loves Sunshine (1999)

Retitled *B.U.S.T.E.D* for the U.S. release, the pairing of Bowie with Goldie—the English drum 'n' bass musician, deejay, visual artist, and actor—in this mostly well-received gang warfare movie is an interesting one. In this very English story set in the gritty, mean backstreets of Manchester, Bowie plays an aging gangster—a "G-man"—called Bernie, while Goldie plays a just-released gangster hell-bent on ensuring that his partner, cousin, and fellow ex-con Ray (Andrew Goth, who also wrote and directed), who wants to go straight, doesn't leave the gang as he wishes to. With the threat of triad gangs increasingly in the mix, it falls to Bernie to try to keep the peace. Visually excellent and with some strong performances throughout, *Everybody Loves Sunshine* is well worth viewing.

Mr. Rice's Secret (2000)

Given star billing in this Canadian film despite the paucity of his on-screen time—he appears in flashback scenes that total around ten minutes' duration—David Bowie impresses in his role as the mysterious Mr. Rice, the deceased neighbor of a twelve-year-old boy who has cancer. It is a story with a fine moral, as Bowie helps the boy, Owen Walters (played by Bill Switzer), find enjoyment in his life. When the film was released, most reviews were negative, including Elvis Mitchell's review in the *New York Times*. Nevertheless, Mitchell praised Bowie's performance, stating, "His work here is smooth and has weight. Mr. Bowie has always displayed a sneaky power in small, supporting roles. He pops right out of the screen, and as the gentle and slightly otherworldly Mr. Rice, he suggests more than just the guy next door in a flannel shirt and chinos."

Zoolander (2001)

Directed by and starring Ben Stiller, *Zoolander* is a mostly effective and generally well-received spoof on the fashion industry. David Bowie plays a cameo role as himself—cast as the epitome of cool—charged with judging a "walk-off" between top model Derek Zoolander (Stiller) and pretender-to-the-top-model-throne Hansel McDonald (Owen Wilson).

The Prestige (2006)

In this Christopher Nolan film about two rival stage magicians whose rivalry ends in tragedy, David Bowie has a small yet crucial role. On the film's release, critic Liz Hoggard wrote a critique in the *Guardian* titled "Why I Love David Bowie's Acting." She enthused, "He is astonishing in Christopher Nolan's *The Prestige* where he plays real-life electrical genius Nikola Tesla, who conducted wild experiments into time travel, death rays and interstellar communication. Nolan says he refused to cast anyone but Bowie. It's not a vanity role, however. Unrecognizable with a walrus moustache and pouchy eyes, Tesla is more Ricky Gervais than Thin White Duke. But you won't see a more magnetic performance this year." Hoggard is right. This late career performance is utterly convincing and adds yet further intrigue to the unanswerable question of what would Bowie's career have been like if he'd forgone music and dedicated himself to stage and screen acting only. The moment in the movie when he emerges from the heart of a huge arcing tesla coil is pure cinematic magic, and with its futuristic science-fiction allusions, it is perhaps the most perfectly apt scene David Bowie ever appeared in on-screen.

SpongeBob's Atlantis SquarePantis (2007)

Delighted to be offered a part in an iconic children's television show, David Bowie took a guest-speaking role in this forty-five-minute *SpongeBob Square-Pants* television special, playing the part of Lord Royal Highness, who rules the lost continent of Atlantis. As he wrote on his blog at the time, "It's happened. At last. I've hit the Holy Grail of animation gigs. Yesterday I got to be a character on . . . tan-tara . . . *SpongeBob SquarePants*. Oh Yeah!! We, the family, are thrilled. Nothing else need happen this year, well, this week anyway. My character in this special longform (I think a half hour special) show is called 'Lord Royal Highness.' Alrighteee!!"

Bandslam (2009)

Notable for being the final film David Bowie ever appeared in, this well-received romantic-comedy musical directed by Todd Graff is also known as *High School*

Rock. Bowie's cameo appearance late in the movie, playing himself, is brief but memorable. Contacting the wannabe band with the Samuel Beckett–derived name of I Can't Go On, I'll Go On, whose formation and journey is the plot of the movie, he overwhelms the band's manager, Will Burton (played by Gaelan Connell), an avid Bowie fan, with his offer to sign them to his new indie record label. With surprise and delight, Will falls down in the hallway of the school, landing in a way that mimics Bowie's bodily configuration on the cover of his *Lodger* album of 1979; held in his outstretched hand, Will's cell phone still glows with Bowie's message. It's a genuinely funny moment and a small but dignified way for David Bowie to close the door on his acting career.

A Selection of David Bowie's Other Screen Roles

The Pistol Shot (1968)

David Bowie made his fleeting television debut in the BBC's *The Pistol Shot* on May 20, 1968. In this drama based on the life of Alexander Pushkin, the Russian poet, playwright, and novelist, Bowie dances a short minuet with his then girlfriend Hermione Farthingale.

The Looking Glass Murders (1970)

Now of considerable historical value for Bowie scholars and fans alike, this Scottish television special renamed and adapted the mime show *Pierrot in Turquoise* by director and deviser Lindsay Kemp, the now-famous-in-his-own-right leader of the mime troupe to which Bowie belonged. With Kemp playing the role of Pierrot, the program aired on July 8, 1970, and featured David Bowie playing the part of Cloud, an extended role requiring both acting and singing. With his original music forming the backdrop to the piece, of particular note is the song "Threepenny Pierrot," the melody of which was recycled for another early release, "London Bye Ta Ta."

Baal (1982)

David Bowie was personally invited by director Alan Clarke to play the lead role in the BBC's production of Bertolt Brecht's first play, written in 1918 and far less well known than his later collaborations with Kurt Weill.

This frequently brutal and cruel story of a self-centered, debauched, wandering minstrel named after a bestial pagan deity was an extremely juicy and in some ways pertinent role for Bowie. Parallels with the excesses of rock stardom abounded in the story line as Baal, a renowned drunk with rotten teeth and a

Bertolt Brecht's *Baal* by David Bowie. A soundtrack EP of the BBC TV film of the same name, 1982   *Author's Collection*

dirty, disheveled appearance who was nevertheless completely irresistible to women and despised by men for it, wallows in alcohol, sensuality, and deceit, abandoning women to destitution or suicide when they fall pregnant, stabbing his best friend to death in a jealous rage, and winding up on the run for his freedom and his life. In the end, he dies alone in a woodcutter's cottage, a dubious testament to a man who lived life his own way without compromise. Bowie performs five songs during the course of the play, accompanying himself on the banjo in the manner of a wandering bard. In reviews at the time, Bowie was credited with having given a very good performance, while the play itself and the BBC's production of it did not fare as well. Typical was the review in the *Sun* newspaper, which declared that Bowie's performance had "confirmed that he is a creditable actor. But what an unspeakable play in which to prove it!"

In an overview of Bowie's on-screen appearances on the website timeout .com in 2013, critic Tom Huddleston summarized his subject's career: "He's played an alien, a vampire, an FBI agent, a Roman general and a goblin with vegetables stuffed down his pants. But somehow he always manages to remain uniquely Bowie." It's a good summation. Because of his own inherent quality of being "different"—the very reason many directors wanted him in their movies in the first place—he was able to inject extra depth and nuances into the roles he played, taking them beyond two dimensions and a script. And that is the mark of a good actor. Of course, because of his fame, it was always abundantly clear to audiences that they were watching David Bowie, mega rock star. Unlike other music stars who try to turn their hand to film, Bowie was able to transcend that initial showbiz impact and be of far more value to the screen roles he took on than being merely a big-name draw card.

The Snowman (1982)

Now an annual favorite of many families at Christmastime, Bowie makes a short, spoken introduction to this twenty-six-minute Channel 4 animation of Raymond Briggs's classic story of a snowman coming to life and taking a young boy to the North Pole to meet Santa Claus. Free of speech, except for the song "Walking in the Air," the music of Howard Blake carries the movie, but Bowie's gentle warmth in delivering the introduction to this children's classic, promising the viewer a "magical day" with a glint in his eye, is a real highlight.

Extras (BBC, 2006)

Quite possibly his best and most loved cameo appearance in a television series and also his last, Bowie stole the episode when playfully mocking the desperately hapless wannabe Andy Millman (Ricky Gervais) by singing his mock-improvised song "Little Fat Man." Straight-faced, Bowie sits at the piano and delivers lines such as "Chubby little loser . . . see his pug-nosed face" to the crowded bar, leaving Millman cut to shreds. It is a masterstroke and epitomizes Gervais and cowriter Stephen Merchant's comedy-of-embarrassment style that had captivated U.K. audiences with their first series, *The Office*, and then *Extras*. Bowie, always an avid fan of his country's uniquely self-effacing comedy, was delighted to fly from the United States to appear in this one-off role and was by all accounts very happy with his final television performance.

15

The Elephant Man

David Bowie's Triumph in Legitimate Theater

While critics and fans alike uniformly utilized the word *theatrical* to describe David Bowie's performance style, it was always within the context in which he was seen to be working: that of rock music and rock concerts. No one considered what he was doing to be "theater" per se; he was instead regarded as a theatrical rock performer. But such was the depth of his acting talent that not only was he given the chance to prove himself in this "purer" and more traditional art form—the legitimate theater—but also, when given that opportunity, he absolutely seized it with both hands and proved to one and all (and almost certainly to himself) that he shouldn't only be considered theatrical within a rock context but also could foot it with the best thespians walking the world's stages.

The Ultimate Test

If ever David Bowie's much-vaunted theatricality was given an acid test, it was when he took on the role of Joseph (aka John) Merrick in the Broadway production of *The Elephant Man*. Merrick (1862–1890) was a British man who had very severe facial and body deformities that continued to develop from age five on. Rejected by his father following the death of his mother, he earned a living as a freak show exhibit (aka a "curiosity") and was given the name The Elephant Man. After a tour of the Midlands, he became an exhibit in a penny gaff (a cheap variety show) in Whitechapel Road, located opposite the London Hospital, where he met a surgeon at the hospital, Frederick Treves, who was intrigued by his extreme condition and arranged to have photographs taken of Merrick. When the penny gaff was closed by order of the London police, Merrick was sent on tour through Europe. While in Belgium, he was robbed and abandoned in Brussels by his road manager. With difficulty, being penniless and unable to communicate properly, Merrick managed to make his way back to London, where he was eventually found by police in an advanced state of exhaustion and bewilderment. When police looked unsuccessfully for identification, all they found on him was a card with Frederick Treves's name on it, and they subsequently called the surgeon. The last four years of Merrick's short life then became his happiest ones, as his benefactor, Treves, who also became his close friend—another first for Merrick—arranged for him to live permanently within the hospital, the only true home of his adulthood, where he was no longer an alienated figure of cruel fun on display for public consumption and ridicule. During this time, having learned to communicate effectively despite his severe speech impediment and having convinced Treves of his intellect (previously, he was assumed by all to be an imbecile), he also enjoyed visits from wealthy and influential members of the London upper classes, both men and women, even including Alexandra, Princess of Wales. At just twenty-seven years of age, however, Merrick died from a dislocated neck, judged by Treves to have been caused by an attempt to sleep lying down as normal people did. The weight of his deformed head, it seems, proved to be too much for his neck to bear.

Given David Bowie's lifelong championing of the outcasts, freaks, and aliens of society, the story of Joseph Merrick was of considerable interest to him. Nevertheless, theater purists, theater critics, rock fans, and rock critics in unison raised their eyebrows high—as high as their skepticism—when his acceptance of the role was reported in the media. In anticipation of the coming challenge, Bowie told the *Daily Mirror*, "It is undoubtedly the biggest single challenge of my career. Going onto Broadway is the fulfillment of a great dream."

Bowie's engagement with *The Elephant Man* began when the director of the play, John Hofsiss, called him during recording sessions for the *Scary Monsters (and Super Creeps)* album. Bowie had watched a performance of *The Elephant Man* while in the United States, with Phillip Anglim in the lead role, and enjoyed it immensely. Hofsiss explained that Anglim would shortly be relinquishing the position and invited Bowie, whom he was convinced had what it took despite his lack of experience and any sort of track record in such demanding theater, to succeed him. Reportedly given just twenty-four hours to consider, Bowie jumped at the chance.

Before the play went on to its highly successful and high-profile run on Broadway, Bowie debuted in the role in Denver's Auditorium Theatre from July 29 to August 3, 1980, where the show completely sold out before opening.

The Accolades Roll In

Reviews were uniformly glowing. The review published in *Variety* on August 6, 1980, is illustrative: "The acting debut on the American stage of rock singer

David Bowie was greeted by a standing ovation in Denver when the singer, noted for his flamboyant musical style, took on the role of physically misshapen John Merrick, the human monster with a liking for culture. Drawing on an early mime background and the resourceful staging of his rock shows, Bowie displays the ability to project a complex character.... Bowie shows a mastery of movement and of vocal projection. Bowie takes the stage with authority to create a stirring performance. Vocally, he is both quick and sensitive. In scene after scene he builds poignantly, crying for the chance to become civilized, though he knows he will always be a freak; pleading for a home; though he knows his presence disturbs; and questioning the rules of society; though his well-being depends on their acceptance. Judging from his sensitive projection of this part, Bowie has the chance to achieve legit stardom."

With this short regional season in Denver completed, the traveling production then moved to Chicago, where it ran and attracted equal acclaim for another three weeks. Following this, it was on to New York and Broadway, where it ran for a full three-month season at the Booth Theatre. The *New York Post* described David Bowie's performance as being "shockingly good." The *New York Daily News* critic regarded his performance as "piercing and haunted," and the *New York Times* regarded him as "preternaturally wise." In short, any and all doubts that David Bowie could make a successful transition from the rock stage to the pretentiously named world of "legit" theater were dispelled. He won *everybody* over with the strength of his acting and the sheer depth and sensitivity of his portrayal of the unfortunate, severely afflicted Joseph Merrick. What made his performance all the more outstanding and memorable was his complete eschewing of the use of any prosthetics. Instead, he used only his own body, the audience "seeing" Merrick's disfigurements and physical disabilities through Bowie's control of gesture and nuance and hearing his severe speech impediments through the artist's carefully devised and rehearsed vocal calisthenics. Reportedly initially skeptical about Bowie's recruitment to the lead role, highly experienced professional actor Ken Ruta, the man who played opposite Bowie throughout the show's duration as the surgeon Frederick Treves, would conclude at its end, "He was incredible. Right on the money." Costar Jeanette Landis was equally impressed, opining, "He was a very pure actor. In fact, more professional than the actor he replaced."

Evidently, although he would never during his life repeat such a performance on the "legit" theater stage, the experience of playing the lead role in *The Elephant Man* was of enormous significance and importance to Bowie as an artist.

The Tragic Ending

Triumphant in every way though David Bowie was in *The Elephant Man*, the experience would end with Bowie relieved that it was over and troubled to the point that he missed several performances during the final weeks. This had nothing to do with the show but was instead due to the assassination of his friend John Lennon, shot by Mark Chapman in the archway of the Dakota Building, where Lennon lived. Unsubstantiated rumors circulated that Chapman had previously attended a performance of *The Elephant Man* and that David Bowie too may have been a target.

16

What's in a Name?

Why David Jones Became David Bowie

No rock artist has been associated with as many names as David Bowie has, and it says much about his approach to his art that any peers he has in terms of adopting multiple roles/names come from theater and the acting fraternity—and perhaps opera and musical theater—and not from popular music. His penchant for inventing and then shedding performative personas knows no equal, and underlying all of the layers is the delightful, true fact that at the heart of it all, even David Bowie is an invented name.

RCA Promotional poster   *Author's Collection*

He was, from the day he was born until the day he died, David Robert Jones. He never changed his name by popular poll to anything else. But in his closet were coat hooks for Major Tom, Ziggy Stardust, Aladdin Sane, Halloween Jack, Thomas Jerome Newton, the Plastic Soul Man, the Thin White Duke, Jareth the Goblin King, Nathan Adler, and many others.

Back at the Start

It was in January 1966 that the still unknown but highly ambitious David Jones changed his name to David Bowie. Although still very early in his career the bands the Konrads, the King Bees, and the Manish Boys were all behind him, and he was now with the Lower Third, a hard-hitting quartet—previously a trio—in the style of the Who. Bowie's talents as a front man were more than ever beginning to separate him from his bandmates, much to their chagrin, and as had been the case with his previous bands, the attention Bowie attracted led to tensions, jealousy, and accusations that he was not a team player. When the Lower Third gained a recording contract to record a single for Parlophone, it was David's songs that featured on both A- and B-sides. "You've Got a Habit of Leaving" backed by "Baby Loves That Way" was released in August 1965 and was credited to "Davy Jones and the Lower Third." The cream was rising to the top, and David Jones was emerging from the pack.

Advertised as the newly titled David Bowie and the Lower Third, a subsequent single, "Can't Help Thinking about Me," backed by "And I Say to Myself," was released on Pye Records. It fared no better than its predecessor, but by this time David Bowie was ready for another change, this time forming a hand-picked band in which he was undisputedly the kingpin: David Bowie and the Buzz. For a short time, Bowie was in both acts, then the Lower Third disintegrated. All too soon, the Buzz would be dispensed with as well, proving that, truly, David Bowie was too big to be contained within a band. (The same would prove true with regard to his Tin Machine experiment much later in his career, when he took time out to recharge his batteries after the trials and stress of global superstardom.) From here on, he would always be David Bowie, solo artist, with David Jones still his official legal name, used for official documents only. To the rest of the world, he was—and would forever remain—David Bowie.

"Nobody's Going to Make a Monkey Out of You"

Just why he changed his name to David Bowie is a question that will result in several different answers if one embarks on a search into the topic. The most common but only partially correct answer is that it was to avoid confusion with

Davy Jones of the Monkees. Certainly, as David soon-to-be-Bowie was taking big strides in his career development, another artist of the same name was coming to prominence. Lancashire-born David Thomas Jones, better known as Davy Jones, was reaping much critical acclaim on the London theater stage as the Artful Dodger in Lionel Bart's musical *Oliver*. The mistake often read and/or heard is that Bowie's name change was to avoid confusion with the Monkees' lead

From his folk singing days in post-Beatle England to his Garboesque image in Madison Square Garden... here is Lady Stard

Presenting
David
Bowie!
by David Douglas

Presenting David Bowie, a book by David Douglas, 1975   *Author's Collection*

singer, but in fact the chronology does not stack up because the Brixton-born David Jones became David Bowie *before* the Monkees ever came to real fame. Nevertheless, Lancashire's famous son was indeed the rival in question, an up-and-coming star who was quite a few rungs farther up the celebrity ladder than the Lower Third's lead singer and was operating in quite a different field of endeavor. It was relatively soon after his theater fame burgeoned that Davy Jones would go on to international stardom through winning the role of lead singer of the Monkees, the world's most famous and deservedly much-loved totally manufactured band. But then, just to confuse matters further, as reported in Melissa Chan's piece in *Time* in 2016, the newly, unofficially named David Bowie wrote when responding to a fan's letter in 1967, "In answer to your questions, my real name is David Jones and I don't have to tell you why I changed it.... 'Nobody's going to make a monkey out of you' said my manager."

Pronunciation

Annoying to fans the world over is the ongoing incorrect pronunciation of the artist's name. It is supposed to be pronounced "Boh-wee." Not "Boo-wee," as some Americans pronounce it. And certainly not "Bow-ee," as British people often pronounce it. It is "Boh (rhymes with go)-wee." To be even clearer, it is not "Boo (as in do)-wee" or "Bow (as in wow)-wee." Often mispronounced, with its architect being ever the gentleman, miscreants were almost never corrected, even on television chat shows. Or perhaps it had nothing to do with being a gentleman. After all, the at-times-mischievous artist always enjoyed presenting layers of meanings and possibilities in his work, so perhaps he rather relished the confusion and disparity that his adopted surname caused.

Why Bowie?

One question remains: when he could have any stage name in the world, why did he choose the surname Bowie? Always fascinated by America and all things American, Bowie reportedly modeled his surname on Texan Jim Bowie—originator of the Bowie knife. Other reports have said that David Bowie was intrigued by Mick Jagger's name and wanted something similarly cutting and dangerous. In *Bowie*, these factors came together. As quoted in Pat Gilbert's *Bowie: The Illustrated Story*, to London's David Jones, *Bowie* represented "the ultimate American knife. It is the medium for a conglomerate of statements and illusions." The selection made, he would never look back.

17

Facts

A Summary of U.S. and U.K. Single and Album Chart Entries

A Summary of U.K. and U.S. Single Releases

Note: Where only one chart placing is provided, the single was released in just one rather than both of these major record markets, or the single was released in both but charted only in one or the other.

1969	Space Oddity U.K. #5
1972	Starman U.K. #10 U.S. #72
	John, I'm Only Dancing U.K. #12
	The Jean Genie U.K. #2
1973	Drive In Saturday U.K. #3
	Life on Mars U.K. #3
	The Laughing Gnome U.K. #6
	Sorrow U.K. #3
	Space Oddity U.S. #15
1974	Rebel Rebel U.K. #5
	Rock 'n' Roll Suicide U.K. #22
	Diamond Dogs U.K. #21
	Knock on Wood U.K. #10
1975	Young Americans U.K. #18 U.S. #28
	Fame U.K. #17 U.S. #1
	Space Oddity U.K. #1
	Golden Years U.K. #8 U.S. #10
1976	TVC15 U.K. #33 U.S. #64
1977	Sound and Vision U.K. #3 U.S. #69
	Heroes U.K. #12
1978	Beauty and the Beast U.K. #39
	Breaking Glass (EP) U.K. #54

1979   Boys Keep Swinging U.K. #7
        DJ U.K. #29
        John, I'm Only Dancing (Again) U.K. #12
1980   Alabama Song U.K. #23
        Ashes to Ashes U.K. #1
        Fashion U.K. #5 U.S. #70
1981   Scary Monsters (and Super Creeps) U.K. #20
        Up the Hill Backwards U.K. #32
        Under Pressure (with Queen) U.K. #1
        Wild in the Wind U.K. #24
1982   Baal's Hymn (EP) U.K. #29
        Cat People (Putting Out Fire) U.K. #26 U.S. #67
        Peace on Earth/Little Drummer Boy (with Bing Crosby) U.K. #3
1983   Let's Dance U.K. #1 U.S. #1
        China Girl U.K. #2 U.S. #10
        Space Oddity U.K. #85
        The Jean Genie U.K. #98
        Life on Mars U.K. #97
        Modern Love U.K. #2 U.S. #14
        White Light/White Heat U.K. #46
1984   Blue Jean U.K. #6 U.S. #8
        Tonight U.K. #53 U.S. #53
        Without You US. #73
1985   This Is Not America (with Pat Metheny Group) UK. #14
        Loving the Alien U.K. #19
        Dancing in the Street (with Mick Jagger) U.K. #1
1986   Absolute Beginners U.K. #2 US. #53
        Underground U.K. #21
        When the Wind Blows U.K. #44
1987   Day In Day Out U.K. #17 U.S. #21
        Time Will Crawl U.K. #33
        Never Let Me Down U.K. #34 U.S. #27
1990   Fame 90 U.K. #28
1992   Real Cool World U.K. #53
1993   Jump They Say U.K. #9
        Black Tie White Noise U.K. #36
        Miracle Goodnight U.K. #40
        The Buddha of Suburbia U.K. #35
1995   The Heart's Filthy Lesson U.K. #35 U.S. #92
        Strangers When We Meet/The Man Who Sold the World U.K. #39
1996   Hallo Spaceboy U.K. #12
        Telling Lies U.K. #76

1997   Little Wonder U.K. #14
        Dead Man Walking U.K. #32
        Seven Years in Tibet U.K. #61
        I'm Afraid of Americans U.S. #66
1998   I Can't Read U.K. #73
1999   Thursday's Child U.K. #16
        Under Pressure (with Queen) U.K. #14
2000   Survive U.K. #28
        Seven U.K. #32

Fanzine poster pinup   *Author's Collection*

2002   Loving the Alien U.K. #41
        Slow Burn U.K. #94
        Everyone Says Hi U.K. #20
2003   Just for One Day (Heroes) (David Guetta vs. David Bowie) U.K. #73
2004   Rebel Never Gets Old U.K. #47
2007   Peace on Earth/Little Drummer Boy (with Bing Crosby) U.K. #73
2013   Where Are We Now? U.K. #6
2014   Sue (Or in a Season of Crime) U.K. #81
2016   Starman U.K. #18
        Space Oddity U.K. #24
        Lazarus U.K. #45 U.S. #40
        Changes U.K. #49
        Blackstar U.K. #61 U.S. #78
        Ashes to Ashes U.K. #62
        Rebel Rebel U.K. #65
        Ziggy Stardust U.K. #76
        China Girl U.K. #97
2017   No Plan U.K. #92

A Summary of UK and US Album Releases

Note: The original studio albums are in bold to differentiate them from compilations, rereleases, sound tracks, or live albums.

1967   **David Bowie** U.K.– U.S.–
1969   **David Bowie** (rereleased in 1972 as **Space Oddity**) U.K.– U.S.–
1972   **Space Oddity** (previously released as **David Bowie** [1969]) U.K. #17
        U.S. #16*
        The Man Who Sold the World U.K. #24 U.S. #105*
        Hunky Dory U.K. #3*
        The Rise and Fall of Ziggy Stardust and the Spiders from Mars U.K. #5
1973   **Aladdin Sane** U.K. #1 U.S. #17
        Pinups U.K. #1 U.S. #23
1974   **Diamond Dogs** U.K. #1 U.S. #5
        David Live U.K. #2 U.S. #8
1975   **Young Americans** U.K. #2 U.S. #9
1976   **Station to Station** U.K. #5 U.S. #3
        ChangesOneBowie U.K. #2 U.S. #10
1977   **Low** U.K. #2 U.S. #11
        "Heroes" U.K. #3 U.S. #35
1978   *Stage* U.K. #5 U.S. #44
1979   **Lodger** U.K. #4 U.S. #20

1980   *Scary Monsters (and Super Creeps)* U.K. #1 U.S. #12

1981   *The Best of David Bowie* U.K. #3

1982   *ChangesTwoBowie* U.K. #24 U.S. #68

1983   *Rare* U.K. #34

Let's Dance U.K. #1 U.S. #4

Golden Years U.K. #33 U.S. #99

Ziggy Stardust: The Motion Picture U.K. #17

The Rise and Fall of Ziggy Stardust and the Spiders from Mars re-release U.S. #89

1984   *Fame and Fashion (Bowie's All-Time Greatest Hits)* U.K. #40

Love You till Tuesday U.K. #53

Tonight U.K. #1 U.S. #11

1986   *Labyrinth* U.K. #38

1987   *Never Let Me Down* U.K. #6 U.S. #34

1989   *Sound + Vision* U.S. #97

1990   *Changes Bowie* U.K. #1 U.S. #39

Hunky Dory re-release U.K. #39

Space Oddity rerelease U.K. #64

The Man Who Sold the World rerelease U.K. #66

The Rise and Fall of Ziggy Stardust and the Spiders from Mars re-release U.K. #10

Aladdin Sane rerelease U.K. #43

Pinups rerelease U.K. #52

Diamond Dogs rerelease U.K. #67

1991   *Young Americans* rerelease U.K. #54

Station to Station rerelease U.K. #57

Low rerelease U.K. #64

1993   *Black Tie White Noise* U.K. #1 U.S. #39

The Singles Collection U.K. #9

1994   *Santa Monica '72* U.K. #74

1995   *1. Outside* U.K. #8 U.S. #21

1997   *Earthling* U.K. #6 U.S. #39

The Best of 1969/74 U.K. #11

1998   *The Best of 1974/79* U.K. #39

1999   *"Hours..."* U.K. #5 U.S. #47

2000   *Bowie at the Beeb* U.K. #7

2002   *Heathen* UK. #5 U.S. #14

The Rise and Fall of Ziggy Stardust and the Spiders from Mars rerelease U.K. #36

Best of Bowie U.K. #1

2003   *Reality* U.K. #3 U.S. #29

2005   *The Platinum Collection* U.K. #53

2007   *The Best of 1980/87* U.K. #34
2008   *Live Santa Monica '72* U.K. #61
2010   *A Reality Tour* U.K. #53
2013   *The Next Day* U.K. #1 U.S. #2
        The Next Day Extra U.K. #89
2014   *Sound + Vision* U.K. #63
        Nothing Has Changed: The Very Best of U.K. #5 U.S. #57
2015   *Five Years 1969–1973* U.K. #45
2016   **Blackstar** U.K. #1 U.S. #1
        The Man Who Sold the World rerelease U.K. #21
        Scary Monsters rerelease U.K. #36
        Lodger rerelease U.K. #64
        Back in Anger Live (with Nine Inch Nails) U.K. #89
        Changes One Bowie rerelease U.K. #32
        Who Can I Be Now 1974–1976 U.K. #21
        Legacy U.K. #5 U.S. #78
        Best of Bowie rerelease U.S. #4
        The Rise and Fall of Ziggy Stardust and the Spiders from Mars rerelease
            U.S. #21
        Hunky Dory rerelease U.S. #57
        The Platinum Collection rerelease U.S. #65
2017   *Cracked Actor (Live in Los Angeles 74)* U.K. #20
        Bowpromo U.K. #38

*Note: *The Man Who Sold the World* (originally released in the United States in 1970 and in the United Kingdom in 1971), *Hunky Dory* (1972), and *Space Oddity* (1972, Bowie's renamed and rereleased second album from 1969, formerly titled *David Bowie*) reached these positions on the charts after the success of the breakthrough album *The Rise and Fall of Ziggy Stardust and the Spiders from Mars* (1972).

18

Let's Dance

Why David Bowie's Most Successful Album Polarizes Fans

If you listen in on any group of David Bowie fans discussing the life's work of their favorite artist for anything longer than a few minutes, it is inevitable that the topic of the divisive *Let's Dance* album (1983) will come up to be chewed over and considered yet again, with the usual familiar brickbats and bouquets abounding. This best-selling album of Bowie's career came after an uncharacteristic two-and-a-half-year gap and followed the release of the critically acclaimed *Scary Monsters (and Super Creeps)* in 1980. *Scary Monsters (and Super Creeps)* had kicked off the new decade in a manner that suggested that his ever-challenging modus operandi, observable throughout an amazing body of no fewer than eleven albums produced during the 1970s, would continue in similar spiky fashion into the succeeding decade. *Scary Monsters (and Super Creeps)* was characteristically prickly and edgy and, as such, effectively business as usual for Bowie. This well-established quality that was so important to long-standing fans even extended to the point, in the song "Ashes to Ashes," of besmirching the name and reputation of that good old career-launching character of Major Tom from the "Space Oddity" days of the late 1960s, who was now evidently just a fallen-from-grace junkie "strung out in Heaven's high, hitting an all-time low."

But as a portent of what was to come in the 1980s, *Scary Monsters (and Super Creeps)* was to prove inordinately deceptive. Between its release and the launch of *Let's Dance*, significant changes had occurred in Bowie-world. RCA Records, which had become synonymous with the artist throughout the 1970s, had been replaced by archrival EMI in a signing coup for the latter rumored to have cost the label somewhere between $10 million and $20 million. While EMI was understandably keen for its new star to produce for it the goods in terms of hit records, it seemed that its new celebrity signing was on a similar wavelength when he overlooked the talents of long-term producer Tony Visconti, who had been expecting to work on the upcoming album and was extremely disappointed to hear of what amounted to his unceremonious shelving. Instead, Bowie sought out New York hit guru Nile Rodgers, who was then riding high on

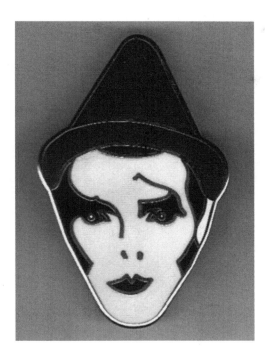

"Ashes to Ashes" badge
Amanda Mills collection

the crest of a wave of hits for Chic ("Le Freak," "Good Times"), Sister Sledge ("We Are Family"), and Diana Ross ("Upside Down"). Approaching Rodgers with the clearly expressed request that he manufacture similarly successful hits for him, Bowie was to find exactly what he sought in his newest collaborator in terms of availing himself of commercial nous and hit-crafting expertise. In addition, an entirely new group of musicians was assembled to assist in the challenge of taking the Bowie name to the top of the charts, most notable among them being a then relatively unknown blues guitarist named Stevie Ray Vaughn. Therefore, in a creative and collaborative sense, the recipe for *Let's Dance* was very different from any that Bowie had previously concocted for the recording of one of his albums. Even for an artist who had thrived on continual change, this evident push for commercial success was a radical shift and one fraught with the potential for misunderstanding and fan mistrust.

David Bowie: Pop Star

The result was, nevertheless, an outstanding album that hit number one in many countries around the world, including in the key U.S. and U.K. markets. It was also, however, thematically and sonically divorced from what Bowie had become known for, even allowing for his changeling nature. Ostensibly a dance pop album, the self-evidently titled *Let's Dance* was sublimely "now" in terms of its super-glossy pop perfection, and the resultant slew of chart-topping hits included the title track, "Modern Love," "China Girl," and (in some countries, including New Zealand, Norway, and Sweden) "Cat People (Putting Out Fire)." A smiling, dancing, bleached-blond, cleaned-up, MTV-friendly pop star called David Bowie was suddenly on TV screens everywhere, while the hits were pumped out on high rotation on radio and in nightclubs for all to enjoy. A new legion of David Bowie fans was spawned. And this is where the eternal debate-creating tension exists for David Bowie's traditional, long-serving fan base, myself included, if I might briefly introduce an auto-ethnographic view. We simply did not want to share him with the mainstream. He was ours, not theirs. However, given the sheer magnitude of this newfound enormously widespread pop fame, we found we had no choice. Seemingly, our alien starman, our gender-bending cage rattler and champion of the outsider, was no longer on the outside looking in on "normal" society—like we were—but was instead now to be found on the inside looking out. This was a turnaround that was hard to come to terms with. Suddenly, kids who bought Phil Collins records were leaving record stores with Bowie's *Let's Dance* under their arms. Maybe they had an Air Supply album at home sitting next to their stereo too. This just wasn't right. It wasn't cool. Ziggy-era Bowie fans muttered into their beer and looked toward one-time Bowie contemporaries Lou Reed and Iggy Pop for a degree of solace.

While accusations of selling out were commonly heard in the music press and in fan debates, it seems, to me at least, and admittedly only with the considerable benefit of hindsight, quite unfair to make such wholesale criticisms of *Let's Dance*. Simply, if I'm honest, I actually feel rather guilty all these years later for coming down on the side of negativity in relation to the album. For an artist renown for change, style fluidity, and risk taking, his time spent within the skin of a pop-hit impresario should be seen better and more fairly as just a case of David Bowie playing another role amid a plethora of such roles. It was Bowie playing at being a pop star, but, characteristically, doing it *so* well (just as he had done when playing the role of an American soul singer on *Young Americans* in 1975 and, with a nod and a wink, referring to himself as a "Plastic Soul Man") and *so* convincingly that he was better at it than most of the "real" pop stars of the day. Yes, it's complicated. But it's also further testament to the depth of talent of the man. If you turned off and away from *Let's Dance* for the reasons I've described above, it might be time to give it another chance.

Let's Dance: Triumph or Tragedy?

The critics were—and remain—as divided over the merits of *Let's Dance* as the fans continue to be. Reviewer for the *Independent* Barney Hoskyns suggests that Bowie lost his distinctiveness on the record, stating, *Let's Dance* "was a record anyone could have made." Nicholas Pegg regards it as "an album on which anything remotely resembling a rough edge has been sanded down and polished up until the glare is dazzling.... [Bowie] plays it safe in every department." Charles Shaar Murray, writing for *New Musical Express*, however, was ebullient on Bowie's change of direction, gushing, "With this album, Bowie seems to have transcended the need to write endlessly about the dramas of being D*A*V*I*D B*O*W*I*E and about all his personal agonies," before going on to describe the work as "powerful, positive music that dances like a dream and makes you feel ten feet tall."

Ultimately, and regardless of whether one is personally in favor of this super-slick joker-in-the-pack album or not, Bowie's new formula and his newfound smash-hit artist status proved unsustainable, and if there is one thing fans can generally agree on in the wake of *Let's Dance*, it is that, for whatever reason, the record marked a watershed in his career, as it was followed by a dire downward spiral in both commercial and critical fortunes. By the time *Tonight* (1984) and *Never Let Me Down* (1987) had been released, Bowie's initial wildly successful flirtation with the mainstream had run its course, and these two albums are almost universally considered to be the creative nadir of his career. Still, not to the taste of his traditional fan base and not strong enough to keep his new fans, it was time for rock's finest shape-shifter to shift shape once again. This time around, he would do so typically in the most unpredictable fashion by relinquishing his solo artist status altogether and attempting to become "just" another member of a band. Tin Machine was about to be born.

So, like it or loathe it, admire it or ignore it, *Let's Dance* is in many ways one of Bowie's most interesting albums and is certainly one of those that will continue to be debated and talked about for a long, long time to come. One thing is certain: it is a significant contributor to the Bowie legend. And finally, many fans who came in on the back of the *Let's Dance* hit machine must have taken the time to check out his back catalog of 1970s albums, discovered the wealth of more challenging and edgy material that they contained, and became lifelong fans because of it. *Let's Dance*, then, can be rightly considered only an enviable success.

The Opposition

Let's Dance had some stiff competition among the other releases of 1983. Michael Jackson's greatest achievement and runaway global smash *Thriller* topped the charts everywhere in that same year. Other notable triumphs included *Colour by Numbers* by Culture Club, *1999* by Prince, *The Art of Falling Apart* by Soft Cell, *Synchronicity* by the Police, *Power, Corruption and Lies* by New Order, *Sweet Dreams Are Made of This* by the Eurythmics, *Murmur* by REM, *Alive She Cried* by the Doors, *Inarticulate Speech of the Heart* by Van Morrison, and *Punch the Clock* by Elvis Costello.

19

"The Prettiest Star"

How David Bowie Made Glam Rock His Own

All That Glitters . . .

In the early to mid-1970s (approximately 1971–1975), glam rock swept all before it and became the preeminent style on the U.K. music charts. On the U.S. popular music scene, where the term *glitter rock* was more commonly used, it never came even close to dominating. Instead, stateside, it remained more of a subversive subculture bubbling away beneath the far safer mainstream rock juggernaut, a curious cultural spin-off embraced by enlightened youth who—like their U.K. counterparts—had overdosed on the 1960s diet of denim, hippies, and bad news. Flower Power had run its tumultuous cultural and political course, and the agent-for-change flag bearers of the countercultural generation either had died (Janis Joplin, Jimi Hendrix, and Jim Morrison) or had lost their potency and relevance, with even the mighty Beatles having dissolved amid acrimony and disillusionment into solo careers. With a new generation of youth disinclined to ride on the worn-out coattails of their incense-smelling, soap-bereft (sorry, hippies) older brothers and sisters, something new was required for the 1970s. And that something was glam rock, the first true music-based youth subculture of the new decade.

David Bowie did not invent glam rock. Yet when one looks around at the vast number of glam-rock–related books, magazines, celebrations, and audio/video compilations that feature him at the forefront of the advertising, the text, and the imagery, you might well be forgiven for thinking that he—especially when performing as Ziggy Stardust—did indeed single-handedly invent this most sparkly of popular music styles. The truth is that glam came from an eclectic combination of sources, stemming primarily from the United Kingdom but with crucial components from the United States completing the blueprint. While David Bowie deservedly can be awarded the crown of King/Queen of Glam through taking the style to its artistic and commercial peak, he did so by appropriating aspects of other glam performers and adding in his own unique mix of theatricality, superb musical talent and nous, and canny awareness of the power of image and persona. Simply, while he wasn't the first, he undeniably did it the best, making the style his own. Therefore, the dominance of his image and name in glam-related publications and references is entirely deserving. Without David Bowie, glam rock would never have achieved the depth and influence it is credited with today. Equally, one might well ponder by what alternative means David Bowie might have achieved superstardom if he had not had glam rock as his vehicle. Certainly, at the time, glam rock and David Bowie were perfect bedfellows.

Glam rock during its heyday is more problematic to describe or define than most other popular music styles because its main characteristics extended far beyond musical style. Reggae, ska, punk, and so on all have musical character- istics so clearly defined and established that acts located within such styles are instantly identifiable through sound alone. By comparison, glam music incor- porated the bubblegum pop of Gary Glitter; the prototype punk of Iggy and the Stooges and the New York Dolls; the art rock of Roxy Music; the football-terrace stomp of Slade; the carefully crafted pop songwriting of the Nicky Chinn and Mike Chapman—aligned acts Sweet, Suzi Quatro, and Mud; the lurking-in-the- shadows danger of Lou Reed; the sneering rip-your-doll's-head-off menace of Alice Cooper; and the cartoon-characters-come-to-life fantasy of KISS (before glam rock, cats didn't play drums)—to name but a few acts of note within the eclectic menagerie that was the glam-rock zoo. Other acts included Wizzard, Cockney Rebel, Mott the Hoople, David Essex, Jobriath, Alvin Stardust, and Chicory Tip, while many more operated with varying degrees of success on the fringes. In the face of such bewildering musical diversity, it was image and attitude that became the most telling delineator. All glam-rock acts placed an emphatic and purposeful emphasis on image, and there was never such a thing as a glam-rock wallflower. All glam-rock acts in some way challenged gender stereo- types, whether it was by the makeup and feather boas of Sweet and Marc Bolan, the platform shoes/boots, spandex, sequins, and lurex of practically everyone involved, or the butch turn-the-tables black leather and legs-apart macho posing of Suzi Quatro. It didn't stop with costuming either because in order to deliver such extremes onstage, one had to "act" the part. Actually, it is more correct to say that one had to "overact" the part, and it was this knowing, winking-to-the-au- dience theatrical quality that was paramount in the glam performance style. The best glam-rock artists possessed an ironic wrist-flapping and head-tossing distancing quality. Knowingly camp, they were in on the joke, and so was their audience. Glam-rock acts did not take themselves too seriously, but that did not mean that they didn't aspire to create great art for the moment—because they did. Qualities of disposability and trashiness, reviled by the 1960s rock audience that was immersed in notions of rock authenticity, were fully embraced within glam rock and underscored by that essential component of irony. Wrapped up in tinsel as a nod to the *Dr. Who* and *Star Trek* science-fiction fantasy generation and sprinkled with glitter, catchy pop hooks, flamboyance, inclusivism, anti-hippy sentiments, and youth rallying cries—these were the essential components of the phenomenon and the reason that so many differing musical styles were able to be lumped under the all-encompassing term *glam rock*.

Under that umbrella label, two subsets have lately come into usage when writers tackle glam rock—high glam and low glam—and it is musical complexity that often determines where an act is deemed to fall within these descriptors. While they are, in some ways, inadequate terms and too simplistic by far, they are nevertheless useful in the way that they imply artistic and musical depth. If one is prepared to imagine a line of continuum with Gary Glitter occupying one end and David Bowie occupying the other, then that accurately describes where David Bowie sits within the glam-rock milieu: he is right at the top of the game. Complex and deeper in what he had to offer than the rest of the pack in almost all facets, Bowie's version of glam is the style's exemplar.

Fanzine poster pinup   *Author's Collection*

The Hype: David Bowie's Glam Rock Experiment

With the end of the 1960s and his succession of early mod-styled bands all discarded behind him, David Bowie began the new decade with an extremely useful experiment. Playing just a handful of gigs in early 1970, most notably at London's iconic rock venue the Roundhouse, the aptly named backing band the Hype was quickly thrown together, paving the way for glam rock and giving birth to what would become Bowie's (still to this day) best-known and most loved collaborators: the Spiders from Mars. In this sparkling, flamboyant lineup that purposely pushed well beyond the boundaries of what was visually acceptable in the rock music of the day, David Bowie, on vocals and twelve-string guitar and dressed in a leotard with several colorful diaphanous scarves sewn to his shirt, became "Rainbowman"; the newly recruited guitar supremo Mick Ronson, resplendent in a gold fedora and gold lamé suit, was "Gangsterman"; Tony Visconti, on bass guitar and vocals, attired in a green cape with a big red *H* on his chest atop a white leotard with silver crocheted briefs, became "Hypeman"; while drummer John Cambridge (to be replaced later by Mick "Woody" Woodmansey) was christened "Cowboyman."

Tony Visconti recalls of his Hype experience with David Bowie at the Roundhouse, "For me this will always be the very first night of Glam Rock. I didn't know it at the time, but when we saw photos taken of us by Ray Stevenson, Marc Bolan was visible resting his head on his arms on the edge of the stage, taking it all in."

In Bowie's words, "I thought it would be really interesting if each of us adopted a persona of some kind because it was all jeans and long hair at the time. I can't remember what I wore, but it was very spacey, and there was a lot of lurex material in it. We got booed all the way through the show. People hated it, they absolutely loathed what we were doing. It was great!"

Marc Bolan

In the United Kingdom, it was Bowie's friend and rival Marc Bolan who spearheaded glam rock. Formerly, Bolan had been a trippy hippy. Through the latter years of the 1960s, he had led a folk duo with the unwieldy name of Tyrannosaurus Rex. Playing bongo drums and sit-on-the-floor-cross-legged–style acoustic guitar, the duo had enjoyed the attentions of a small but enthusiastic fan base but always remained on the fringes of the commercial mainstream. At this time, their performances, both recorded and live, featured fictional, mystical song themes describing Tolkien-type worlds and a curious unique bleating-like singing style. By 1970, however, Bolan's act had undergone a magical transformation. Trading acoustic instrumentation for electric and expanding to a full band size, the name was truncated to the much simpler and more punchy T Rex, and Bolan began to write far more accessible pop-format songs that owed more to Chuck Berry than to folk music. At the end of 1970, one of these newly styled songs, "Ride a White Swan," reached the top ten of the U.K. singles chart, and as 1970 gave way to 1971, it achieved its peak position of number two at the end of January. This was the beginning of what came to be known in the United Kingdom as T Rextacy, with Marc Bolan becoming the number one pop star pinup boy of the new decade while launching a string of eleven top ten singles, including "Hot Love," "Jeepster," "Get It On," "Telegram Sam," "Twentieth Century Boy," and "Metal Guru," and releasing top-selling albums such as *Electric Warrior*, *The Slider*, and *Tanx*.

On Britain's iconic *Top of the Pops* television program, Bolan revolutionized the look of rock 'n' roll for a new generation with his boyish good looks, his corkscrew black locks falling down on his sparkle-adorned face, and his clothes brightly colored and shiny in satin, silk, velvet, and sequins. Marc Bolan put a "look" to the music, and it was a look that many, including David Bowie, would seek to emulate and build on further. Suddenly, putting on a show was back in fashion.

Whether the result of having a mainly preteen/early teen audience with fickle and rapidly changing taste or else Bolan's oft-criticized reluctance to deviate from his tried-and-proven songwriting style, fame was not lasting for Marc Bolan and T Rex. By 1974, further commercial success was proving elusive. Just a couple of years later, however, with the advent of punk rock and in particular the enthusiastic endorsement of top British punk band the Damned, T Rex began enjoying a resurgence of popularity, and Marc Bolan even gained his own television show. On *Marc*, he would showcase his own music and that of invited guests, such as Thin Lizzy, Eddie & the Hotrods, the Bay City Rollers, Generation X, the Boomtown Rats, and the Jam. But on September 16, 1977, the T Rex story would come to an abrupt and tragic end when Bolan was killed in a car crash just two weeks before his thirtieth birthday. The final episode of *Marc*, which had been recorded just ten days before his death, was broadcast in tribute two weeks after he died, on September 28. Fittingly, his main guest artist on that last show was David Bowie, who performed "Heroes." Following this, in a tragicomedic ending to the show, the two friends then performed a jammed duet side by side that ended suddenly with Bolan tripping and falling off the front of the stage, at which point the end credits rolled amid amusement, farce, and confusion.

In terms of musical style, Bolan had little influence on David Bowie's work; however, in terms of providing incentive and encouragement for the young, not-yet-a-star Bowie, Marc Bolan was a very big influence as a prime and telling example that childhood dreams could come true. Born, like Bowie, in London in 1947, Marc Bolan (real name, Mark Feld), through the potent mix of self-belief, talent, innovation, and a blinkered, relentless pursuit of his goal, became everything that he had aspired to be: a pop star sensation replete with fame and fortune. In an interview in 1969, reprinted in Mark Paytress's excellent biography *Bolan: The Rise and Fall of a 20th Century Superstar*, Bowie described Bolan as "the only friend I have in the business." Later, he would expand on this relationship to say, "There was quite a bit of rivalry between Marc and myself. We had a sparring relationship. We both knew we were going to do something in the future, but he was a few rungs up—he was really starting to happen."

The Sparkly Americans: Lou Reed and Iggy Pop

Two other artists made vital contributions to Bowie's performative palette. Americans Lou Reed and Iggy Pop both possessed intrinsic qualities of total artistic commitment and uncompromising confidence, delivered with an edgy, aggressive, and dangerous vibe that Bowie found inspiring. Not only would he befriend each of these artists, but he would work with them closely on two of their classic albums: Reed's *Transformer* and Iggy and the Stooges' *Raw Power*. Other acknowledged influences on Ziggy Stardust, Bowie's state-of-the-art glam rocker, included 1960s rocker Vince Taylor, U.S. fringe performer the Legendary Stardust Cowboy (aka Norman Carl Odham), Eddie Cochran, and the infamous and villainous Alex character from Stanley Kubrick's *A Clockwork Orange* (1971). Yet another artist Bowie much admired was Bryan Ferry, lead singer with Roxy Music, who oozed class, sex appeal, and sophistication. All of these qualities from such sources (and more) Bowie would consciously imbue within the constructed persona that was Ziggy Stardust. Possessing a radical and knowing approach to such assemblage, something he utilized in both personal and professional realms, Bowie told *Rolling Stone* in 1976, "When I heard someone say something intelligent, I used it later as if it were my own. When I saw a quality in someone that I liked, I took it. I still do that. All the time. It's just like a car, man, replacing parts."

While Bowie's glam-rock career began most obviously with *The Rise and Fall of Ziggy Stardust and the Spiders from Mars* album (1972) and his critical reinvention both on- and offstage as the perfect glam-rock star of the same name, many of his earlier songs seamlessly fitted the new direction—particularly several from *Hunky Dory*. It is in some of these songs that Bowie's absolute mastery as a songwriter shines through the most strongly, a mastery that sets him well apart from the far more perfunctory and formulaic glam-rock offerings of acts such as Gary Glitter, Alvin Stardust, and so on. None of these other acts could ever have written "Life on Mars," "Changes," or "Oh! You Pretty Things." The flamboyance, depth, and sophistication of the Ziggy Stardust character were therefore brought to musical life in such cleverly written songs, providing high-end glam with a far more expansive, musically and visually aligned platform that few other glam acts could get near. Even "Space Oddity," Bowie's breakthrough single of 1969, was given new life once he'd become a superstar through Ziggy Stardust, the song featuring in all of his concerts and going on to reach number fifteen in the United States in 1973, his first charting song stateside. In addition, it reached the lofty heights of number one in the United Kingdom in 1975 despite the fact that by that point, Bowie had stylistically moved on. Tellingly, within the glam era, the only others who could approach anywhere near such depth were those very same acts that Bowie had expressed his admiration for and that had been of influence to him, especially Lou Reed, Iggy Pop, and Brian Ferry's Roxy Music. Other acts to show a depth beneath their shiny glam veneer included Steve Harley and Cockney Rebel and, at times, Alice Cooper.

Lady Stardust
Hang On To Yourself
Ziggy Stardust
Life On Mars
Supermen
* Changes
* Five Years
Space Oddity
Andy Warhol
My Death
Width of Circle
John I'm Only Dancing
* Starman
* Moonage Daydream
* Queen Bitch
* Suffragette
* White Light
* Waiting For The Man

Set list written by Mick Ronson for Robin Lumley   *Robin Lumley Collection*

The best glam rock contained an air of decadence and escapism vaguely comparable to Weimar-era German cabaret. It existed in the cross-dressing aspects of the costuming of many of the artists and in the subject matter visited by some. Apocalypse, anyone? Care to "Walk on the Wild Side"? Bowie recognized this link and freely admitted that the image of his Ziggy Stardust character owed a partial debt to Liza Minnelli's portrayal of Sally Bowles in the *Cabaret* movie (1972). Weimar cabaret possessed a live-for-today-for-tomorrow-we-may-die quality, and such sentiments lie at the heart of Bowie's *Aladdin Sane* (1973) and *Diamond Dogs* (1974) albums. The bracketed dates (1913–1938–197?) that accompany the title track "Aladdin Sane" invite the listener to consider war and apocalypse, with the first two dates indicating the years immediately prior to World War I and World War II, and thus the 197? is surely an invitation to the viewer to speculate as to just when the world will once again be at war. Such heavy subject matter is a far

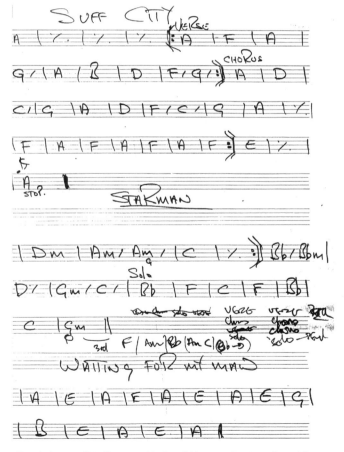

Chord charts of "Suffragette City" and "Starman" written by Mick Ronson for Robin Lumley   *Robin Lumley Collection*

cry from Slade's "clap your hands and stamp your feet" good-time dance music or Mud's endearing but essentially throwaway "Tiger Feet."

While glam rock is widely regarded as a singles genre, in Bowie's hands albums mattered the most. Sure he had hit singles just like other glam-rock stars, some of which—such as "Rebel Rebel," "Starman," and "The Jean Genie"— became signatures of the era, but, in addition to standing alone on the singles charts, Bowie's hits also helped deliver the larger stories told on his 33-rpm twelve-inch vinyl records. The *Ziggy Stardust*, *Aladdin Sane*, and *Diamond Dogs* albums were all conceptual, telling stories and painting pictures in the listeners' minds of dystopian societies, fallen heroes, and technology gone wrong.

Survival beyond Glam

When glam rock came to its inevitable end as the dominant force in U.K. popular music (such is the transient nature of popular music subcultures), Bowie's tactic of presenting Ziggy—the "leper messiah"—and his allied glam-rock alter egos (Aladdin Sane on the album of the same name and Halloween Jack on his final glam album, *Diamond Dogs*) as constructions allowed him simply to shrug off the role(s) and carry on reinventing himself as he pleased. The next role was a complete and utter about-face as he became the Plastic Soul Man of *Young Americans* (1975). Other glam rockers were not so lucky, having been typecast as glam rockers and nothing more and thereby lacking the stylistic depth and performative variety to move on convincingly. The careers of Slade, Sweet, Suzi Quatro, Gary Glitter, and so on all took markedly downward turns even as Bowie's fortunes continued to rise, their fans having grown up and moved on, while the bands that had once stirred their prepubescent and pubescent hormones offered nothing sufficiently new to warrant the fans taking them with them. In contrast, Bowie was able to keep the interest of his fans through being virtually a rock 'n' roll tour guide. Lou Reed and Iggy Pop, Bowie's glam-rock peers, were similarly able to take off the makeup, strip off the glittery clothes, and carry on.

In summation, it is simply impossible to imagine glam rock without David Bowie. Not only the artist responsible for taking the style to its creative, artistic, and commercial peak, he is the one artist whom rock music fans the world over associate with the style. Recognized today as a crucial link between the 1960s countercultural generation and the safety-pin–festooned rebellion of mid-1970s punk rock, glam rock would unlikely be considered the potent force it was had it not been for Bowie's startling, cage-rattling, glam incarnation(s).

20

A Stylistic Smorgasbord

David Bowie's Tour of Musical Styles

David Bowie's career-defining taste for reinvention went far beyond the periodic reworking of his image. Each time he came up with a new persona or look, this would be reflected in a newly adopted musical style through which he would express himself. During interviews with the music press, he would frequently admit to a low threshold for boredom, and so, in part at least, the constant changing can be seen as a natural reflection of his personality. Others have suggested that the eternally changing "package" (Bowie's amalgam of image and music) was a ploy to maximize audience potential by drawing in enthusiasts of multiple styles. Regardless of whether the motivation was driven by personal quirk or commercial nous—the real truth probably incorporates a combination of both mixed with a large dollop of simple curiosity for trying new things—no other artist who achieved anything like David Bowie's level of success and global popularity ever produced such a wide-ranging body of work. He provided a veritable guided tour of musical styles for his fans.

Unfortunate Beginnings, Style Shopping, and Getting It Right with Glam Rock

His first album, the self-titled *David Bowie* (1967), was one of the strangest and most eclectic bunch of songs that has ever been committed to vinyl and owed far more to music hall than rock 'n' roll despite the photograph on the front cover that depicted him as a typical young Swinging London mod. The fact that *David Bowie* was released on exactly the same day as the Beatles' *Sgt. Pepper's Lonely Hearts Club Band* was certainly unfortunate (and is explored in chapter 7) but not the main reason for its abject failure. Any popular music fan shelling out his or her hard-earned wages or pocket money on the promise of the unknown but seemingly cool mod on the front and justifiably expecting a fine dose of rhythm and blues, à la the Who, would have been sorely disappointed on getting home and placing the vinyl on the turntable. With orchestral instrumentation, brass bands, and quirky un-hip story songs that told tales of twisted, tragic characters who were mostly middle-aged and all washed up, the contents were far more at home on the music hall stage than the rock stage. Despite the cover image and a brief, misleading biography on the back cover written by his manager that boasted of the artist's prowess in the rhythm-and-blues bands that he'd belonged to previously, David Bowie wasn't "Talkin' 'bout My Generation" at all. Rather, in his unfashionable and highly affected and exaggerated cockney accent, he was the embodiment of music hall star Anthony Newley or Bernard Cribbens and—bar one or two songs that stood out as anomalies, most notably the genuinely catchy "Love You till Tuesday"—a whole world away from being hip and happening.

Quickly abandoning the song vignettes of troubled characters presented in outdated musical styles, on his second album (1969)—also self-titled before being rereleased under the title *Space Oddity* following the success of the single of the same name—Bowie's style was that of the 1960s singer-songwriter, à la Bob Dylan and Donovan. With acoustic guitar to the fore, the instrumentation was entirely consistent with the mid- to late 1960s wear-flowers-in-your-hair hippy festival vibe.

Just one year later, however, the flowers also were abandoned as *The Man Who Sold the World* (1970) served up prototype heavy metal. Its dark and distorted sonorities were such that today many commentators consider the album to be one of the formative works that helped establish the heavy metal style. Typically, it was to be Bowie's only such record.

The fourth studio album, *Hunky Dory* (1971), presented fans with a carefully crafted and much lighter piano-and-voice–led vibe where the emphasis was on melody and harmony rather than driving, heavy rhythms. In this format, Bowie's increasingly masterful songwriting was allowed to shine unencumbered by the swathes of dense sound of just a year earlier.

It was on the fifth studio album that everything came together and Bowie's career took off. For *The Rise and Fall of Ziggy Stardust and the Spiders from Mars* (1972), Bowie had assembled a tight, stripped-back, but highly talented band in Mick Ronson, Woody Woodmansey, and Trevor Bolder. With Bowie at the front, the powerhouse quartet of vocals, guitar, bass, and drums was the perfect vehicle for the sharply honed rock songs that told the story of the Starman coming to save a doomed Earth. The band's appearance on television's top-rated *Top of the Pops*, their number augmented by Robin Lumley on keyboards, superbly sold the song to the public both visually and aurally, and the album literally took off from that point on. Straightforward rock without flab or excess and sitting perfectly within the hottest style of the day, glam rock, the album established its creator as the next big thing in the rock world.

Stylistically, things changed little in *Aladdin Sane* (1973), as the Ziggy Stardust concept was continued through a set of songs that documented Bowie's recent touring experiences through the United States. With its flagship single

"The Jean Genie" going all the way to number two on the U.K. singles charts (it performed significantly more poorly in the United States, where it reached only 71), *Aladdin Sane* took David Bowie to the top of the U.K. album chart and into the top twenty in the United States (#17). A little more rough and abrasive than its predecessor and with the introduction of avant-garde jazz stylings from piano player Mike Garson, *Aladdin Sane* and its star-making predecessor are nevertheless albums of similar ilk.

Pinups followed in the same year, with almost the same band lineup at the core once more. Although the songs here were cover versions of Bowie's favorite rhythm-and-blues tracks from his teenage years, the vibe remained once again firmly fixed in the Ziggy/glam mold.

Diamond Dogs (1974) retained the sound (if not the personnel) of the previous three glam-era works. Having disbanded the Spiders from Mars, Bowie performed much of the instrumentation himself on this album along with contributions from session musicians. Still, the glam sonorities ensured a continuation of style. The album also contained one of David Bowie's best-loved songs, "Rebel Rebel," a virtual paean to youth estrangement, youth power, and the glam-rock generation.

Bye-Bye to Glam Rock and Hello to Soul and Ambient-Electronic Music

With four albums firmly situated within the glam camp, things were about to change dramatically. In 1975, Bowie entered his self-named and very fleeting "Plastic Soul Man" phase, relocating to the United States and recruiting a band of top Philadelphia soul musicians and convincingly swapping the guitars of glam for the brass of soul. It was his first big stylistic change since becoming a star, and while it bamboozled his glam fans, so convincing was his white-boy-from-London facsimile of the soul style that it brought him to the attention of a whole raft of new fans. It especially brought him significant success in the United States, where the album reached the top ten—far higher than any of his previous efforts stateside—and even more notably provided him with his first number one hit in "Fame."

As quickly as he'd reinvented himself as a soul singer, he dropped both the role and, for the most part, the style in the following *Station to Station* (1976).

On an album consisting of only six songs, Bowie became the Thin White Duke and began his European canon. Dense, long, technologically driven songs, such as the title track and "TVC15," are juxtaposed against beautiful ballads, such as "Wild Is the Wind" or the beautifully crafted "Word on a Wing."

If the technology evident in the instrumentation of *Station to Station* warned of a future direction, then it all came to pass on *Low* (1977). Here, in the most

STATIONTOSTATIONDAVIDBOWIE

Station to Station album, 1976   *Author's Collection*

daring stylistic change ever made by any rock artist, Bowie entered the world of ambient electronic music. In collaboration with electronic whiz kid Brian Eno, the album suggested music-for-robots-performed-by-robots and bleak, impersonal postapocalyptic wastelands, especially on the remarkable second side of the record. The human voice was mostly secondary and subsumed, used only sparingly in the traditional role of singer-of-words and more as just another sound flavor, often found making unintelligible utterings and strange colors to enhance, not dominate, the ambient instrumental soundscapes. Having recently featured in the leading role of Thomas Jerome Newton in Nicolas Roeg's groundbreaking science-fiction movie *The Man Who Fell to Earth* (1976), David Bowie had also worked on a potential sound track. While this music wasn't used in the movie in the end (see chapter 14), the experience certainly influenced the music of *Low* and beyond.

"*Heroes,*" released in the same year, offered more of the same, although it contained a higher percentage of more traditionally styled songs. While in the subsequent *Lodger* (1979), the third installment of what is commonly termed Bowie's "Berlin trilogy," the balance swung back even further from ambient electronica to traditional song form.

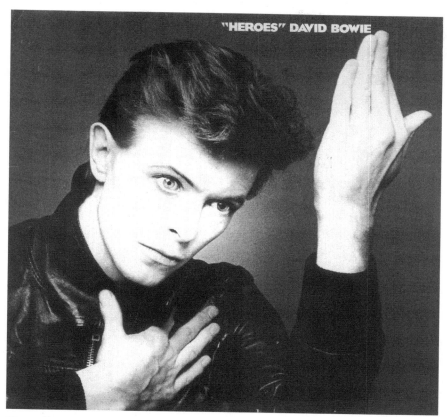

Heroes album, 1977   *Author's Collection*

 Thirteen albums into his career, David Bowie had by now firmly established one thing: if you were a fan, then you must be prepared to ride his roller coaster of stylistic changes and never get too comfortable with any one style because it would be sure to change. This change might come abruptly between consecutive albums (the first and second albums or *Station to Station* and *Low*), or he might linger within a style for a brace of albums (the four of the glam era and the Berlin trilogy), but no one should ever be in any doubt that he was—as his previous album so strongly inferred—only ever a Lodger within any musical home. That he would exit, slam the front door behind him, and walk off into an undetermined future when he was ready to move on was by now a given.

The Unexpected Return of Major Tom and the Divisive Pop Years

In 1980, *Scary Monsters (and Super Creeps)* revived Bowie's commercial fortunes, which had dropped markedly during the Berlin years.

Scary Monsters (and Super Creeps) album, 1980   *Author's Collection*

A spiky, heavy, and, at times, angry album that in part reflected on his past, including the startling admission that Major Tom was now a junkie as told in the extraordinary "Ashes to Ashes," it was a fine way to begin the new decade. Whereas *Low* had found Bowie introspective, passive, and purposely overshadowed by technology, here he returned to rock 'n' roll, raging at the sky with frequently angst-ridden songs. *Scary Monsters (and Super Creeps)* is the favorite David Bowie album of many fans.

An uncharacteristic three-year hiatus followed, and when *Let's Dance* was released in 1983, it caused more than a sharp intake of breath among Bowie fans. Just as *Young Americans* had introduced a whole new set of fans to Bowie's work with its sublime success in a style very different from that which had preceded it, with the Nile Rodgers–produced *Let's Dance*, the gloriously spiky David Bowie of *Scary Monsters* had evidently left the building. *Let's Dance* offered a string of hits and glossy pop/dance perfection. Soon the title track, "China Girl," "Modern Love," and "Cat People (Putting Out Fire)" were being heard in every disco; Bowie's songs were sitting at the top of the pop charts; and, instead of being a champion of the outsiders, he was the darling of the insiders. Selling in numbers that far exceeded any previous Bowie album, this was mainstream success on a massive scale. *Let's Dance* was pop perfection.

David Bowie, pop artist, lasted for two more albums: *Tonight* (1984) and *Never Let Me Down* (1987). But neither effort would come close to emulating the commercial heights of *Let's Dance*, and they are frequently cited as the low points of his career.

Stepping Away from the Treadmill and Taking On the New Breed

His newfound status as a mainstream pop star never sat easily with David Bowie, and with industry and record company pressure to resurrect his pop fortunes too heavy a burden to bear, he responded with a controversial and surprising twofold tactic. He joined a band, Tin Machine, attempting to become just another guy in a band, and the band's music was purposely a very long way from pop. It worked. The pressure was off. His new band's music was raw, aggressive, brash and celebratory garage style and noncommercial and had middle finger extended. Bowie himself was making a point. He belonged on the outside looking in, not on the inside looking out.

The year 1993 found Bowie solo again, rejuvenated, and releasing his twentieth studio album, *Black Tie White Noise*. While rock based, jazz is a major inflection on the album, and hip-hop and funk elements are also frequently to be heard. With three instrumentals on the album as well, *Black Tie White Noise* is a potpourri of styles and refuses to be pigeonholed.

Following suit in the same year is *The Buddha of Suburbia*, David Bowie's lost album. Wrongly categorized as a sound track album due to Bowie providing the theme song for the BBC television series of the same name, the ten songs run a stylistic gamut that ranges from retro-glam rock to *Station to Station* and the Berlin trilogy.

If the preceding two albums refused to be categorized stylistically, *1. Outside* (1995) was not so reticent. The new and highly contemporaneous sounds of techno, industrial, and jungle permeate the work, helping Bowie tell his tale in what is his most obviously conceptual album since *Ziggy Stardust*. Just like the murderous story itself, the sounds are frequently ugly and aggressive.

On *Earthling* (1997), those techno, industrial, and jungle influences from *1. Outside* combine into fully fledged drum 'n' bass. Heavy and uncompromising and true to his Lodger nature, Bowie inhabits and employs the new current style with ease and class, the album stacking up easily alongside the giants of drum 'n' bass, such as Nine Inch Nails and the Prodigy.

"Hours..." (1999) shifts style once more. Far gentler than *Earthling*, the album in some ways harks right back to *Hunky Dory* with its emphasis on beautiful melodic phrasing and with its vocals exposed and right at the forefront of the mix, the accompaniment supporting the tracks and not driving them relentlessly. But there are also stylistic surprises in store. "The Pretty Things Are Going to Hell" is pure 1970s glam, while the instrumental track "Brilliant Adventure" could easily have come from *Low*.

Like No One Else Could

For his first post-millennium album, *Heathen* (2002), Bowie achieves a fine balance of instrumentation that amounts to a veritable powerhouse of traditional rock instruments and synthesizers that impeccably serve his ever-strong songwriting. The style is big, bold, and completely his own. No longer seemingly a Lodger inhabiting or assembling the styles of others, *Heathen* offers no comparisons to other artists. Particularly notable is the return of producer Tony Visconti, with whom Bowie had worked extensively in the 1970s.

Reality (2003) is stylistically much the same. With the same cast of musicians and Visconti once again at the helm, it is essentially *Heathen* part 2: the work of a man with no need or desire to do anything but his own thing, and that thing is big, bold, proven, and confident.

The Next Day (2013) is the album that took everyone by surprise. Most people believed that David Bowie had retired without ever announcing it. Just how he managed to keep this comeback album a secret until announcing it on his sixty-sixth birthday on January 8 is anyone's guess. But there it was. "Boo!" David Bowie had a new album out. Despite the red herring of the album's cover, with its clear reference to *"Heroes,"* once again the vibe and feel of the music sits with its post-millennium predecessors, *Heathen* and *Reality*. The central core of musicians with whom Bowie was working had by now been together a long time, and this settled combination, along with the presence of Visconti, flavors the album. Once again, the music is big, aggressive, and spiky and could have come from no other artist.

Blackstar completes the full set of David Bowie's studio albums. While jazz elements had been evident in previous works, especially on *Aladdin Sane* and *Black Tie White Noise*, here it is more present than ever, its soulful sounds adding poignancy and emotion to Bowie's deeply philosophical lyrics. Elements of hip-hop, rap, acid house, drum 'n' bass, and even folk music can also be heard, but in truth, *Blackstar* is both experimental and new. The rule book has been torn up. The work of a man who knew that he had cancer and was operating on limited time, depth, freedom, and gravitas permeates the work. An exemplar of musical self-reflection, the songs are full of mood and swirling emotion.

Fan art by Tanja Stark

Tanja Stark Collection

According to producer Visconti, both he and Bowie wanted to avoid rock 'n' roll, and this was clearly achieved, as *Blackstar* is by far his least rock 'n' roll record since his self-titled debut of 1967. Eschewing any categorization other than experimental or perhaps avant-garde, the album is a highly fitting end to a career that has been founded on stylistic change.

Uniquely, David Bowie was capable of immersing himself in any musical style he wished to and producing work the equal of any of the top artists operating within that style. He frequently and successfully did just that, and his body of recorded work is a virtual tour of musical styles from music hall to Dylanesque troubadour, heavy metal to glam rock, soul to electronic ambient, glossy pop to techno, industrial and jungle to drum 'n' bass—and just about everything in between. Equally, however, he was quite capable of extending his arm with his hand up and his palm outward and refusing to follow any existing path. The former tactic served him extraordinarily well throughout his career, but it was with the latter that he so emphatically signed off. No other artist could have made *Blackstar*. It is a highly experimental groundbreaking masterpiece.

21

"Fa Fa Fa Fa Fashion"

David Bowie's Influence on the World of Fashion

David Bowie's reputation as the most stylish, most fashionable, and most oft-imitated rock star in history is richly deserved, and his legacy in the world of fashion burns as brightly as his other legacies. Off-duty rock stars have often been snapped by the press in unflattering clothing and unflattering situations, their hair unkempt and their personal grooming a tragedy. Anyone surfing the Internet in the hope of finding photographs of David Bowie caught with his pants down, so to speak, will almost certainly come up empty-handed. A keen follower of Andy Warhol's notion of living one's life as if always starring in a movie, throughout his career Bowie remained fully aware of the importance of a carefully constructed, presented, and scrupulously maintained image. David Bowie was always "onstage," always aware that he was being looked at and critiqued, and always ready to oblige by, as the saying goes, "keeping up appearances."

Vogue, the world's fashion bible, has long considered David Bowie to be one of their own, a fashionista through and through. By the very definition of the term, fashionistas lead fashion; they don't follow it. They set trends; they don't follow the trends of others. In 2016, British *Vogue* writer Ella Alexander described Bowie as "unarguably fashion's king of self invention." Alexander supported her claim by explaining that "Bowie changed his style more dramatically than any other musician in history. His transformations brought about seismic cultural shifts, changing the definition of what it meant to be a popular rock star. For Bowie clothes were a way of projecting self-expression, a powerful tool in communicating individuality at its most extreme, glittering and creative."

David Bowie was seemingly always aware of the power of unified clothing and costuming, as, again, any Internet search for images of the young and early career artist will show. His look was never haphazard or ill considered; his poses were always carefully choreographed and, presumably, rehearsed, to convey simultaneously meaning and cool. As a teenage mod with his early bands such as the Buzz, he dressed immaculately in tailored suits, and when he went through his hippy-looking phase during his Beckenham Arts Lab days (around 1969), his long hair was always well groomed and his clothing immaculate. And once he started performing in his succession of invented personas (Ziggy Stardust, the Plastic Soul Man, the Thin White Duke), the manner of his dressing up to inhabit these roles was probably the most carefully thought-out approach to costuming that rock music has ever seen.

Getting the Right Help

David Bowie also had the not-to-be-underestimated talent of surrounding himself with the right people who could help him achieve the vision he had with regard to his image. Hairstylist Suzi Fussy, who was initially the stylist for Bowie's mother Peggy and who would go on to marry Spiders from Mars guitarist Mick Ronson, was one such ally. Quickly recruited by Bowie, it was Fussy who came up with the now iconic Ziggy Stardust haircut that was so much a part of the Ziggy look. A scarlet cut with a razored-back and stick-up blow-dried front, the "rooster cut" became *the* youth haircut in the United Kingdom during the glam rock era of the early to mid-1970s. During his early career, he wore clothes designed by the uber-trendy Michael Fish (aka Mr. Fish), most notably on the front cover of *The Man Who Sold the World* album, where he infamously attired

The Man Who Sold the World album, 1971   *Author's Collection*

himself in a Mr. Fish "man's dress" as he lounged languidly on a chaise longue, Pre-Raphaelite femme fatale style.

The Freddie Factor

Fellow Londoner Freddie Burretti also designed for the rising star. An early associate of David Bowie's, Burretti performed with him in the short-lived, pre–Ziggy Stardust and the Spiders from Mars experimental band Arnold Corns before both realized that Burretti's true talent lay not in music but in design, the role for which he was gratefully retained on the David Bowie upward trajectory. The most iconic Bowie costumes that bore the Burretti name were the ice-blue satin business suit he wore in the "Life on Mars" video and the bright and shiny gold, blue, and red quilted jumpsuit he wore on *Top of the Pops* for his unforgettable performance of "Starman." The association between the two men continued beyond Ziggy Stardust, through the *Diamond Dogs* (1974) late glam era and into the *Young Americans* (1975) Philly Soul period. In the mid-1970s, the two men parted ways, however, and never worked together again, with Burretti fading into relative obscurity. After Burretti's death from cancer in 2001, David Bowie remembered his former collaborator in a touching tribute, since reported on the fashionunited.uk website in a remembrance piece written by Jackie Mallon and titled "Fashion's Unsung Designers; Bowie's Freddie Burretti": "I am so sad at this particular passing, as he was generally one of the nicest, most talented spirits that I have had the honour of working with. Freddie and I changed our world, small as it was, to what we thought it could be. He lives on for me through his creative genius. I kept all your stuff, Fred. I lost very little. I've got all the best things. I'll look after them for you, God bless."

Kansai Yamamoto

Perhaps most famously, during his Ziggy Stardust/glam rock era, David Bowie secured the services of the then up-and-coming Japanese designer Kansai Yamamoto, an association that would work equal wonders for the success and profile of each of them. The two men met in 1971 when Yamamoto found out that Bowie was wearing some of his women's designs onstage. The two quickly established common ground and a friendship, and the designer's avant-garde kimonos and other Japanese-inspired garments added much to the androgynous and "other" qualities of Bowie's glam-era work, especially on the Ziggy Stardust and Aladdin Sane tours. For a piece titled "Dressing David Bowie as 'Ziggy Stardust'" in the *Cut* in February 2018, interviewer Mary Dellas asked Kansai Yamamoto to elucidate why the two of them clicked so well. He responded, "David was a true vanguard—he was making waves in the musical landscape of the time. His energy resonated with my own desire to venture out into the world. I think David felt that the energy in my designs contributed to his own energy. He knew that when he wore my clothing onstage, he could elicit a strong reaction from the audience." Among the most well-known of the Yamamoto designs worn by David Bowie are the knitted asymmetric multicolored leotard with bare left arm and right leg worn with matching bangles and the wide-leg vinyl jumpsuit worn with a white cape featuring *kanji* lettering that the artist would dramatically strip off onstage during his Ziggy Stardust shows.

Beyond Glam

Later, as the Thin White Duke, David Bowie's stage outfits of choice veered toward oversized suits by the likes of Yves Saint Laurent. Other designers to contribute to the Bowie fashion legacy include Will Brown, Alexander McQueen (who created one of his most strikingly memorable garments, the Union Jack greatcoat worn on the cover of *Earthling*), and, toward the end of his life, Paul Smith.

Elsewhere in this book, I explore Bowie's endeavors in the arts beyond music and film—those media for which he clearly and justifiably is best known.

Fanzine poster pinup

Author's Collection

But Jess Cartner-Morley, the *Guardian*'s fashion editor, makes an excellent point when she argues that "Bowie made art out of his clothes."

Fan Emulation

Anyone who has ever attended a live David Bowie concert anywhere in the world will have seen amid the throngs of fellow concertgoers a multitude of little Ziggy Stardusts, Aladdin Sanes, Thin White Dukes, Halloween Jacks, and so on, of all genders and probably across a broad spectrum of age-groups. Perhaps you, the reader, also dressed up in such fashion when attending a David Bowie concert. While such fan emulation at concerts is common today—and for decades, this has been evident among the fans of many acts, especially fans of certain visually over-the-top flamboyant acts (Alice Cooper, KISS, Madonna, and Lady Gaga, to name but four obvious contenders)—when David Bowie hit the heights of stardom in the early 1970s as Ziggy Stardust, such a thing was not common at all. Sure, kids might have had Beatles haircuts, worn a Rolling Stones T-shirt or badge, or shown mod/rocker clothing allegiances (parkas or leather jackets, respectively). But going all the way in order to look as much like your idol as possible was a David Bowie thing; he is largely responsible for a trend that has lasted ever since. Hairdressers across the United Kingdom quickly had to learn how to perform a "Bowie cut"—also called a "rooster cut"—on swarms of girls and boys, and sales of orange hair dye soared. Many a mom and dad were appalled, threatened, or alarmed at the sight that greeted them when little Johnny or Sharon returned home from the hairdresser in 1972–1974. Back in 1979, as the rather famous (in academia at least) sociologist Dick Hebdige pointed out in his own groundbreaking popular culture textbook *Subculture: The Meaning of Style*, "Every Bowie concert performed in drab provincial cinemas and Victorian town halls attracted a host of startling Bowie look-alikes, self-consciously cool under gangster hats which concealed (at least until the doors were opened) hair rinsed a luminous vermilion, orange or scarlet streaked with gold and silver. These exquisite creatures, perched nervously on platform shoes or slouching (just like the boy himself in that last publicity release) in 50s plastic sandals, cigarette held just so, shoulders set at such and such an angle, were involved in a game of make-believe which has embarrassed and appalled some commentators on the rock scene who are concerned for the 'authenticity' and oppositional content of youth culture." While Hebdige is wrong to assume that such dressing up negates the possibility of "oppositional culture" (tell that to the punk rockers with their safety pins and zips and spiked mohawks!), he is otherwise correct in his observation that David Bowie inspired the kind of dressing up among his fans that flew completely in the face of the 1960s notions of rock authenticity.

Fashion often is seen as inauthentic, as contrived and artificial, but fashion also speaks volumes about one's worldviews and public and personal allegiances across multiple fields. David Bowie used fashion as a vital part of his reinventive tool kit to display what he stood for, something his fans were quick to pick up on and apply to themselves. If you were spotted in town dressed in Ziggy Stardust regalia in 1972–1973, you wouldn't even have had to open your mouth to tell people what you stood for. They could take one look at you and know. Your adoption of Bowie fashion had you marked out as someone who was in his camp: an outsider and proud of it. At the very least, you were the coolest kid on the block.

The Best-Dressed British Citizen in History!

Tellingly, in a BBC poll conducted in 2013, David Bowie was voted the best-dressed British citizen in history, winning 48.5 percent of the vote and beating back the challenge of none other than Queen Elizabeth I into second place. "Fashion icon" is thus yet another of his well-deserved descriptions and another area of endeavor in which he inspired others. That he one day became married to supermodel Zara Mohamed Abdulmajid (aka Iman) should come as no surprise. For certain, they must have understood better than most couples each other's fields of endeavor. That his "look" is around to this day and acknowledged as his speaks volumes. A Bowie haircut, a Bowie-esque garment, Bowie makeup, and the Ziggy flash—these signatures and many more still exist and help to ensure that the influence and efforts of the best-dressed British citizen in history will forever be remembered, imitated, and celebrated.

22

The Managers and Coco Schwab

The Important Nonmusical Connections

David Bowie benefited from the help, expertise, and even love and devotion of many people during his career and his life. At the top of the heap is his personal aide, Coco (Corrine) Schwab, who was at his side for the majority of his career and whose critical importance he acknowledged glowingly and frequently, even right at the very end of his life. Early in his career, he benefited to varying degrees from the assistance of four managers, all of who recognized his prodigious talent but, perhaps with the exception of the last and most contentious of these, Tony Defries, struggled to align their efforts to their charge's own vision. To be fair, in the early days, even David Bowie didn't seem to quite know what he wanted, so it is important to acknowledge the difficult task that faced these four very different individuals.

Leslie Conn (1964)

Noteworthy more for the fact that he was David Bowie's first-ever manager than for any spectacular innovations or successes despite evidently being passionate and hardworking in his task, Leslie Conn joined forces with Bowie in mid-1964, when Bowie was still performing with one of his early bands, the King Bees. Conn certainly had some impressive credentials that would have attracted the young artist, as he was a talent scout for the Dick James organization (publisher to the Beatles), had worked with the Shadows and other big-name acts, and ran a music publishing company for superstar Doris Day. He was not, however, it should equally be noted, known as a manager. When David Bowie wrote to a local wealthy entrepreneur, John Bloom, seeking financial support for his band, his letter was passed on to Conn, bringing the two together. While Bloom declined to give support, he had arranged for Conn to organize bands for his wedding anniversary party on February 12, 1964. Conn included the King Bees in the lineup of acts, but when they actually played at the event, Bloom did not like them at all and insisted that they be removed from the stage only a few songs into their set. Nevertheless, Conn was sufficiently impressed to continue the association, although no official contract between he and Bowie was ever signed. Around this time, Conn also began championing one of his new charge's friends and rivals, Marc Bolan, who would go on to massive fame—before Bowie achieved his—with his band T Rex.

Despite having booked performances for David Bowie and negotiated a handful of failed single releases, the relationship between the two men was foundering by 1965, with Conn reportedly becoming increasingly disillusioned. When addressing his lack of success with both Bowie and Bolan in Paul Trynka's excellent book *Starman: David Bowie, the Definitive Biography* (2010), Conn explained, "I was going broke looking after them. And I was getting very depressed with the music business—so I had to say goodbye."

Ralph Horton (1965)

A road manager for the Moody Blues and booking agent at the Kings Agency in London, Ralph Horton was greatly impressed with David Bowie. Although it would once again turn out to be a liaison heavy on enthusiasm but light on results, it was during Horton's tenure—acting as his first official contracted manager—that David Bowie would abandon trying to be part of a band and instead embark on his solo career. While still with the Lower Third under Horton's management, it became clear to the other band members that the new manager had far more interest in their lead singer than in the rest of them, leading to accusations of preferential treatment and favoritism that were uncomfortable for all concerned, not the least Bowie himself. While this feeling would end in the band's breaking up, Horton first achieved a modicum of success in convincing record producer Tony Hatch of Bowie's quality, securing a recording deal with Pye, and getting the band into a studio. While the resultant singles ostensibly failed, at least in a commercial sense, David Bowie was compiling more valuable experience in the industry, and momentum was growing. When the Lower Third dissolved, Horton and Bowie recruited a backing band titled the Buzz and recorded a single, but Horton, for his part, realized that he would need help. Little did he know that this decision would lead to his downfall in terms of his involvement with the artist in whom he was so personally and professionally invested.

Kenneth Pitt (April 1967–May 1970)

Brought into the Bowie fold by Horton, who preferred to deal with the artistic side of things rather than business side, Kenneth Pitt was renowned for his expertise as a publicist, with a track record of conducting public relations for famous clients, including Stan Kenton, Billy Eckstine, Billy Daniels, and Liberace. By the time Horton approached him to consider David Bowie, Pitt's portfolio of acts had expanded to include the then high-flying Manfred Mann. Neither Horton nor Pitt—nor probably David Bowie himself—would have foreseen at the time that before long, Pitt would end up taking responsibility for all aspects of Bowie's career, with Horton soon to be left completely out of the equation. Even before he was officially taken on as manager (on April 25, 1967), Pitt made his mark in the David Bowie story, strongly recommending to Horton and Bowie that the latter change his surname from Jones because of the potential for confusion with others of the same common name, especially his namesake at the forefront of the Monkees. Thus it was that David Bowie was born.

Kenneth Pitt oversaw David Bowie's career for three years, a critical formative period that included his first flush of success with the release of the "Space Oddity" single (1969), which reached number five on the U.K. singles chart following the successful Apollo 11 mission that put man on the moon. Right from the start of their association, Pitt had absolute belief in Bowie's talent yet, much like the artist himself, struggled to know in which direction it was to be best channeled, at one stage even encouraging a career in cabaret. Pitt released his own account of their time together in *Bowie: The Pitt Report*, published in 1985. For hard-core fans, it is a must-read. Several accounts have Pitt cast as an old school–style theater manager with not much of a taste or any particular instinct for rock 'n' roll. Even David Bowie himself was reportedly at times a little embarrassed at the comparative squareness of his manager: in David Buckley's Bowie biography, *Strange Fascination*, Bowie's producer and friend Tony Visconti recalls, "When I saw the two of them together I sensed an awkwardness between them. I remember Pitt telling me his plans for Bowie but none of it registered with me. It all seemed like he really didn't have anything concrete." Pitt himself, however, believes that had the artist stayed with him instead of signing to a new manager in May 1970, Bowie would have enjoyed the same level of subsequent success and that it would have happened even more quickly than it did. One can never know, of course, but certainly in Pitt, David Bowie had a manager who believed in him completely and who worked tirelessly for him during their time together, investing large amounts of both time and money.

Of all Bowie's managers, it is Pitt, with more rock 'n' roll nous than he is often credited for, who deserves considerable respect and sympathy in equal measures for taking his charge to the very edge of success and then seeing someone else get the bulk of the credit. During their time together, Pitt came to understand extremely well the nature of the artist he was representing even if the biggest step on the ladder of success was destined not to transpire under his watch. Closing his account in *Bowie: The Pitt Report*, he perceptively observes, "Those who judge him and me and, in doing so, take as their yardstick rock and roll, fail to understand that David never was a devotee or exponent of rock and roll. Whenever he rocked and rolled he did so in the context of theatre, as an actor." During the three years he spent with the theatrically oriented Kenneth Pitt, David Bowie was able to experiment with roles, musical styles, and images; hone his talents and goals; and get a brief taste of success in his mouth with "Space Oddity." As the 1960s rolled over into the 1970s, this was exactly what Bowie needed in order for him to be able to achieve what he did shortly after leaving his third manager behind.

Tony Defries (May 1970–January 1975)

David Bowie's fourth and last manager, Tony Defries, is the one who is most talked about and controversial, with their relationship ending as it did in legal action, friction and confusion, acrimony, and bitterness. Formerly a solicitor's clerk, Defries was an astute businessman only slightly older than David Bowie himself. He had worked with industry legends Alan Klein and Mickie Most during the 1960s and had recently formed a company named Gem with then business partner Laurence Myers. To this highly ambitious, sharp-as-a-tack wheeler and dealer, the chance to manage a nascent but obviously sublimely talented star-to-be such as David Bowie must have seemed like the quintessential golden opportunity that had dropped from heaven.

Dissatisfied with progress under Pitt, a situation that came to a peak during the recording of *The Man Who Sold the World*, Bowie met with Defries and Myers in March 1970. The meeting was arranged by Olav Wyper, the general manager of Bowie's record company at the time, Philips, in which Bowie had confided his dissatisfaction with his then current management. Excited by the enthusiasm of Defries and Myers, it was not long until the artist drafted and sent a letter to the unsuspecting Pitt informing him that his services would no longer be required. With David Bowie on board, the new association led to the establishment of another company, MainMan, under which Bowie's activities were conducted with Defries at the management helm and Myers's involvement much reduced. MainMan's wider scope of operations included artists associated with David Bowie, such as Lou Reed, Iggy Pop, Mick Ronson, and Mott the Hoople. When Myers left Gem in 1972, David Bowie became the concern of Defries alone.

The flamboyant Defries had a significant and commanding presence about him. Almost all accounts describe him as a superb talker who was sublime in any negotiation scenario, who was adept at boosting the confidence of his artists, and who was both fearless and extremely shrewd in his business dealings. David Bowie believed in him utterly and was delighted to be able to focus on his art and leave the business and, more tellingly, the money side of things in

Defries's seemingly very capable hands. A firm believer in the power of hype—a factor that must have immediately struck a chord with David Bowie given his own penchant for it—Defries would treat his charges, especially David Bowie before his achievement of true superstardom, as top-tier megastars even when they had yet to achieve anywhere near such status. It was all limousines and swanky hotels and flashbulbs in order to create the all-important illusion of success. Proof of the seriousness of intent behind this marketing strategy is evident in the following excerpt reproduced from a management memo, dated October 22, 1972, sent to Bowie's entire entourage regarding the U.S. tour in progress at the time. Defries wrote, "If we are to remain inaccessible then we must maintain a degree of privacy.... People should stay in the hotel provided for them and should be available at all times.... Please try and remember that I am feeding, clothing and paying everybody in a style to which they are not accustomed for the one specific purpose called SUCCESS!!! It is important that you pick the right kind of hotel. We prefer no Howard Johnson/Holiday Inn type. I feel a Royal Coach Inn where possible would be excellent. Something with charm."

Photographer Mick Rock, who accompanied David Bowie on his British and American tours during 1972–1973, recalls another ruse designed to make David Bowie look larger than life. In the compact disc liner notes of the 2003 rerelease of Aladdin Sane (EMI), Rock recalled, "The whole game was theatre. It was, like, David going to America with three bodyguards. When he got to America, yes, there was interest in certain areas, but if you went to the Midwest, you couldn't drag people off the streets to see him. It was part of the theatre to treat him like a star. And there I was; I came very cheap—in fact I came for nothing! DeFries could then start talking about David having an 'exclusive photographer.' People were saying, 'David Bowie's got an exclusive photographer. Who the fuck is David Bowie?' The people reasoned: 'If he's got an exclusive photographer and bodyguards, there must be something going on.' That was a piece of living theatre, if you like, part of the whole thing that Tony and David cooked up between them."

But what David Bowie didn't know until 1974, by which time he was a bona fide superstar, was that the nature of the contract he had signed with Defries meant that his manager was earning as much as he was. Even worse, while Bowie believed that he and Defries were partners in MainMan, he was, in fact, Defries's employee. Feeling betrayed and hurt and unsure of his financial situation, David Bowie began legal action to extract himself from Defries and Main-Man. An extraordinarily messy undertaking, however, a full and final separation wasn't concluded until 1982, with Defries still earning off his famous employee right up until that point.

Biographer Paul Trynka suggests that Defries has been judged harshly over the years and effectively cast as something of a villainous shyster. There is perhaps some truth to this, as, like Pitt before him, he was completely devoted to furthering David Bowie's career and ultimately succeeded quite spectacularly. On this, Trynka attests that "those who were there testify that, not only was Defries the key figure in helping Bowie's rise to fame, he was also an integral part of that period's unforgettable magic." In addition, Defries undeniably made some good business decisions that played a large role farther down the road in allowing Bowie to take control of his career. For example, during the 1970s, he negotiated the deals with RCA Records that ensured that the recording copyrights would be retained and not signed away, something almost unheard of at that time. Nobody knew then how valuable recording rights would one day become, especially how valuable David Bowie's would be. According to an estimate published in *Billboard* in January 2016, his recordings and publishing rights at the time of his death had a value of at least $100,000,000.

Still, back in 1974–1975, there existed for David Bowie only the feeling of having been severely burned and betrayed through his experience with Tony Defries. Having learned the hard way some vital lessons about career management and the business side of the entertainment industry, following the parting of ways between the two, he elected to manage himself from that point on. He proved to be extremely adept at management, and for an artist so intent on forging his own way, this was both a sound and a highly pragmatic decision. With that said, he retained one very important figure from his Tony Defries/ MainMan days who would prove herself invaluable to this new self-determination: his ever-faithful and devoted personal assistant, Coco Schwab.

Coco Schwab: Assistant Extraordinaire

David Bowie has credited his (almost) career-long assistant, Coco Schwab, with many things, but perhaps the most important of all is being responsible for curing him of his out-of-control cocaine addiction during the mid-1970s. Quoted in the *Telegraph* in an article by Bernadette McNulty, Bowie acknowledged, "She became the most important person in my life in the mid Seventies. My whole lifestyle at that time made me quite bonkers, and I had a complete breakdown. Coco was the one person who told me what a fool I was becoming and she made me snap out of it." Coco was with David Bowie for no less than forty-three years—a full two-thirds of his life—and given the closeness with which they worked together, it's not unreasonable to suggest that she probably knew him better than anyone on the planet. In general, however, people know very little about Coco herself. She almost never gave interviews, and she has been the subject of much speculation—frequently spurious and speculative—from (probably jealous) fans and media over the decades. During a rare exception to her policy of declining to be interviewed, in a Q&A interview with fans on bowie.net conducted between June 27 and July

13, 2001, she explained, "I found it hard to learn that often my actions were misinterpreted or misunderstood, or simply slandered. I took a long time to understand that people believe in what they want. . . . However, David's friendship and understanding, and the importance of what he does, helped me to distinguish [between] the fear and envy of others and not react."

Coco's career-long journey with David Bowie began in 1973, when she answered an advertisement for a "girl Friday for a busy office" placed by Bowie's management, MainMan, in the *London Evening Standard*. With no clue as to what the job entailed or any idea regarding whom she would be working for or with, the young, enthusiastic, multilingual, and extremely smart American woman applied and was given the position. Reportedly anything but a fan of rock music, she worked in the MainMan management office for six months before announcing her intention to leave and go on a bus trip through the United States with a friend. As revealed in the above-mentioned Q&A interview on bowie.net, on hearing of her intended termination, Bowie invited her to become his personal assistant and have a limousine tour through the United States instead. Accordingly, she began her new role by accompanying him on the *Diamond Dogs* tour. From that point on, they became inseparable.

Coco the Protector

Coco quickly gained a reputation for being single-mindedly and ferociously loyal, completely and utterly devoted to her famous employer. Such was her devotion to Bowie and to her role that she polarized people because of the extent she would go to in protecting him. For anyone who wanted to get close to Bowie for whatever reason, it became a case of "getting past Coco" first. Biographer David Buckley describes her as a "gatekeeper, sometimes savagely restricting access to the superstar," and suggests that her always well-executed duties expanded even to the point of "hiring and firing and organising Bowie's diary." Bowie's first wife, Angela (Angie), went so far as to accuse Coco of breaking up her marriage to Bowie, and when she went to visit her husband in Berlin in 1976 to discuss the details of their divorce, she was incensed to find Coco living in the same apartment building. (Iggy Pop was also living there.) As Angie herself put it, "I found all her stuff in his apartment so I rearranged it—straight through the bedroom window. I heard it landed on the car below." Perhaps there is some justification for the act because, as Bowie's friend and producer Tony Visconti said in 1986, "Coco kept the irritating people out of his life and Angie had become one of them." There is also much speculation that Bowie and Schwab did indeed have an affair in the early days of her employment, but the most important fact of the matter is that they became great friends, confidantes, and colleagues, and any such brief dalliance—if true—is rendered rather immaterial.

If it is indeed true that Coco was not a fan of rock music before she began her career with David Bowie, the exploits of her employer clearly changed her view. On bowie.net, she claimed the following songs as her Bowie favorites: "Memory of a Free Festival," "Rock 'n' Roll Suicide," "Silly Boy Blue," "Queen Bitch," "Can You Hear Me," "Beauty and the Beast," "Sound and Vision," "Red Sails," "Always Crashing in the Same Car," "This Is Not America," "I'm Afraid of Americans," and "Something in the Air."

Coco on Film

Coco made her sole appearance in a David Bowie video for the song "Wild Is the Wind" in 1982, released as a single from the compilation album *ChangesTwoBowie*. In the video, which also features producer/bassist Tony Visconti miming on upright bass, Mel Gaynor from Simple Minds miming on drums, and Andy Hamilton playing the part of the saxophonist, Coco mimes in the shadows, strumming away as the guitarist.

David Bowie's Very Public Gratitude

In 1987, Bowie dedicated the song "Never Let Me Down"—the title track of his album of the same name—to Coco. The lyrics seemingly point to and give thanks for her intervention in the mid-1970s that helped him beat his drug addiction: "When I needed soul revival, I called your name. When I was falling to pieces, I screamed in pain. Your soothing hand that turned me round." If ever conclusive proof was needed that Bowie held his friend, constant companion, and assistant in the highest possible esteem, it came when his will was made public after his death. He stated that should his wife Iman not survive him, Coco should be appointed guardian of his daughter Lexi (Alexandria). In addition, he left to her $2 million from his estate in gratitude for all she had done for him over more than four decades.

Without the devoted attentions of Coco Schwab, his best friend, confidante, and ever-dedicated assistant, perhaps the David Bowie story would not have unfolded as it did. Certainly, the artist himself believed so.

23

The *Low* Album

David Bowie's Biggest Gamble and RCA's Nightmare

Turning a Blind Eye to Trendiness

The *Low* album (1977) found David Bowie at his most fearless and daring, effectively putting everything on the line in his desire to try something new. At a time in popular music history when punk rock held sway—especially in the United Kingdom, where the likes of the Sex Pistols and the Clash were the new safety pin–festooned, spitting rock royalty and the darling of rock critics and fans alike—existing rock stars (or "old farts," as they were frequently irreverently referred to) struggled to retain credibility. But not so David Bowie, whose spiky glam-era albums the young punks had grown up on, being emboldened enough in the process to beg, steal, or borrow a cheap guitar, learn three chords, and head on out to the garage to (as Bowie sang in "Star" from the *Ziggy Stardust* album) "play the wild mutation as a rock 'n' roll star." Instead of trying to compete with this prickly new breed that he had helped spawn, Bowie more than ever went his own way. As an advertising campaign slogan trumpeted later in 1977 on the release of the subsequent *"Heroes"* album, "There's Old Wave. There's New Wave. And There's David Bowie."

Instead of frenetically paced songs carried by the sounds of thrashing guitars, testosterone, snarling/sneering vocals, war-like drum aggression, and intentional studio-created primitivism, David Bowie eschewed all traces of trendiness and withdrew completely to come up with a beautifully crafted introspective prototype electronica-meets-ambient album. Incredibly, given that Bowie's fame was that of a singer, more than half of the album was instrumental, with side 2 the most remarkable of all, consisting of four tracks made up of lengthy free-time textures and electronic instrumental colors that evolved in their own time instead of following any kind of popular song form in their structures. Even on side 1, if rather more upbeat and conventional in comparison, the seven shorter tracks—bookended by instrumentals—sounded like mere unfinished fragments:

songs that had been started and then abandoned without explanation. Frankly, *no* other established rock artist would have dared try anything like *Low* in 1977 (or, indeed, probably since). Kris Needs summed up Bowie's bravery in his review in *ZigZag* on the album's release: "Bowie has gone right out on a limb with this album. He'll probably lose a bunch of fans, but I admire him for having the courage to put it out. He could have cruised on churning out *Ziggy Stardust Part 22* forever, instead, he battles on, donning new styles and guises, widening his scope and improving all the time. And that's part of the reason he's so exciting … you never know what he'll get up to next but can rest assured he won't stay trapped in the same bag, regardless of how successful it may be."

RCA's Trauma and Fan Confusion

While his motivation was personal catharsis, through the process of working out his problems through his art, David Bowie virtually invented a new musical language on *Low*. Coming at a time when he was burned out, drug weary, and looking to clean himself up after the cocaine-fueled though wonderful *Station to Station* (1976), even the most ardent of his fans, who'd stuck with him through the unexpected transitions from glam (*Ziggy Stardust* [1972], *Aladdin Sane* [1973], and *Diamond Dogs* [1974]) to soul (*Young Americans* [1975]) to motorik rock (*Station to Station*), didn't see this one coming. Small wonder, then, that his record company, RCA Records, collectively wrung their hands in horror on hearing the tapes for the first time. As Bowie writer Nicholas Pegg remembers, "Horrified RCA executives expecting another *Young Americans* or *Station To Station* pulled the album from the 1976 schedule and, as David later recalled, one of them offered to buy him a house in Philadelphia 'so he can write some more of that black music.'" Record companies don't like a successful artist changing their style, and, while based on previous experience, one might have quite rightly expected Bowie's record company to be more forgiving than most in that regard; such was the magnitude of the stylistic change in *Low* that they fully expected it to flop. Badly. It didn't, however, going on to reach highly respectable chart placings of number two in the United Kingdom and number eleven in the United States. Despite this, though, by comparison to what had gone before, it was still a poor result in RCA's eyes, with Thomas Jerome Seabrook, a specialist in Bowie's Berlin-era work and author of *Bowie in Berlin: A New Career in a New Town*, pointing out that "for the accountants at RCA it was nothing short of a failure. Initial chart peaks were comparable to those of *Young Americans*, but that only tells part of the story. The album's overall long-term performance was much less impressive. *The Rise and Fall of Ziggy Stardust and the Spiders from Mars* spent a total of 172 weeks on the British album chart: *Low* only managed 24."

Things were similarly patchy on the singles charts. The lead single from the album, "Sound and Vision," reached an impressive number three on the U.K. singles chart while also reaching the top ten in Germany, the Netherlands, and Austria. In the United States, however, it reached only a disappointing sixty-nine. From an album clearly almost completely bereft of songs that fitted normal pop chart single criteria, "Be My Wife" was released as a follow-up single but failed to chart.

To say that *Low* confounded fans and critics alike at its time of release is a huge understatement. Referencing the 1976 movie *The Man Who Fell to Earth*, in which David Bowie made his movie-acting debut in a lead role and which was released a year prior to the *Low* album, esteemed music critic Charles Shaar Murray, in his album review, humorously but cuttingly renamed *Low* as *The Man Who Fell to Bits*. He also wrote that the album consisted of "music and sounds so synthetic and depersonalised as to imply that the instruments did the playing after the band had gone home . . . an album so negative that it doesn't even contain emptiness or the void. . . . This is passive, inward-looking and—despite its ostentatious depersonalisation—profoundly selfish and ego-tistical, encouraging each individual to lay on his ass and listen to his wounds fester rather than go out to help and be helped. It's decadent in the sense that it glamorises and glorifies passive decay and I don't give a shit about how clever it may or may not be—David never makes minor errors, only fundamental ones—it stinks of artfully counterfeited spiritual defeat and futility and emp-tiness. We're low enough already, David. Give us a high or else just swap tapes with Eno by post and leave those of us who'd rather search for solutions than lie down and be counted to try and find ourselves instead of lose ourselves. You're a wonderful person but you've got problems."

This damning critique from a leading critic was a far cry from being a lone voice in the wilderness. Robert Christgau in the *Village Voice* decreed the instru-mental tracks on side 2 of the album to be mere "movie music" and regarded them as "banal." Such reactions led to a, at times, defensive response from the artist. To Tim Lott in *Record Mirror* in 1977, David Bowie responded archly, "I was disappointed in the reception *Low* got from the press—I gave them more credit than that." Some critics, however, found positivity even in the depths of their bafflement. Bud Scoppa, in *Phonograph Record*, wrote, "The new Bowie album doesn't make much sense. . . . [But] *Low* is the most intimate and free recording this extraordinary artist has yet made. This haunting, oddly beautiful music, strewn with recesses to be delved into gradually and a few at a time, is affecting in a strikingly subtle and powerful way. . . . Bowie's instincts are uncanny: he seems to stay on-course by continually veering off-course and he has a knack for making music that (as a friend says) 'feels exactly the way I feel right now.' There's something about *Low*'s textures, moods, and energies that gets under the skin and keeps working deeper, but I couldn't begin to explain how or why it works. I don't want to try—there are times when it's better to acknowledge than attempt to analyze, and this music is governed by a mystery that exists not to be penetrated but to be accepted as mystery."

The album's nonconforming mystery starts from the opening of the very first track. "Speed of Life" fades in with its synth-driven saw-like ambience from silence like someone has forgotten to turn the volume knob up on the stereo and then suddenly remembered. You wait for vocals that never arrive, although the track infers that they will at any moment, and just as you realize it's an instrumental after all, the track ends. Track 2 nods more toward conventionality, but its minimalist lyrics expose the fact that the album is in fact Bowie's own self-therapy, that all is not well with his mind-set or his behavior because he admits in the opening line, "Baby I've been breaking glass in your room again." The more energized "What in the World" follows, and the description of the damaged protagonist hiding away "deep in your room" is transparently all about Bowie himself. Containing the only real pop hooks on the album, what has become a virtual Bowie signature tune follows in fourth position on *Low*, but in "Sound and Vision," the gloomy introspective message stays the same, with "pale blinds drawn all day—nothing to do, nothing to say." The next track, "Always Crashing in the Same Car," is magnificently bleak too, with its message of repeated behaviors and an inability to break free of them no matter how destructive, as Bowie here is reduced to "going round and round the hotel garage." If the title of track 6, "Be My Wife," sounds more positive on the surface, then Bowie's emotionless, joyless vocal delivery soon punctures any hint of respite. "Sometimes you get so lonely," he opines, and the proposal of the song's title is thereby reduced to a mere ploy to relieve loneliness rather than a declaration of love and devotion. As far as conventional lyrics go, these are, however, the last to be heard on *Low*, as "A New Career in a New Town" then completes side 1 in the same manner it began: instrumentally. The track sounds like two ideas thrust together: the first a robotic Kraftwerk-esque slice of electronica and the second a more organic piano and harmonica–driven—almost honky-tonk— jam. Mysterious indeed.

Side 2 is the side that first pushes and then breaks asunder popular music in 1977. "Warszawa," "Art Decade," "Weeping Wall," and "Subterraneans" are like nothing previously heard in popular music, and certainly nothing came remotely close by any major top-tier artist of David Bowie's caliber. Willfully breaking all the rules of melody, harmony, rhythm, and instrumentation that governed and corralled what popular music was thought to be—that safeguarded it, if you like—here Bowie acts like he's never heard of such limitations and constraints. There is suddenly no rule book governing anything. The tracks are without exception beautiful and evocative. When Bowie uses his voice— something he does only rarely—it is to add color and texture but not to sing in any conventional sense. There are no words, and sound alone carries the message. The ambient electronic soundscapes drift onward completely on their own terms, and the effect suggests that human supremacy has given way to technological dominance. It is eerie but compelling, disturbing but masterful.

The Opposition

The 1977 was a watershed one peppered by the release of many great albums by pop and rock acts, making David Bowie's risk-laden diversion to the avant-garde world of ambient electronica stand out even more. How the RCA record company executives must have gnashed their teeth seeing the following list of releases: *Rumours* by Fleetwood Mac, *Animals* by Pink Floyd, *Never Mind the Bollocks* by the Sex Pistols, *The Clash* by the Clash, *Aja* by Steely Dan, *The Stranger* by Billy Joel, *My Aim Is True* by Elvis Costello, *Bat Out of Hell* by Meatloaf, *Out of the Blue* by Electric Light Orchestra, *News of the World* by Queen, *Saturday Night Fever* by Various Artists, *Let There Be Rock* by AC/DC, *Even in the Quietest Moments* by Supertramp, *I Robot* by the Alan Parsons Project, *Slowhand* by Eric Clapton, *Damned, Damned, Damned* by the Damned, *Rattus Norvegicus* by the Stranglers, *Running on Empty* by Jackson Brown, *Seconds Out* by Genesis, *In the City* by the Jam, *New Boots and Panties* by Ian Drury and the Blockheads, *Songs from the Wood* by Jethro Tull, *Bad Reputation* by Thin Lizzy, *Foreigner* by Foreigner, *In Color* by Cheap Trick, and *Decade* by Neil Young.

The Link to *The Man Who Fell to Earth*

When David Bowie accepted Nicolas Roeg's invitation to play the leading role of Thomas Jerome Newton in his film adaptation of Walter Tevis's 1963 novel of the same name, the understanding between both men was that he would also provide a unique, purpose-written sound track for the movie. Ultimately, the music David Bowie wrote and recorded for the project—created with the assistance of Paul Buckmaster, who had done the wonderful string arrangements for "Space Oddity" eight years earlier—was not used; at the eleventh hour, John Phillips of the Mamas and the Papas was asked by Roeg to compile a sound track. Phillips did so very successfully by combining existing successful popular music tracks, including Louis Armstrong's "Blueberry Hill" and the Kingston Trio's "Try to Remember," with more obscure Americana and a selection of various highly evocative and atmospheric instrumentals written by Phillips and by Japanese composer Stomu Yamashta. Rolling Stones guitarist Mick Taylor guest-starred on the sound track. Several contrasting explanations exist for this unplanned change in the arrangements for the movie's sound track. These include an alleged dispute over money, Bowie withdrawing his work in the belief that other candidates might have been asked to submit work despite his standing agreement with Roeg and that his work was not considered good enough or appropriate enough by Roeg for the task. In the *Guardian* in September 2016, in a piece by Chris Camion titled "Bowie and the Missing Soundtrack: The Amazing Story behind The Man Who Fell to Earth," Paul Buckmaster suggested that when he and David Bowie presented the handful of demos to Roeg, un-synched to the film and therefore heard well out of context, the director's reaction to these "disparate pieces" was, "What the hell is this?"

Whatever the actual facts may be—possibly the truth lies somewhere within a combination of these explanations—the experience of attempting to write a sound track for *The Man Who Fell to Earth* proved to be a vital, eye-opening, and rewarding one for David Bowie. The *Low* album released the following year was imbued with music of the same nature—the final track, "Subterraneans," actually utilizing one of the unused movie demos as its basis—and the subsequent *"Heroes"* was, in part, of a similar vibe.

Creating the Stuff of Legend

With the passing of time, the groundbreaking brilliance of *Low* has been widely recognized as a virtual line in the sand, and the album's stature has grown to the point where it is seen as one of the most important and defining works in the history of popular music. Toward the end of 1977, RCA would proclaim, "Tomorrow belongs to those who can hear it coming," as they began to realize that their most troublesome superstar was, for all their commercial qualms, breaking new musical ground. To their credit, it was a good advertising slogan that completely and succinctly summarized the nature and importance of David Bowie's work in 1977 with *Low* and, subsequently, with *"Heroes."*

24

The Musical Family

Identifying Some of David Bowie's Most Important Collaborators

While David Bowie is rightly considered to be one of the most creative artists of the twentieth and twenty-first centuries, being a fine performer and songwriter, an actor, and so on, he had an additional talent of considerable worth that is often overlooked. That is, he was extraordinarily adept at identifying talented collaborators with whom he could work and who possessed talents that enhanced his own. Of course, given the constant changing of musical style that David Bowie enjoyed, these collaborators would sometimes come and go relatively quickly according to Bowie's needs of the moment, and other specialists would be identified and brought in to help bring the next vision to life. Others would come and go throughout his career. The first of these invaluable allies to enter his realm was Tony Visconti, the American musician and producer who came to international prominence initially through his hit-laden work with Marc Bolan and T Rex.

Tony Visconti

Tony Visconti produced David Bowie's second album, the self-titled *David Bowie* (1969), released in the United States as *Man of Words/Man of Music* and rereleased as *Space Oddity* in 1972 in the wake of the success of his breakthrough album *The Rise and Fall of Ziggy Stardust and the Spiders from Mars.* Oddly enough, the album's standout track and Bowie's first-ever hit, "Space Oddity," was the exception on the album, being produced instead by Gus Dudgeon due to Visconti's personal distaste for the song. This blip aside, the recording of the album was the starting point of a career-long relationship—albeit with a lengthy two-decade break through the 1980s and 1990s—that saw Visconti at the studio controls for many other David Bowie album projects, including most of those that are considered to be his landmark works.

Visconti's credits are *The Man Who Sold the World* (1970), *David Live* (1974), *Young Americans* (1975), *Low* (1977), *"Heroes"* (1977), *Stage* (1978), *Lodger* (1979), *Scary Monsters (and Super Creeps)* (1980), *Heathen* (2002), *Reality* (2003), *The Next Day* (2013), and *Blackstar* (2016).

When asked in a 2002 interview on livewire.com what approach made their relationship so successful and special, David Bowie replied, "I'm not sure that Tony and I have much of an approach really. It never feels like work." Reading this and other interviews conducted across the significant breadth of David Bowie's career, it becomes clear that both men allowed each other significant free space to experiment and bring their own ideas, strengths, and creativity to their collaborations in an easy, unpressured vibe. Bowie's songs would not be even close to completely written going into the studio, so the two of them would enjoy sculpting and reshaping the works until both agreed they were finished. Such flexibility, freedom, friendship, and an extremely high regard and respect for each other seems to have been the foundation of the Bowie/Visconti magic formula.

Mick Ronson

Another highly significant early collaborator was guitarist Mick Ronson. Gaining the trust and full cooperation of the down-to-earth, Hull-born Ronson paid testament to the power of Bowie's personality and talent for persuasion. Ronson needed much persuasion to, first, move down to London to join the Spiders from Mars and then, especially, to don the makeup and gender-bending glam costuming of the Ziggy Stardust glam-rock era. But once he agreed, Bowie found that he had the perfect onstage partner. As he explained in 1994, "Mick was the perfect foil for the Ziggy character. He was very much a salt-of-the-earth type, the blunt northerner with a defiantly masculine personality, so that what you got was the old-fashioned Yin and Yang thing. As a rock duo, I thought we were every bit as good as Mick and Keith or Axl and Slash. Ziggy and Mick were the personification of that rock n roll dualism."

It was with the engaging, flamboyant, and attractive blond-haired guitarist that Bowie would create one of the most challenging gender-bending rock images of the era as he performed mock fellatio on Ronson's guitar during the band's live shows to the delight of the audience and the clicking of press cameras. But Ronson was more than a guitarist. He was a talented arranger and producer in his own right, fully on the same wavelength as Bowie and therefore able to help bring to life some of most iconic pieces of their early 1970s glam-era work, including *The Rise and Fall of Ziggy Stardust and the Spiders from Mars* (1972), *Aladdin Sane* (1973), and *Pinups* (1973).

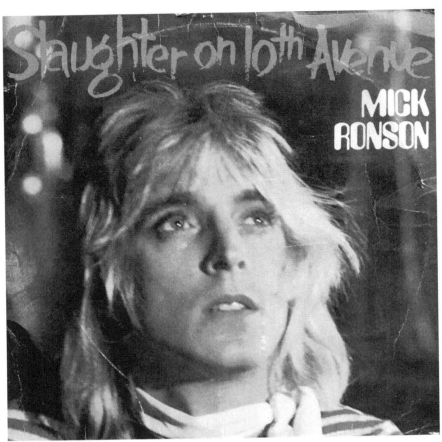

Slaughter on 10th Avenue album by Mick Ronson, 1974   *Author's Collection*

Ronson had fleeting success of his own as an artist, with his 1974 album *Slaughter on 10th Avenue* reaching an impressive number nine on the U.K. album charts, although subsequent albums did not fare so well.

Mike Garson

Having toured with Bowie during his Ziggy Stardust period, extraordinarily versatile American keyboardist Mike Garson was to prove a crucial ally on the *Aladdin Sane* album, imbuing the work—especially the title track—with a decadent avant-garde quality perfect for the subject matter and going well beyond rock norms. During the recording of the album, Bowie requested something very unusual of Garson, as the keyboardist told interviewer Maarten de Haan on artistinterviews.eu in 2008: "I had told Bowie about the avant-garde thing.

When I was recording the *Aladdin Sane* track for Bowie, it was just two chords, an A and a G chord, and the band was playing very simple English rock and roll. And Bowie said: 'play a solo on this.'... I played a blues solo, but then he said: 'No, that's not what I want.' And then I played a Latin solo. Again, Bowie said: 'No no, that's not what I want.' He then continued: 'You told me you play that avant-garde music. Play that stuff!' And I said: 'Are you sure? 'Cause you might not be working anymore!' So I did the solo that everybody knows today, in one take. And to this day, I still receive emails about it. Every day." Effusive in his praise for the way David Bowie brings out the best in the performers he chooses to work with, Garson concluded, "I always tell people that Bowie is the best producer I ever met, because he lets me do my thing."

In addition to working extensively with Bowie on concert tours and appearing on resultant live recordings, Garson would feature on many other studio albums after *Aladdin Sane*, including *Pinups* (1973), *Diamond Dogs* (1974), *Young Americans* (1975), *Black Tie White Noise* (1993), *The Buddha of Suburbia* (1993), *1. Outside* (1995), *Earthling* (1997), and *Reality* (2003).

David Bowie gave a telling tribute to Mike Garson that heads up Garson's own website, MikeGarson.com. He said, "It is pointless to talk about his ability as a pianist. He is exceptional. However, there are very, very few musicians, let alone pianists, who naturally understand the movement and free thinking necessary to hurl themselves into experimental or traditional areas of music, sometimes, ironically, at the same time. Mike does this with such enthusiasm that it makes my heart glad just to be in the same room with him."

Brian Eno

Bowie had admired another keyboard player, Brian Eno, throughout the glam-rock days, when he, along with Eno's band Roxy Music, epitomized the high-art end of the genre. By the time Bowie had left glam behind, had flirted convincingly and successfully with soul on *Young Americans* (1975), and was ready to embark on his groundbreaking Berlin-era albums, Eno had assembled a showcase of daring experimental solo albums, having left Roxy Music in 1973. These piqued Bowie's interest even more, with the out-of-left-field creativity of Eno, along with his mastery of all things synthesizer and electronic related, making him the perfect collaborator as Bowie looked to dehumanize his work and allow highly experimental technology to dominate. Brian Eno thus became the perfect partner for Bowie's new and controversial musical direction, and the resultant ambient/electronic *Low* (1977) is now regarded as a hallmark in the development of popular music. The two albums that followed, *"Heroes"* (1977) and *Lodger* (1979), built further on the pair's legacy, and after a lengthy hiatus, the collaboration would continue with the similarly left-field conceptual album *1. Outside* (1995).

In an interview with Paul Gorman at the time of the *1. Outside* album, reproduced on his website, paulgormanis.com, in 2013, David Bowie was asked if it was easy slotting into working with Brian Eno again. His enthusiastic answer spoke volumes about the relationship and connection between the two men: "Oh, I can't tell you how easy it was. It was almost as though no time had been wedged in, like we were carrying on from the third album together. The chemistry between us is just tremendous. I'm not quite sure what it is, but it's probably about the differences between us. Where Brian will take things from low-art and elevate them to high-art status, I tend to do exactly the opposite, which is to thieve from high art and demean it down to street level!"

Carlos Alomar

Guitarist Carlos Alomar's name has become synonymous with David Bowie's, the two having worked extensively together since their first alliance on *Young Americans* (1975). Like Mike Garson, Alomar has appeared in Bowie's work both live and recorded across a four-decade span (1970s–2000s), an extraordinary feat given Bowie's penchant for evolution and change. Other album credits include *Station to Station* (1976), *Low* (1977), *"Heroes"* (1977), *Lodger* (1979), *Scary Monsters (and Super Creeps)* (1980), *Tonight* (1984), *Never Let Me Down* (1987), *1. Outside* (1995), *Heathen* (2002), and *Reality* (2003).

Robert Fripp

With a guitar style both angular and unorthodox and a personality to match, the King Crimson guitarist who had previously worked with Brian Eno on his solo projects, including the albums *Here Come the Warm Jets* (1973) and *Another Green World* (1975), proved to be a highly distinctive element on two of Bowie's best and most critically acclaimed albums: *"Heroes"* and *Scary Monsters (and Super Creeps)*. His signature is all over, in particular, the title tracks of both albums and elsewhere. Fripp provided a colorful highlight on the excellent *Five Years* documentary (BBC, 2013). Recalling being asked by David Bowie and Brian Eno in the *"Heroes"* recording session to play some "hairy rock 'n' roll" on the title track, Fripp asks of the BBC interviewer, "What is the difference between pop and rock and roll?" Pausing for wonderful dramatic effect before superbly answering his own question, he utters, with gravitas saturating his voice, "You might get fucked." While in relative terms Fripp's contribution to Bowie's work is small, it is significant enough on these landmark works that he should be considered one of Bowie's most vital collaborators—a quality, not quantity, measure.

Earl Slick

One of rock's great guitarists and a significant contributor to Bowie's work both on record and onstage, Slick made notable contributions to four early career albums—*Diamond Dogs* (1974), *David Live* (1974), *Young Americans* (1975), and *Station to Station* (1976)—before the two parted ways for a lengthy twenty-six years, only to reunite post-millennium and work on *Heathen* (2002), *Reality* (2003), and *The Next Day* (2013). An integral member of Bowie's touring band, he also appeared on the *A Reality Tour* album (2010).

Nile Rodgers

While some might question the inclusion of Rodgers in a compilation of Bowie's most important collaborators because of the brevity of their association and the way the resultant album, *Let's Dance*, polarized fans, the selection of the hit-proven producer is comprehensive proof of Bowie's ability to recognize in his chosen creative partners precise qualities that he needed at a given time. In short, Bowie sought out Rodgers for one specific reason—to provide smash hits—and Rodgers obliged magnificently.

Reeves Gabrels

Worn out from the personal and commercial demands of being a mainstream pop celebrity and feeling drained of creativity, by the end of the 1980s, Bowie needed to draw on something new and edgy in order to reinvigorate himself. When publicist Sarah Gabrels gave him a tape of her husband's work during a 1987 tour, Bowie was intrigued enough by what he heard to contact the stylistically unusual and experimental guitarist. This introduction initially led to the two men working together in the band Tin Machine (covered in chapter 25). Following Bowie's subsequent return to his solo career, the Tin Machine venture having provided the breathing space that he'd needed, he continued to work with Gabrels, and the guitarist's sound duly permeates Bowie's 1990s-era work, performing with his distinctive approach to guitar playing on *1. Outside* (1995), *Earthling* (1997), and *"Hours…"* (1999).

Gail Ann Dorsey

Like Carlos Alomar and despite having performed onstage and in the studio with a plethora of other artists, multi-instrumentalist (but primarily bassist and vocalist for Bowie) and solo artist Gail Ann Dorsey's name has become synonymous with David Bowie's through her extensive late career work with him. Joining the artist's live band on the 1995–1996 1. *Outside* tour, she remained a core member of the touring lineup for the rest of Bowie's career in addition to performing on the albums *Earthling* (1997), *Reality* (2003), and *The Next Day* (2013).

Drawing the Best from his Many Short-Term and Long-Term Collaborators

As stated at the beginning of this chapter, David Bowie had an extraordinary gift for choosing the right collaborators. Sometimes they were with him a long time, sometimes a short time; some were big, already established performers in their own right, and others were plucked from seeming obscurity. But all nevertheless left their mark within the Bowie chronology. Among others well worthy of mention are Woody Woodmansey, Trevor Bolder, Robin Lumley, Mark Plati, Sterling Campbell, Aynsley Dunbar, Adrian Belew, Stevie Ray Vaughn, and Pete Townshend, and there are surely many others deserving of mention as well. For the last word on David Bowie's acclaimed prowess in first choosing and then getting the best from his pool of collaborators, Gail Ann Dorsey commented in a tribute piece in the *Guardian* some months after his death in 2016, "David had an uncanny ability to choose just the right people, with just the right chemistry, and all the skills necessary to execute his vision. Rarely did I see him get it wrong. He believed that once the perfect cast was in place, so to speak, the play would virtually perform itself … the most important work was done. Because of that philosophy there was an incredible amount of freedom for the musicians to 'play,' and by that I mean to play as a child plays—fearless and free. For David, there were treasures to be found in the unexpected. He would feed off the energy around him, and with grace, humour and enthusiasm he would effortlessly guide and shape our efforts into something inevitably awesome."

Often praised for his musical genius as a performer and songwriter, this aspect of David Bowie's modus operandi has perhaps not received the recognition it deserves. It is a rare superstar who can completely subsume his own ego in pursuit of presenting an open canvas to his collaborators with the goal of allowing them to bring to the table their own creative ideas. It is a tactic that worked superbly for him throughout his career.

25

Tin Machine

David Bowie's Attempt at Becoming One of the Boys

By the time 1987 came to an end, David Bowie was tired and disillusioned, wrung out by the never-ending expectations brought about by having sat on the top rung of the ever-hungry, all-devouring music industry. Now a global superstar and genuine pop giant who'd been launched into the mainstream on the technically brilliant, uber-successful, but creatively divisive *Let's Dance* album—followed by the much weaker *Tonight* and *Never Let Me Down* albums—he was a bona fide stadium-filling act to whom countless thousands of the MTV generation flocked to hear his impressive bevy of hits. The pressure on him was huge to keep the momentum going at all costs. At no other stage of his career had he more resembled a puppet rather than his rightful role as a supreme puppeteer. As he related to *Uncut* magazine in 1995, "After *Let's Dance*, I succumbed, tried to make things more accessible, took away the very strength of what I do." No longer seen primarily as the edgy, fringe-aligned artist renown for pushing the boundaries with every successive album, the 1987 global Glass Spider tour (eighty-six concerts over six months) had very effectively delivered him to his new worldwide mass audience. But it had also brought on the Bowie name the double-edged sword of commercial success tinged with a huge decrease in critical/aesthetic acclaim. Accusations of selling out and becoming a "greatest hits" kind of artist abounded in the reviews and music media. This was, surely, overly harsh, and a kinder view was that Bowie-as-pop-star was just another brilliantly conceived and achieved role played by rock's finest thespian. Nevertheless, the combination of beige public and critical perception, his own increasing boredom with his new career direction, and the grueling greatest-hits treadmill he had found himself on served to instill in him a very strong desire for change. And when it came, it was to be a typically big and unexpected one.

Spotting an Escape Route from Pop Stardom

While on the North American leg of the Glass Spider tour, David Bowie was given a demo tape to listen to by Sarah Gabrels, one of the public relations people accompanying him on the tour. It contained music made by her husband's band, guitarist Reeves Gabrels, and Bowie was immediately intrigued by its experimental and rule-breaking nature. He'd met Reeves briefly during the tour when he visited his wife and had enjoyed talking matters of art with him, the guitarist having had an art school background, which immediately established common ground between them. After hearing the tape, Bowie quickly made personal contact with the oblique guitarist, gently chiding him in the process for not having mentioned the fact that he was a guitarist (Bowie had assumed he was a painter), and the two decided to try working together. At this time, the pair looked to expand the creative palette by experimenting with composing with multi-instrumentalist Erdal Kizilcay, but Kizilcay ultimately would not join the nascent band.

Back in the late 1970s, when accompanying his close friend Iggy Pop on tour, Bowie had enjoyed performing with two of Pop's other backing musicians, brothers Tony and Hunt Sales. The sons of famous comedian Soupy Sales, Tony was a bassist and Hunt a drummer, the two of them combining to form a rather unique rhythm section. It was to the Sales brothers that Bowie and Gabrels turned to complete the new lineup as plans for their new band firmed up. As Tony Sales recalled in the *Music Paper* in 1989, David Bowie was "thinking about getting a band together—*something* together. He didn't know exactly what he wanted to do, but he wanted Hunt and I to meet Reeves and maybe we could all write together, come up with something."

Because of David Bowie's reluctance to play guitar in the live setup on tour, they were joined at first by Kevin Armstrong and later by Eric Schermerhorn (who would go on to play with Iggy Pop), but neither were core members of the band. As Gabrels put it in an interview with *guitar moderne*, "If David was a little more responsible, guitar-wise, we could have done it with just the two of us, especially the first record. On the second record some of the chord voicings were more complicated. At one point I tuned his guitar in all roots and fifths and said, 'You just play with one finger and it will be okay.' But he was only going to play guitar when he felt like it."

In *Spin* magazine, Gabrels would reveal the attraction of the band's name, which was taken from a song they had collectively written. Tin Machine, he said, "worked on a number of levels for us. The archaic—the idea of tin, which is still everywhere: tin cans, when you go to the supermarket; when you walk down the street you find rusting tin. It's such a supposedly archaic material, but it's everywhere. Sort of like the idea of us playing this music and not using drum machines and sequencers and things like that. There's a point at which it connects. At least for us. And the final thing, for lack of a better name."

Bowie was adamant that the band was to be a four-way democracy, and the notion of being regarded as David Bowie with a backing band was not what any of them wanted. Even the band's album covers and publicity photographs were purposely designed to buy into this totally egalitarian notion, with the four of them dressed alike and no one allowed to stand out. According to Gabrels, Bowie put it to them like this right at the beginning: "I think this has got to be a band. Everybody's got input. Everybody's writing. You guys don't listen to me anyway . . . the band will cease to exist the moment it ceases to be a musical experience for any of us."

The raw music of Tin Machine was in complete contrast to the glossy, careful, and calculated production and songwriting perfection of Bowie's most recent albums. Encouraged by the Sales brothers not to spend too long in crafting the music and lyrics at either the writing or the recording stages, the music turned out rough, heavy, angry, and punk/grunge in style. Recording basically live in the studio and with overdubs kept to a minimum, it was a massive U-turn from what Bowie had been delivering to his record company, EMI, and while they released the debut self-titled album *Tin Machine*, they were clearly displeased at his new direction. Despite initially reaching number three on the U.K. album charts (and number twenty-eight in the United States), sales faded quickly, and the label subsequently began searching for another record company to take on their errant artist's contract. As a result, *Tin Machine II*, which performed poorly in contrast to the first album (U.K. #23, U.S. #126), was released on Victory Records.

The low-fi approach of the band's songwriting and recording stretched to their tours. Concerts were held in small clubs and intimate venues far removed from the vast stadiums of *Let's Dance*–era solo Bowie. They sold well, with audiences largely made up of Bowie fans taking the rare opportunity to witness their idol performing up close and personal. However, those fans hoping to hear "Rebel Rebel" or "Ziggy Stardust"—let alone "China Girl" or "Blue Jean"—were left frustrated as Tin Machine stuck to Tin Machine originals or, now and then, cover versions of other acts. Of David Bowie's vast back catalog, there was nothing to be seen.

The Financial Sacrifice

Between the two Tin Machine studio albums (1989 and 1991), Bowie found himself financially challenged—the price of stepping off the superstar roller coaster—and therefore, to replenish his funds, he released the *Sound + Vision* boxed set, which sold very well. On the proviso that it would be the last time he performed his back catalog, the attendant concert tour was also a great success. The coffers duly restored, it was back to Tin Machine and the second—and final—studio album. Whether due to its poor reception or the revitalization of his solo career through the *Sound + Vision* experience (possibly both), this was the end of the band experiment, and David Bowie would instead turn his attention to creating the critically acclaimed "comeback" album *Black Tie White Noise* (1993).

In Retrospect

It is all too easy to look on David Bowie's Tin Machine experience as a glitch in the matrix, some kind of a blip on a stellar career. But while a relative failure in a commercial sense and certainly leaving many fans bewildered, even disappointed, at what seemed to be an obvious and uncharacteristic retreat, the truth was that, at this moment in his career, Bowie needed a kind of artistic cleansing, something that would stand in opposition to the superstar shallowness he had experienced through much of the 1980s. Without Tin Machine, perhaps none of the challenging work he created through the 1990s and post-millennium might ever have been made. As he put it in *Uncut* magazine in October 1999, "The whole being-in-a-band experience was good for me . . . it really is a strange thing to think about now, that I actually did that to myself . . . but it was very useful. All three of them were very canny, masters of the put-down—the Sales brothers, being the sons of Soupy Sales, were born stand-ups. So I wasn't allowed to lord it, which I recognised as a situation I wanted. To be part of a group of people working towards one aim. Success was rather immaterial. I needed the process, to acclimatise myself again to why I wrote, why I did what I did—all those issues that an artist going through 'a certain age' starts to think about . . . I had to kick-start my engine again in music. I look back on the Tin Machine years with great fondness. They charged me up. I can't tell you how much."

However valuable it was to him on a creative level, it always seemed inevitable that Tin Machine was not destined to last, and sure enough, the band came and went in two years. The band had served its purpose admirably, allowing Bowie to cut the industry strings that had rendered him more a puppet than a puppeteer and making him hungry and uncompromising once again—just like the David Bowie of old whom both he and fans the world over longed for. Unsurprisingly, then, artistically and spiritually renewed and refreshed, David Bowie moved on with his career. As the experiences in the earliest days of that career had shown, with a string of bands joined and then left in quick succession, the unique talent that was David Bowie was never destined to be held within a band. In rock 'n' roll, not everyone is created equal. But Tin Machine had served its purpose well. And in a significant development, David Bowie was to retain the services of Reeves Gabrels on the resumption of his solo career, the two continuing to write and perform together until 1999. Of their decade-plus time together, Gabrels told *Mojo* in February 2016, "Whether it was the Tin Machine albums, Outside, Earthling, 'Hours...' or any of the other projects we worked on, my role never seemed clearly defined. It was co-writer, co-producer, confidant and of course, guitarist. Being art-school boys David and I settled into a conspiratorial friendship early. Throughout the following 13 years, the studio was our Buckminster Fuller sandbox, our safe place to create where time stopped and art was made. There was no careerism, or attention to a 'market-place' but, instead, a desire to tell a story... leave a trail of good work."

Gabrels is currently (since 2012) guitarist with the Cure, ironically having first met Robert Smith at David Bowie's now legendary fiftieth-birthday concert, which featured a plethora of rock star friends as guests joining him onstage at Madison Square Garden on January 9, 1997.

The Tin Machine Albums and Chart Placings

Tin Machine, 1989 (U.K. #3, U.S. #28)
Tin Machine II, 1991 (U.K. #23, U.S. #126)
Tin Machine Live: Oy Vey, Baby, 1992 (U.K. #–, U.S.#–)

26

The Art of Pretense

Becoming a Real Star by Acting Like One

Among his many innovations, David Bowie brought hefty dollops of pretense, play, and make-believe into rock 'n' roll, wonderfully so in the eyes of his legions of supporters and fiendishly so in the eyes of his many detractors who feared the foundational changes to the rock 'n' roll landscape that would transpire. Sure enough, David Bowie did rewrite the rule book, or, more correctly, he completely threw it out of the window. The notion that a star could be an artificial construction was the antithesis of the traditional rock values that had been carefully honed and solidified throughout the 1960s. With a wave of David Bowie's theatrical hand, everything was about to change.

Puncturing the Myth of Authenticity

In the 1960s, rock stardom was intrinsically bound up in a myth of authenticity. How a star looked and acted on the rock stage was supposed to be inseparable from how that same star looked and acted in all other facets of his or her life. Further, whatever was being sung about or portrayed during a performance or on a recording was supposed to reflect the true innermost feelings, morals, politics, emotions, and personality of the singer and/or band in question. Should any hint of obvious theatricality, masking, or "showbiz" appear, then the myth of authenticity could be pierced, and—to rather appropriately paraphrase David Bowie—then the others might see the faker. Simply, the 1960s ethos of rock authenticity demanded that there be no division between the person and the performer. The Rolling Stones, Jimi Hendrix, Jim Morrison and the Doors, Janis Joplin, and so on—these artists were seen as truly authentic performers, divinely chosen as if a lightning bolt from the heavens had bestowed on them limitless God-given talent so that they might soar above the heads of mere mortals and take their rightful place as the flag bearers of the countercultural generation. The motivations and trajectories of these chosen few were regarded as pure and transparent, untainted by commerce, and unmanipulated by industry concerns. In short, these stars were supposed to be naturally occurring entities, not constructed in any way, shape, or form; they were perceived to be as 100 percent natural as Woodstock's mud puddles were. That they might be the result of any kind of construction was antithetical. Okay, the mighty Beatles might be seen as having pushed the envelope a little with the release of *Sgt. Pepper's Lonely Hearts Club Band* (1967) in the way that it presented to the world a new and totally fictitious band. But really this did nothing to puncture the myth of authenticity because they were so well established and adored as Paul, John, George, and Ringo—the lovable, cheeky mop-tops from Liverpool—that everyone knew it was just the lads having a bit of dress-up fun. It was still, for all intents and purposes, "real."

Enter David Bowie

Despite the significant but fleeting brush with fame afforded by the success of "Space Oddity" back in 1969—a song largely written off as a novelty designed to cash in on the successful Apollo 11 space mission—by the opening years of the 1970s, David Bowie's achievements remained relatively modest. From the time of his first single release, "Liza Jane," on June 5, 1964, a succession of early bands had all sunk without trace with record companies coming and going in quick succession, and this was a pattern that would repeat through both singles and albums when he became a solo artist. Seemingly, everyone recognized that David Bowie had talent, but neither Bowie nor those charged with assisting him seemed to know quite what to do with that talent and how to package it. By 1972, a full eight years after his debut, he was still not "a name" in the upper echelons of rock in either the national or the international popular music industries. Perhaps, then, it was time to make a bid for success with the assistance of a new name and a new bag of tricks. If it wasn't going to happen organically, what could a bit of genetic engineering do?

The Experiment Begins: Hype and Arnold Corns

The invention of characters had already featured heavily in Bowie's early work. While Major Tom and his doomed space mission of 1969 is certainly the most well-known early example of the artist's penchant for inventing and playing a role, his failed self-titled debut album of 1967 featured a different character in practically every song. There was the chilling child killer of "Please Mr. Gravedigger"; the tragic "Little Bombardier," run out of town because of suspicions of pedophilia; the heartbroken soldier in "Rubber Band," who returned from fighting in World War I to find that his sweetheart had married the leader of the local brass band; and "Uncle Arthur," a thirty-two-year-old man who, on finally meeting a woman and falling in love, at last plucked up the courage to move away from his mother, only to find his new life all too much, admitting defeat and moving back in with her. While none of these characters was particularly endearing, empowering, or successful and certainly none of the constructions were in the least bit "star-like"—quite the opposite, in fact—it is very clear that here David Bowie was playing with visions of the world seen through the eyes of others beyond himself. He was beginning to cast his net.

The clearest portent for what was to come was a handful of performances, between February and May 1970, by the hand-selected, Bowie-fronted band Hype. Each member of the four-piece band adopted a character, brought to life by flamboyant costuming. Bowie himself was Rainbowman, guitarist and future Spider from Mars Mick Ronson was Gangsterman, bassist and future Bowie producer Tony Visconti was Hypeman, and drummer John Cambridge was Cowboyman. Having tried bringing characters to life on vinyl, he was now trying the same thing on the live rock stage. Performing a disparate mix of original songs from his career to date along with a light sprinkling of covers, the onstage image of the musicians did not have much to do with the band's music, and by all accounts, the experiment bombed as the denim-clad audiences looked on this theatrical spectacle with a mix of suspicion and derision. While the 1960s myth of rock authenticity still held tenuous sway, then, one notable exception in the crowd at the February 22 performance at London's Roundhouse was the soon-to-be-glam-idol himself, Bowie's friend and rival Marc Bolan, who attended dressed as a Roman soldier complete with plastic breastplate. But David Bowie would not be held at bay for much longer.

Almost ready to make his bid for stardom, one additional piece of the preliminary experiment remained in the form of another temporary "pretend" group, a band with the most unlikely and unlovable name Arnold Corns. But this time around, it was a band that would actually release music into the marketplace, albeit to no avail. The original Arnold Corns band—the name reputedly inspired by the Pink Floyd song "Arnold Layne"—was a preexisting act from Dulwich College that David Bowie had agreed to write some songs for. He had also agreed to write songs for Freddie Burretti (aka Rudi Valentino), who would later stake his own place in Bowie history as a fashion designer (see also chapter 21). David Bowie decided to combine both tasks and have Burretti front a revamped Arnold Corns that featured replacement musicians hand-picked by himself, a lineup that was really the Spiders from Mars in waiting, as it featured Mick Ronson on guitar, Woody Woodmansey on drums, and Trevor Bolder on bass. In his book *Strange Fascination: David Bowie, the Definitive Story*, biographer David Buckley refers to Arnold Corns as "an early answer to Milli Vanilli," and it's not a bad comparison given that Burretti/Valentino was cast as the lead singer, but actually it was David Bowie's voice that featured in the ill-fated debut (and only) single "Moonage Daydream"/"Hang on to Yourself," released on May 7, 1971. A total flop, a second single, "Looking for a Friend"/"Man in the Middle," was planned but withdrawn before it saw the light of day, although it was to appear many years later in various rarity and outtake compilations destined for the collections of Bowie completists. Burretti's voice was only ever to be heard on the unreleased "Man in the Middle." Arnold Corns was summarily folded up and deposited in a trash can, having made zero impact on the music scene. Nevertheless, the songs David Bowie had written for the project would resurface very soon and meet with great success, while the lineup of musicians assembled, sans Burretti, became the last piece of the puzzle. Arnold Corns, therefore, proved to be the final dress rehearsal for the tumultuous events that were to follow.

Enter Ziggy Stardust

With the Hype and Arnold Corns experiences behind him but tellingly absorbed and analyzed, Rainbowman was refined and reinvented until he ultimately reemerged in 1972 as Bowie's most famous character of all: Ziggy Stardust. And this time, the invented persona was not a down-on-his-luck, unlikable character like the sad and lonely souls who inhabited the debut album; rather, this was a fully fledged *star* character, oozing confidence, sex appeal, social relevance, and oodles of X factor. And now, rather than having an image divorced from the music being performed onstage, Ziggy Stardust had his own concept album full of songs to assist in pushing home the message. Sure, it was still a pretense if you really wanted to boil it down, but it was so well realized and carried off with such aplomb that it was in most ways even better than the real thing. David Bowie's plastic star, Ziggy Stardust (it was even right there in the name), shone brighter than anything else on the pop/rock horizon in 1972. It was a sound/vision/fantasy fait accompli.

Ziggy Stardust was a potpourri of pop music and wider pop-cultural influences, all assembled with great care and forethought by Bowie. Rocker Vince Taylor was in there, and so was Gene Vincent. American fringe performer the Legendary Stardust Cowboy was there, and so was Liza Minnelli's Sally Bowles from *Cabaret*. Japanese fashion designer Kansai Yamamoto played a key role, while Stanley Kubrick's droogs from *A Clockwork Orange* also received a nod. Ziggy Stardust was packaged from a radically new take on a bunch of used parts. As he would retrospectively put it himself, reprinted in Nicholas Pegg's *The Complete David Bowie*, "What I did with my Ziggy Stardust was package a totally credible, plastic rock & roll singer—much better than the Monkees could ever fabricate. I mean, my plastic rock & roller was much more plastic than anybody's. And that was what was needed at the time."

The true magic of Ziggy was the extent to which his creator threw himself so completely into the role, progressing well beyond the studio recordings and the stage. So personally and professionally empowering was the Ziggy Stardust role that Bowie extended it well beyond these traditional performative media. As Angie Bowie, his wife at the time, confirmed about her husband in her frank personal account *Backstage Passes*, "By creating Ziggy to go out and front for him, David never had to act like himself in public if he didn't want to." And as the man himself attested in a 2003 interview with Chris Roberts in *Uncut* magazine, "I was having a blast at first . . . I was doing great, having a helluva time. And I'd play up to the Ziggy persona, I enjoyed it. I was basically an extremely shy person. I really was. I found it hard to get it up for a conversation with anyone. I was very reticent, and felt incredibly insecure about my own abilities of communication on a one-to-one level. So that flamboyant front was very useful to me. It gave me a platform: I talked to people as Ziggy. Some of me came through, but it was kinda twisted through the persona of Ziggy, who was a crazed mirror, one of those funny fairground mirrors. David Jones was in there somewhere. But not much."

The Name of the Game Was Hype

When Bowie-as-Ziggy toured the United States for the first time in September 1972—an experience that he would channel into the *Aladdin Sane* album, which was basically a *Ziggy Stardust* part 2—he and his then manager, Tony Defries, set about creating their own myth in order to further their joint prospects, a myth not of authenticity but one of a stardom not yet achieved. It was to prove a masterstroke. In the liner notes to the anniversary release of *Aladdin Sane* on compact disc, the wonderfully named photographer Mick Rock, who accompanied Bowie on both his British and his American tours, recalled the ruse designed to make Bowie look larger than life: "The whole game was theatre. It was, like, David going to America with three bodyguards. When he got to America, yes, there was interest in certain areas, but if you went to the Midwest, you couldn't drag people off the streets to see him. It was part of the theatre to treat him like a star. And there I was; I came very cheap—in fact I came for nothing! DeFries could then start talking about David having an 'exclusive photographer.' People were saying, 'David Bowie's got an exclusive photographer. Who the fuck is David Bowie?' The people reasoned: 'If he's got an exclusive photographer and bodyguards, there must be something going on.' That was a piece of living theatre, if you like, part of the whole thing that Tony and David cooked up between them."

The pretense flowed into the band's inflated manner of touring, as can be seen in the following memo written by manager Tony Defries and distributed to the entourage, reprinted in Bowie and Rock's collaborative book *Moonage Daydream* (2005). Defries wrote, "If we are to remain inaccessible then we must maintain a degree of privacy. . . . People should stay in the hotel provided

Flyer for V&A Museum Exhibition *David Bowie Is*, 2013   *Author's Collection*

for them and should be available at all times.... Please try and remember that I am feeding, clothing and paying everybody in a style to which they are not accustomed for the one specific purpose called SUCCESS!!! It is important that you pick the right kind of hotel. We prefer no Howard Johnson/Holiday Inn type. I feel a Royal Coach Inn where possible would be excellent. Something with charm."

Amazingly, the contract that Bowie had with Defries—or, more correctly, with his management company MainMan—included probably the most amazing even outrageous clause (clause #19, to be pedantic) ever seen on an entertainment industry contract. Reprinted in David Buckley's excellent Bowie biography *Strange Fascination* (1999), it was basically a license to lie for what was seen as their common good: "[The] Employee grants to company the exclusive right to use or simulate his name, photograph, likeness and voice and to use his biography (fictionalized to the extent the company desires) for credits in connection with advertising or publicizing Employee's services hereunder."

Hype might have been a short-lived band name, but its ethos lived on more strongly than ever during the Ziggy Stardust and the Spiders from Mars adventures that followed. Of such subterfuge and trickery, Bowie would later reveal to *Melody Maker* writer Roy Hollingworth in May 1973, "I never believed a hype could be made of an artist before he got anywhere. That's what happened and I don't like it. But when I saw that our albums were selling … that's when I knew the hype was over. Well it wasn't over but at least we'd done something to be hyped about." While such ruefulness seems somewhat out of character, it was a brilliant strategy and surely one that has been copied by rock managers ever since.

The Dangers of Blurring Fantasy and Reality

Ultimately, the amalgamation of David Jones, David Bowie, and Ziggy Stardust would prove to be a potent cocktail that its architect would struggle to keep under control. As he revealed in *Bowie in His Own Words* by Miles in 1980, "I fell for Ziggy too. It was quite easy to become obsessed night and day with the character. I became Ziggy Stardust. David Bowie went totally out the window. Everybody was convincing me that I was a Messiah … I got totally lost in the fantasy."

The End

Ziggy Stardust's stratospheric trajectory could never last, however, and at the Hammersmith Odeon Theatre on July 3, 1973, David Bowie would retire the creation that launched him to superstardom via a public announcement from the stage, surprising everyone, including most of his own band. Before the final song of the night, the perfectly titled "Rock 'n' Roll Suicide," he famously proclaimed, "Of all the shows on this tour, this, this particular show will remain with us the longest because not only is it, not only is it the last show of the tour, but it's the last show that we'll ever do. Thank you."

For David Bowie, then, it was mission accomplished—for now. But it was certainly not the end of the invented characters because Halloween Jack, the Plastic Soul Man, the Thin White Duke, and so on were still to come. The difference was, though, that whereas Ziggy Stardust had seemingly come from nowhere, because of his unprecedented success, all of Bowie's future personas would start with superstar status already bestowed.

Surely the most wonderful and innovative aspect of David Bowie's achievement of finding fame and fortune through Ziggy Stardust is the way that—in a complete turnaround from the normal scheme of things—life followed art instead of vice versa. It was the old "I pretend therefore I am" notion writ large. And it was brilliantly done. David Bowie had become a real star by acting like one. The 1960s myth of rock authenticity had taken a fatal blow, but rock music had suddenly become a whole lot more open, expansive, and exciting because of it. A new wave of up-and-coming performers had a new blueprint to follow; rock's audience widened to include the more theatrically and visually minded, and popular music was a changed medium. And it was David Bowie's doing.

Part 2

The Man

27

Family Life

Peggy, John, Terry, Angie, Iman, Duncan, and Alexandria

David Bowie was born David Robert Jones on January 8, 1947, in the London suburb of Brixton. The strained family dynamics of his early life left a lasting impression on him, while all of the important relationships in his life contributed much to his life and work, a notion epitomized nicely in an article in the *Telegraph* in 2016 titled "The Cruel Grandmother, Shamed Mother and Psychotic Half-Brother Who Shaped David Bowie's Life and Work." This chapter concentrates on providing overviews of his closest relationships: those with his parents, Peggy and John Jones; his half brother, Terry Burns; his two wives, Angie and Iman; and his two children, Duncan (Zowie) and Alexandria. (David Bowie also had two half sisters, Annette and Myra-Ann, but due to the complexities and complications of his family life when he was a child, he had little to do with the former and nothing at all to do with the latter.)

Peggy Jones

David Bowie's mother was Margaret Mary Jones (née Burns; 1913–2001), known as Peggy, the oldest of six children. Following an affair, she had a son, Terence (Terry), in 1937. Terry was handed over when just six months old to be raised by Peggy's (reportedly draconian) mother, also named Margaret, until he was ten years old, at which point he was returned to Peggy. After an affair with a married man during World War II, she also had a daughter, Myra-Ann, but this child was quickly put up for adoption and subsequently vanished from the Jones/Burns family circle. While working as a waitress in the Ritz Cinema café in Tunbridge Wells during 1946, she met the man who would become David's father, John Jones, and the two quickly set up home together, something considered somewhat scandalous for the era. Quickly becoming pregnant with David, the two married the following year, 1947, eight months after David's birth, a delay that was required by law as John Jones served the time required to secure a divorce from his previous wife.

David's relationship with his mother was at times a strained one, and her fondness for speaking to the press about their relationship caused tension between the two of them. At the peak of his 1970s success, she very publicly complained that her son never made contact with her, and when David did not attend the funeral of his half brother Terry, another all-too-public spat ensued. To David's mind, he did not want to turn the event into a media circus, but clearly his own thoughts and those of his mother varied greatly over his nonattendance.

Relations are reported to have improved markedly following David's second marriage, to Iman in 1992, and mother and son were in regular contact from then until her death in 2001. Peggy, who reached her late eighties, died at a nursing home in St. Albans, Hertfordshire, while her son was in the United States. While David himself did not comment publicly at the time, his spokesperson, Alan Edwards, said, "I can confirm it is sadly true. It's just come out of the blue."

John Jones

David Bowie's father was Haywood Stenton Jones (1912–1969), known to all as John. John had been married previously to a nightclub singer named Hilda Sullivan, who performed under the stage name of the "Viennese Nightingale." He had a daughter, Annette, who was born in 1938 in a relationship that occurred outside his doomed on-again, off-again marriage to Sullivan. When the two finally separated for good, however, Hilda, who was unable to have children of her own, agreed to keep Annette and raise her as her own. John was seemingly a fairly affable middle-class man if rather emotionally remote and undemonstrative, but he was reportedly very supportive of David's artistic endeavors.

In response to the *Economist's* obituary of David in 2016, Jones's cousin, Kristina Amadeus, wrote a letter to the newspaper. In it, she recalled how Bowie as a young child was given a plastic saxophone, a tin guitar, and a record player and went on to describe how the two of them would "dance like possessed elves" to Elvis Presley records. While thankful for the "insight and sensitivity" of the obituary overall, she took issue with one part, stating, "It is not true that he 'grew up as David Jones, a sharp-toothed kid from dull suburban Bromley whose parents held no aspirations for him. David's parents, especially his father, 'John' Jones, encouraged him from the time he was a toddler. His mother, Peggy, spoke often of our deceased grandfather, who was a bandmaster in the army and played many wind instruments."

Never seeing his son achieve even a modicum of the success that awaited him, John, a heavy smoker, died of lobar pneumonia in August 1969, just a few weeks before the breakthrough single "Space Oddity" launched David's career. Indeed, Bowie was actually recording the song at Trident Studios in Soho when he received the news that John had passed away. It was a heavy blow for David, the emotional hit complicated further when he found out that Peggy had opted to care for her husband at home longer than many thought she should have instead of seeking further professional medical help.

Terry Burns

Peggy's firstborn had a troubled life, stemming from his earliest days when passed over to his grandmother to bring him up for the first decade of his life. To be born out of wedlock was still a domestic scandal at this time despite the way World War II had ravaged British society, and Terry inevitably was tarred by this resultant stigma. Reportedly harshly treated and shown little affection by his mother's mother, when he returned to the home of his birth mother at age ten—who was by then with John Jones and had recently been joined by the newborn David, the apple of his parents' eyes—John Jones did not warm to him at all; over the years that followed, he treated Terry very differently and more harshly than he did David. Accounts suggest that for him, Terry was a constant reminder of Peggy's past love life and was, seemingly, a major and unwelcome complication within the newly constituted family unit. David reportedly had a very different view of his intriguing and much-maligned older brother. When Terry returned from a term of compulsory conscription in the British air force and took up lodgings near the family home—he was not allowed to return to the Jones household—his interests in literature (especially the beat poets) and in jazz, in particular, were a constant source of wonderment and enlightenment to the teenage David. Terry would sneak him into clubs, buy him Cokes, and allow him to savor the nightlife—exotic and heady stuff for the young teen.

But Terry, formally diagnosed with schizophrenia, was plagued by mental illness and spent much time in and out of institutions—mental asylums, as they were called then—including London's somewhat infamous Cane Hill Hospital. Such problems were not at all unknown in the Burns family, as Peggy's sister Vivienne was diagnosed with schizophrenia; a second sister, Una, was treated with electroshock therapy for depression and schizophrenia; and a third sister, Nora, had a lobotomy in order to cure what was described as "bad nerves."

By all accounts, David and Terry were a very close-knit unit, and through the formative days of his youth, David looked on Terry with a mixture of love and hero worship tinged with sadness at how he was treated for being "different." Visiting his half brother held captive in intimidating, impersonal, stark white institutions such as Cane Hill left a big impression and cemented in him a life-long desire to champion the outsider.

As David's career went into the stratosphere, the fates of the two siblings could not have been more contrasting. In the late morning of January 16, 1985, then age forty-seven, Terry slipped out of London's Cane Hill Hospital—which by then had been his home on and off for the past sixteen years—and made his way to the nearby South Coulsdon train station, where he stood waiting on the platform. Just after midday, as the Littlehampton-to-London express approached the station, Terry stepped down from the platform and lay down across the tracks, facing away from the train, with his neck on the rail. The driver saw him but had no chance of stopping in time, and Terry was killed instantly.

A few years before his suicide, Terry had tried to end his life by jumping out of a window at Cane Hill, fracturing his arm and leg in the process. And just three weeks before his death, he had gone to the same train station with the same intention but had changed his mind at the last minute, climbing back onto the platform as a train approached.

Bowie rather infamously did not attend Terry's funeral, which led to a fairly unsavory and very public mudslinging match involving family members, including Peggy, in both the mainstream and the music media. Bowie was accused of being heartless and of not doing more for his brother over the years. Interviews with Cane Hill staff and patients confirm that Terry had always held the hope that one day David—of whom he was enormously proud—would come and get him out of there. While he did not attend the funeral, Bowie sent a card and a bunch of flowers. The flowers were either red roses or pink and yellow chrysanthemums, depending on which biography you read. But the wording on the note is not in debate. It read, "You've seen more things than we could imagine but all these moments will be lost, like tears washed away by the rain. God bless you—David." There were eleven attendees at Terry's funeral—mostly from Cane Hill Hospital.

Angie Bowie

On March 20, 1970, David Bowie married Mary Angela (Angie) Barnett at the Beckenham Registry Office in a private ceremony to which no family were invited, which did not stop Peggy going along anyway and notifying the press. Born in 1950, Angie, a vivacious Cyprus-born American woman, was outgoing, cultured, smart, attractive, outwardly confident, theatrical, and highly strung with an X factor that would turn heads when she entered a room. The two met in 1969 and were instantly attracted to each other, although rumors have always persisted—sometimes purported by the proponents themselves—that their official union was as much a marriage of convenience (so that Angie could get a work permit) as it was a romantic liaison. Actively bisexual, Angie enjoyed the experimental nature of their open relationship as much as David did, and the two at times shared lovers, including, as Angie enjoyed relating, on the eve of their wedding day, when they had a threesome with an unnamed mutual friend.

Angie encouraged David to be outrageous, to ignore those who would knock his art, and to actively court publicity. In her autobiography *Backstage Passes*, she seems intent on taking credit for a very large chunk of her husband's celebrity, which has annoyed many Bowie fans. In truth, however, her impact and influence on the then nascent star has been rather underacknowledged, and she is certainly deserving of credit to a degree. That he had such a flamboyant and uber-supportive partner during the heady days of his rise was surely a major factor in maintaining both his confidence and his courage, especially since most reports and his own appraisals suggest that he was quite shy in some circumstances at this time. Certainly, for a time at least, David Bowie very much appreciated Angie's better qualities and in particular what she brought out in him through his association with her. In response, he immortalized her in the song "The Prettiest Star." Released as a single in 1970—with none other than friend and rival Marc Bolan of T Rex featuring on guitar—the song flopped in that initial guise but was remade during the recording of songs for *Aladdin Sane* and is one of the unheralded highlights of that album. To Angie, he sang, "One day, though it might as well be someday, you and I will rise up all the way. All because of what you are, the prettiest star."

The relationship was doomed to failure, however. As reported in the *Telegraph* in January 2016, Bowie said of his fiery and unpredictable wife, "Living with her is like living with a blow torch. She has as much insight into the human condition as a walnut and a self-interest that would make Narcissus green with envy." After the birth of their son Zowie (Duncan) in 1971, things quickly turned acerbic and nasty. While David Bowie was destined for immense and enduring stardom, as the lyrics to "The Prettiest Star" foretell, the "you and I" quickly fell by the wayside as Angie was excised from his life.

Angie gave her view to the *Daily Mail* also in January 2016. At their peak, she says, "We were a great team. He made music and I kicked down industry doors and sorted his problems out ... I'd spent seven years at boarding school in Switzerland so I knew how to cook and sew. If I wasn't looking after him or running up costumes for his stage shows on my sewing machine, I'd be off to Amsterdam, Frankfurt and Paris on a £60 ticket to promote Ziggy Stardust And The Spiders From Mars.... When we divorced I only wanted two things: a relationship with our son Zowie and enough money to live on until I had established my own career. I got neither ... I was doubly punished when we split—I lost my work which was David, and my family."

Iman

On April 24, 1992, Bowie married Iman, a Somali American supermodel, in a private ceremony in Lausanne, Switzerland, followed by another wedding ceremony later that year on June 6 in Florence. They had one child together, daughter Alexandria (Lexi) Zahra Jones, born in August 2000, while Iman also has a daughter named Zulekha from a previous relationship. David Bowie and Iman resided primarily in New York City and at times in London and also owned an apartment in Elizabeth Bay in Sydney, Australia, and at Mandalay Estate on the island of Mustique, formerly known as Britannia Bay House.

According to all accounts, David Bowie's years with Iman—a superstar in her own right—were the happiest of his life, and on the birth of their daughter, he described how he had inexplicably finally "stumbled into bliss." Shortly before David's death, Iman was interviewed by Oprah Winfrey for her *Where Are They Now?* program, and the interview was broadcast some months later. Seldom one to speak publicly of such personal matters, Iman revealed some very rare insights into her long and happy marriage with David: "We both understand the difference between the person and the persona. When we are home we are both just Iman and David. We're not anybody else. You have to be at the right time of your life that you're ready for an everlasting relationship, that it becomes a first priority in your life. If your career is important to you, don't get married and have children, because something will give. I know as women we want to be able to have it all, but we can't have it all at the same time. So, make your priority of what you want at that time."

Duncan (Zowie) Jones

Zowie Bowie was immortalized in the song "Kooks" from the *Hunky Dory* album. In what is surely the most delightful and empowering song ever written by a father to a son, he is told, "Cos we believe in you—soon you'll grow so take a chance on a couple of kooks hung up on romancing." Born on May 30, 1971, Angie and David's son immediately brought something both stabilizing and very special to David's life. As Bowie told *Melody Maker* on October 29, 1977, "I think having a son made an enormous difference to me. At first it frightened me, and I tried not to see the implications. Now it's *his* future that concerns me." Given the catchy, rhyming name Zowie Bowie by his parents (a name soon to be emulated by the one that friend and rival Marc Bolan chose for his son, Rolan Bolan), Zowie began using his first name, Duncan, and his father's real surname, Jones, once he was old enough to choose for himself. He goes by the name Duncan Jones to this day.

Duncan recalls his childhood as being anything but run-of-the-mill and yet certainly happy, lacking in nothing for all its unconventionality, especially in the first decade of his life, and he regards his famous parent as being a very good father. Speaking to podcast interviewer Marc Maron on February 22, 2018, he remarked, "He was a great father. I had an unusual upbringing, but not a negative one." Nevertheless, estranged from his mother Angie following his parents' divorce when he was nine years old, Duncan was brought up mainly by his Scottish nanny, Marion Skene. David Bowie acknowledged the vital role played by Skene, leaving her $1 million in his will; unfortunately, Skene passed away not long after her grateful benefactor. Following the divorce, in which David was granted custody of his son, Duncan was sent to Gordonstoun, his father's school of choice, a very strict and traditional boarding school in Scotland, previously attended by Prince Charles. His presence there gives ample proof that David wanted anything but an indulged, privileged, and cushy upbringing for his son—no pampered-rock-star's-kid scenario. Of his mother, whom he chose to stop speaking to at age thirteen, Duncan told the *Sun* newspaper in 2018, "She was a corrosive person."

Always encouraged by his father to pursue his passion, Duncan Jones spent three years studying at the London Film School in Covent Garden and is today an award-winning and successful movie producer. Very much a name in his own right, his credits include *Moon* (2009), *Source Code* (2011), *Warcraft* (2016), and *Mute* (2018), the latter dedicated to his father. However, he was never tempted to follow his father into music. As he told the *Daily Mail*, "I was always interested in making films. Music didn't feel like a natural fit."

Extremely proud of being his father's son, Duncan is not slow to criticize if he feels his father is being disrespected or if a tribute falls short of what he believes his father's memory warrants. When Lady Gaga performed a medley of ten of his father's classic songs at the 2016 Grammy Awards ceremony, including "Space Oddity," "Changes," "Ziggy Stardust," "Suffragette City," "Rebel Rebel," "Fashion," "Fame," "Under Pressure," "Let's Dance," and "Heroes," his disapproving response was to post on Twitter an unflattering definition of the word *gaga* taken from the *Oxford English Dictionary*: "Over-excited or irrational, typically as a result of infatuation or excessive enthusiasm; mentally confused." Lady Gaga—an avid David Bowie fan—was reportedly very upset at this.

Duncan can see the humorous side of his background. He laughingly told the *Sun* that he was part of a "weird little group" of celebrity children that included Jacob Dylan, Stella McCartney, and Julian Lennon, who were trying to forge their separate careers away from the spotlight spillage of their uber-famous parents.

Alexandria Jones

The daughter of David Bowie and Iman, born in August 2000, when her father was fifty-three years old, Lexi afforded her father the considerably later-than-usual experience of being able to enjoy something approaching a normal fatherhood role. At the peak of his career during Duncan's childhood, when he had a nomadic, whirlwind, and at times outright dysfunctional lifestyle, David Bowie was unable to dedicate himself to the task of fatherhood in anything like the manner he was able to do with his second-born child. If his fathering of Duncan was sporadic—albeit well intentioned and as dedicated as possible under extremely trying and unusual circumstances—the slower pace of his later career exploits allowed him the luxury of being largely a stay-at-home dad. The *Daily Express* put it very well shortly after his death when they rightly suggested that "away from the crowds, spotlight and music, David Bowie lived out his final days in perhaps his most conventional persona as a loving dad to his two children Duncan, 44, and Lexi, 15."

Lexi was carefully and purposely kept out of the media spotlight by her parents so as to afford her as normal an upbringing as possible—given that her parents were a supermodel and a globally famous rock icon. Photographs of the family almost never surfaced, and requests for interviews and photo sessions were never granted. When occasional snippets did surface, usually a lucky paparazzi photo or a rare tweet or Facebook one-liner, they revealed an extremely normal domestic family life with David helping on the school run, visits to playgrounds or the local park, or the three of them sitting in a café. Now twenty years old, Lexi has truly been granted the most normal childhood possible.

28

Drugs

David Bowie's Cocaine Years

During the years 1974–1976, after moving from London and taking up residency in the United States—initially in New York but then more permanently in Los Angeles—cocaine was Bowie's ever-present companion.

The grueling *Diamond Dogs* tour, the *Young Americans* album, and the following *Station to Station* album were all completed within this time frame, and the shadow of drug addiction hung heavily over them all. By his own account, as he told *Rolling Stone* writer Cameron Crowe, "I like fast drugs. I hate anything that slows me down." This admission, coupled with the testimony of others around him at this time who witnessed his behavior, point to that fact that his usage of the drug was primarily to keep him awake and stimulated so that he could work and create in the prodigious fashion that he wished to. He even boasted that he could stay awake for up to six days at a time. Nevertheless, the intake of the drug took an inevitable and heavy toll on him, the cocaine psychosis making him almost schizophrenic and certainly delusional, paranoid, and unhappy in equal measures. In *Strange Fascination: David Bowie, the Definitive Story* author David Buckley states unequivocally, "By mid-1975 Bowie's cocaine intake was astronomic." Bowie himself has recalled, "I blew my nose one day in California and half my brains came out." In a 1996 interview with Mick Brown of the *Telegraph*, he elaborated further: "I was in a serious decline, emotionally and socially. I think I was very much on course to be just another rock casualty—in fact, I'm quite certain I wouldn't have survived the Seventies if I'd carried on doing what I was doing. But I was lucky enough to know somewhere within me that I really was killing myself, and I had to do something drastic to pull myself out of that. I had to stop, which I did."

While producer Tony Visconti recalls Bowie dabbling with cocaine as early as 1973, by the middle of the decade, Bowie's increasingly large drug dependency was no secret, the United Kingdom's *Record Mirror* newspaper even bestowing on him in 1975 the nickname "Old Vacuum Cleaner Nose." There are a couple of documented and now infamous examples of Bowie appearing in public when his cocaine addiction was at its worst and where the effects of the

Young Americans album, 1975   *Author's Collection*

drug are very plain to see. In 2017, *Rolling Stone* declared that his appearance on the top-rated U.S. television program *The Dick Cavett Show* in 1974 was an "unforgettable moment" in Bowie's career—although for all the wrong reasons. As they put it, "An absurdly wasted-looking Bowie visits the talk show to introduce his new soul band. He also sits down for a chat, sniffling, twirling his cane and mumbling incoherent coke babble at his terrified host." More telling than a thousand words, watching this footage graphically brings home to the viewer just how far his descent into cocaine addiction had gone at this time. Similarly, the excellent Alan Yentob documentary *Cracked Actor*, which aired on the BBC in January 1975, showed a plainly unhealthy, stick-thin, and pale-as-a-ghost

Bowie cocooned in the back of his limousine drinking milk from a carton, paranoid about police sirens in the distance, struggling to focus, and sniffing relentlessly in the manner of any serious cocaine addict. Both pieces of footage are hard to watch, and Bowie's assertion that he would not have survived the decade if he had not changed his drug-taking ways seems all too true.

In the middle of this dark and dangerous period of Bowie's career, a three-month hiatus occurred when he cleaned up considerably to feature in the lead role of Nicolas Roeg's movie *The Man Who Fell to Earth*, which was filmed on location in New Mexico. While still unhealthily thin and reportedly living on a diet of little more than milk, his cocaine usage was ditched or at least greatly reduced for the entire shoot. On his return to Los Angeles, however, and the beginning of his next project, the *Station to Station* album, his old drug habits quickly resurfaced. Indeed, it was during the recording of *Station to Station* that his cocaine use hit its peak, and such was its effect that Bowie recalled almost nothing of his time in the studio. Bowie's band, too, was using the drug, as guitarist Carlos Alomar recalled to David Buckley: "The coke use is driven by the inspiration ... if there's a line of coke which is going to keep you awake until 8am so that you can do your guitar part, you do that line of coke because it basically just keeps you up and keeps your mind bright."

On March 21, during the American leg of the 1976 *Station to Station* tour, Bowie, Iggy Pop, and two friends were arrested by Rochester police after eight ounces of marijuana were allegedly found on them. Given the much heavier drugs the group was into, there is some irony in this, and the whole affair ended up eventuating in little more than a light slap on the wrist for all concerned. Having each paid $2,000 bail, they were released, and, subsequently, the charges were dropped.

Fed up with his Los Angeles lifestyle and worried for his health and sanity, Bowie moved to Switzerland in 1976, purchasing a chalet in the hills above Lake Geneva's northern shoreline. His cocaine use decreased somewhat, and he engaged in some far healthier pursuits, such as painting and visiting galleries. By the end of the year, with his residency in Switzerland only sporadic and sandwiched in between other commitments, he yearned for change—to establish himself with more permanence somewhere and afford himself the opportunity to clean up his act completely.

A fan of German electronic music from the likes of Kraftwerk and Neu! and seeking a location with as much anonymity as he could manage, he deemed Berlin, a location he had always been fascinated by, the place in which to do so. "Nobody gives a shit about you in Berlin," he told a reporter at the time. In 2001, in an interview with Stephen Dalton in *Uncut* magazine, he elaborated on why Berlin had attracted him: "Since my teenage years I had obsessed on the angst-ridden emotional work of the expressionists, the Die Brücke school in particular ... and Berlin had been their spiritual home."

When questioned about his move to Berlin in a 1980 interview with *New Musical Express* writer Angus MacKinnon, Bowie credited the move with helping him turn his life around. He stated, "Oh yeah, it was best thing that could have happened to me. I'd come out of the American thing with smashed ideals inasmuch as I'd found that the ideals I did have weren't worth a shit anyway.... And so yes, Berlin was definitely the best place I could have gone."

His close friend, fellow musician, and sometime collaborator Iggy Pop, who had more than enough of his own drug demons to deal with and was equally motivated, became his roommate at this time. The two men lived comparatively spartanly (compared to the excesses of Los Angeles) in an apartment on Hauptstraße in Schöneberg along with Coco Schwab, Bowie's personal aide from 1973 until his death. Their lodging was close to Hansa Tonstudio, the recording studio Bowie had chosen to work in with Brian Eno and producer Tony Visconti; the studio was located on Köthener Straße in the suburb of Kreuzberg, right next to the Berlin Wall. In this atmosphere of simplicity and frugality within a welcome cocoon of anonymity and drawing from the wealth of cultural and artistic inspiration available to them at locations such as the Brücke Museum, both artists would create some of the finest work of their careers: Bowie's *Low* and *"Heroes"* albums and Pop's *The Idiot* and the aptly named *Lust for Life*.

In a rare and very frank interview in 2013 at age sixty-six on the release of his unexpected comeback album *The Next Day*, Bowie told Garth Pearce of the *Sun* newspaper that he'd ignored advice about drugs as far back as when he was a teenager. He admitted, "Before I took them, when I took them and afterwards. Every time, that advice was right." He continued, recalling that during his worst period drugs took over his life and crediting his personal assistant Coco Schwab for helping him to get well, "I really did think that my thoughts about not making thirty would come true. Drugs had taken my life away from me. I felt as though I would probably die and it was going to be all over. My assistant, Coco, got me out of it. Thanks to her, I got myself out of America to Berlin."

According to most accounts, Bowie kicked the habit completely during his time with Iggy Pop in Berlin, although some suggest he still dabbled on and off and didn't shrug them for good until the early 1990s. Some accounts have Bowie replacing cocaine with very large amounts of alcohol during the early days of living in Berlin, while Iggy initially struggled with the ready availability of heroin. Regardless, the Berlin experience unequivocally worked for both men, and they eventually left the city in far better shape than when they arrived. As is the case with many rock stars who survived the tumult and dangers of their younger years, David Bowie lived a healthy and drug-free lifestyle throughout the last couple of decades of his life. And as for Iggy Pop, when asked in 2017 by *Rolling Stone* interviewer Andy Greene if he missed taking drugs, his reply was, "Oh, God, no. No no no no no. I've had a wonderful relationship with my body late in life. Even the thought of smoking weed gives me the creeps."

29

Religiosity

Just What Did David Bowie Believe In?

Setting the Scene Early

In Bowie's career-launching "Space Oddity" single of 1969, the last words uttered by Ground Control to astronaut Major Tom before the engines of his rocket ignited and blasted him beyond the Earth's gravitational pull and into space were, "And may God's love be with you." This raised an inevitable question in the minds of the general public and Bowie fans alike: Did David Bowie have a faith of some kind?

Other References in Lyrics and Beyond

Often the subject of speculation and enquiries from interviewers, pinning down David Bowie's religious stance and/or beliefs was not an easy task throughout most of his career. At times, he was capable of what seemed to be outright worship of God. The song "Word on a Wing" from the *Station to Station* album is virtually a prayer. It finds Bowie seeking divine guidance in an impassioned heavenward plea: "Lord I kneel and offer you my word on a wing." Elsewhere, he cries, "Lord, my prayer flies like a word on the wing" and "I don't stand in my own light... I walk beside you, I'm alive in you."

Blatant religious symbolism can be observed in Bowie's stagecraft. There's no better or more graphic example than the crucifixion pose that he would strike at the end of the song "Ziggy Stardust," his "leper messiah" glam-rock alter ego. Indeed, this is one of the artist's most iconic poses. On the same album, the track "Soul Love" provides a searching critique of belief systems, addressing love, politics, and religious faith. The third verse addresses the latter, "The priest that tastes the word" being set up cleverly by musical word painting; an upward key change mimics the action of looking to the heavens for answers—to "God on high" who is "all love."

"No confessions—no religion," sang Bowie in "Modern Love" from his best-selling album *Let's Dance*, while all the while, the refrain heard throughout the song emphatically joins "God and man" together. He would later say, "A lot of my songs seem to be prayers for unity within myself." Nowhere is this more evident than in the confusion and the dilemma of modern life, problematized in the lyrics of "Modern Love."

In "The Wedding Song" from *Black Tie White Noise*, Bowie celebrates his recent marriage to Iman with religious imagery. He sings, "Heaven is smiling down, heaven's girl in a wedding gown . . . I believe in magic, angel for life."

Much later in his career, on the provocatively titled *Heathen* album, the song "Sunday" pits religious beliefs against secular beliefs, with the former winning the day. At the song's conclusion, following descriptive imagery of souls rising up through clouds, Bowie looks to God for deliverance: "All my trials, Lord will be remembered." Supporting the religious theme is a monastic-styled chant that sits beneath Bowie's voice. The listener can almost see a procession of hooded monks walking slowly by, swinging incense as they pass.

With regard to his album art, while obvious religious imagery cannot be said to be a common fixture, the front cover of *Tonight* carries clear religious connotations with its church-like stained-glass windows dominating the image and Bowie's eyes cast heavenward as if searching for enlightenment and deliverance. The cover of *Hunky Dory*, too, found him in a similar searching-for-answers pose.

The Lord's Prayer at Wembley Stadium

Lyrics and album covers aside, Bowie's religiosity can be readily observed in other media and in other actions during his career. During the 1992 Freddie Mercury tribute concert at Wembley Stadium in London, he controversially recited the Lord's Prayer, surprising everyone by kneeling onstage before the audience of 72,000 and beginning the "Our Father who art in heaven" recitation. In their review of the concert, *Classic Rock* magazine reported several different takes on Bowie's action. Promoter Harvey Goldsmith suggested, "Bowie delivered the performance of the day. Even The Lord's Prayer, I felt, was right." Audience member Mark Cox, however, experienced it differently: "Seeing David Bowie was a big deal. But when he dropped to his knees and starting reciting The Lord's Prayer I couldn't believe what I was seeing. It was meant to be an emotional moment, but a lot of people around me were laughing." David Bowie himself reported, "I felt as if I were being transported by the situation. I was so scared as I was doing it. A couple of my pals were sitting near Spinal Tap and they were speechless with disbelief."

In an interview with *Arena* magazine the following year, Bowie explained his actions on that day far more fully before going on to give what is surely his clearest explanation of his faith. He explains, "I decided to do it about five minutes before I went on stage. Coco [Schwab, Bowie's long-term personal assistant] and I had a friend called Craig who was dying of AIDS. He was just dropping into a coma that day. And just before I went on stage something just told me to say the Lord's Prayer. The great irony is that he died two days after the show.... In rock music, especially in the performance arena, there is no room for prayer, but I think that so many of the songs people write are prayers. A lot of my songs seem to be prayers for unity within myself. On a personal level, I have an undying belief in God's existence. For me it is unquestionable.... Looking at what I have done in my life, in retrospect so much of what I thought was adventurism was searching for my tenuous connection with God. I was always investigating, always looking into why religions worked and what it was people found in them. And I was always fluctuating from one set of beliefs to another until a very low point in the mid-Seventies where I developed a fascination with black magic.... And although I'm sure there was a satanic lead pulling me towards it, it wasn't a search for evil. It was in the hope that the signs might lead me somewhere."

David Bowie and Buddhism

One of the beliefs outside Christianity that he enthusiastically explored as a young man stayed with him his entire life. Buddhism had always fascinated him to the point where, around 1967–1968, friends recall, he even contemplated becoming a Buddhist monk. That he retained an interest became clearly evident on the reading of his will at the end of January 2016. In this document, prepared in 2004, he wrote that he wanted his ashes to be scattered on the Indonesian island of Bali "in accordance with the Buddhist rituals."

The Last Word(s)

The last word(s) on David Bowie's religiosity must be left to the man himself and to his wife Iman. On the highly autobiographical and extremely moving "Lazarus" from his final album *Blackstar*, released just two days before he died, he sang, "Look up here, I'm in Heaven." Then, on Sunday morning at 9 a.m., thirteen hours before Bowie's death was publicly announced, Iman tweeted, "The struggle is real, but so is God."

While not part of any organized religion, David Bowie, it seems, had his own faith, perhaps spanning belief systems, both Buddhist and Christian.

Bowie T-shirt

30

The Eyes Have It

The Story behind Bowie's Alien Eyes

The Windows to the Soul

In Bowie's career-long engagement with themes of alienation and otherness, his own image played a vital supporting role. While costuming and makeup achieved much, it was his eyes that gave off the most convincing suggestion of all that he was legitimately "different" to mere mortals. Without artificially doctoring them, Bowie's eyes were different colors, one blue and one brown.

Given that the eyes are widely regarded as being windows to the soul—the common phrase "The eyes have it" readily comes to mind—the natural order of things was disrupted at a very basic and disturbing core level. Could he actually be, in fact, an alien—a starman? Ridiculous though it sounds, in the early 1970s during the Ziggy Stardust period, some legitimately pondered that very question. Long before the ready availability and convenience of colored cosmetic contact lenses, such as those that served Marilyn Manson so well, the Bowie/Ziggy look certainly was disturbing. But David Bowie was from Brixton, not from Mars. And the reason for his ill-matching eyes too had a very earthbound cause. Bowie simply suffered from a condition known as anisocoria, an eye affliction that can have several different causes. Bowie's specific version of the condition is known as mechanical anisocoria. The cause? Trauma affecting the eye—an accident.

When George Hit David

The backstory to Bowie's famously mismatched eyes is now an oft-visited part of Bowie history. His left eye was damaged in a school-yard fight with his best friend, George Underwood, over the attentions of a girl. During an interview with *Mojo* in 2007, Underwood clearly recalled the occasion: "It was coming up to David's 15th birthday. We both liked the same girl, Carol Goldsmith, so I invited her to a party. David got absolutely rat-arsed, but I stayed sober and asked Carol out, and she said, 'Yes, next Wednesday at the youth club.' David

Fan Art by Tony Kelly

Author's Collection

was a competitive sort, and he was furious. On the day, he phoned me and said, 'She doesn't want to go out with you; she asked me to tell you.' I thought, 'Oh well,' but went out anyway, and another friend said, 'You're late. Carol waited and then left.' David's call was complete bollocks, and when I later heard him boasting about how he'd got off with her, I saw red. I hit him. I didn't know until a week later that he'd been rushed to hospital, so I went to see him and said, 'It's not worth it over a girl,' and we stayed friends."

When Bowie was taken to Farnborough Hospital after the fight, doctors observed that the blow to the eye had damaged and paralyzed the muscles controlling the iris, which left Bowie with a permanently dilated pupil. This gave the impression that his eyes were different colors because his left eye could no longer react to different lighting and the pupil was permanently big and dark. Underwood still doesn't quite understand how the damage occurred. As he explained in Paul Trynka's Bowie biography *Starman*, "It was just unfortunate. I didn't have a compass or a battery or various things I was meant to have—I didn't even wear a ring, although something must have caught. I just don't know how it managed to hurt his eye badly.... I didn't mean it to be like that at all."

Reaping the Benefits

The dilated pupil creates something of an optical illusion when one looks at it: although the two eyes look to be different colors, they are actually not. As Bowie himself responded to a question about the famous incident in a televised interview on Italy's *Roxy Bar TV* in 1987, "They're really the same color. It's just the pupil itself is larger." Asked whether there was any lasting damage to his sight, he replied, "I see something, but it's kinda hazy." He then points to his other eye and reassures the interviewer, "*This* one's very good."

With the condition being far from debilitating, the fact that rock's most famous alien had two different colored eyes was a perfect, if fluky, enhancement of his inherent quality of difference. His album covers reflect this, with the color and/or pupil size discrepancies particularly noticeable in the portrait-style close-ups of his face on his second album, *David Bowie* (1969) (aka *Space Oddity* in the United Kingdom and *Man of Words/Man of Music* in the United States), *Pinups* (1973), *"Heroes"* (1977), and *Black Tie White Noise* (1993). Given the chance to artificially exacerbate the difference, David Bowie takes full advantage of the opportunity. For example, on the *Scary Monsters (and Super Creeps)* (1980) cover, which blends a photograph by Brian Duffy with a painting by Edward Bell, the difference could not be more strikingly rendered. The same is true of the cartoon-anime caricature of him by Rex Ray on the ironically titled *Reality* (2003) and the montage portrait on the *Best of Bowie* greatest-hits compilation of 2002. On these three covers, the difference becomes more than just a discrepancy for the careful observer: it is elevated to a purposeful defining feature.

Even beyond his music-related iconography and allied imagery, the kinds of roles he played in his movies—for example, an alien, a prisoner of war, a vampire, a goblin king, and so on—were almost universally characters who existed outside society, so once again, this visual reinforcement of his otherness became a distinct bonus. It is particularly noticeable in *The Man Who Fell to Earth* (1976), where, in many scenes, there are close-ups that focus on the eyes of his character, the alien Thomas Jerome Newton, to ensure that the audience notices the difference. Even in the advertising poster for the movie, its leading man is pictured close enough for the anomaly to be clearly discernible. The same is true for the advertising poster for *Labyrinth* (1986), where, as Jareth the Goblin King, his eyes are clearly observable to even the most casual of appraisals.

Bowie would go on to acknowledge how useful this fluke accident was to his career. On the *London Tonight* program on ITV1 in 2012, Underwood was yet again interviewed about the incident, remembering, "I was so aggrieved I just walked over to him basically, turned him around and went whack, you know, without even thinking. As time went by and people became more intrigued with it, he said to me 'Actually you did me a favor George.' So I don't feel so bad about it."

31

Words of Wisdom

A Selection of David Bowie's Best Quotes

David Bowie was a highly intelligent man and a very deep thinker. He valued the same kind of qualities in others and found inspiration in the great works of art, read the great works of literature, and devoured philosophical teachings from both contemporary and historical times. Extremely well-read across a very broad range of disciplines, friends, musical colleagues, interviewers, and critics quickly came to recognize this quality in him. Equally at home discussing the great artists, sociologists, or philosophers throughout history—and critiquing their attendant theories and doctrines—he was capable of exposing those who sought to venture into such areas in interviews but who had not done their homework beforehand. Whether discussing the art of Gabriel Rossetti or Erich Heckel, the philosophies and social theories of Friedrich Nietzsche or George Steiner, or the work of the beat poets, such as Jack Kerouac, Allen Ginsberg, or William Burroughs, David Bowie could more than hold his own in any forum. As befitting such a learned man, he was highly adept at providing deep readings of his own personal and artistic philosophies and motivations and making salient comments on all manner of other things, including the music industry in which he was working, the society in which he lived, and even the state of humankind. With the exception, perhaps, of some of the interviews he gave during his cocaine years of the mid-1970s, where he was at times evasive, struggled to stay on topic, and even occasionally bordered on incoherent, in general it is fair to say that David Bowie gave many of the most insightful and intelligent interviews of any popular music artist in history. These interviews removed any doubt that here was an artist fully comprehending of what he was doing and why, a far cry from many others who would often be found wanting in interview situations when pressed about their motivations and artistic raisons d'être.

In this chapter, a broad selection of memorable interview quotations, drawn from right across his lengthy career, displays this depth of intelligence and the insightfulness he brought to bear on all aspects of his life and career.

Comments on Life

Disc, 1969 "I'm really a born idealist. I worry and I don't think before leaping in, but I believe there are only three things worth talking about—love, hate and communication. Even talking is ridiculous—you have to put things into practice."

Playboy, 1976 "The only kinds of drugs I use, though, are ones that keep me working for longer periods of time . . . I hate downs and slow drugs like grass. I hate sleep. I would much prefer staying up, just working, all the time. It makes me so mad that we can't do anything about sleep or the common cold."

Rolling Stone, 1976 "Maybe I am insane, too—it runs in my family—but I always had a repulsive sort of need to be something more than human. I felt very very puny as a human. I thought, 'Fuck that. I want to be a superman.'"

Telegraph, 1996 "I was virtually trying anything. . . . And I think I have done just about everything that it's possible to do—except really dangerous things, like being an explorer. But anything that Western culture has to offer—I've put myself through it."

Fiftieth Birthday Concert, Madison Square Garden, 1997 "I don't know where I'm going from here but I promise it won't be boring."

New York Times, 1998 "Once something is categorized and accepted, it becomes part of the tyranny of the mainstream, and loses all its potency."

Golden Years documentary, Radio 2, 2000 "The worst thing would be to . . . look back and think of all the things that one could have tried and could have done, and think—why didn't I do that?"

beliefnet.com, 2003 "My priority is that I've stabilized my life to an extent now over these past 10 years. I'm very at ease, and I like it. I never thought I would be such a family-oriented guy; I didn't think that was part of my makeup. But somebody said that as you get older you become the person you always should have been, and I feel that's happening to me. I'm rather surprised at who I am, because I'm actually like my dad! [laughs] That's the shock. All clichés are true. The years really do speed by. Life really is as short as they tell you it is. And there really is a God—so do I buy that one? If all the other clichés are true. . . . Hell, don't pose me that one."

beliefnet.com, 2003 "Questioning my spiritual life has always been germane to what I was writing. Always. It's because I'm not quite an atheist and it worries me. There's that little bit that holds on. Well, I'm almost an atheist. Give me a couple of months." [laughs]

Esquire, 2004 "Make the best of every moment. We're not evolving. We're not going anywhere."

Esquire, 2004 "Confront a corpse at least once . . . the absolute absence of life is the most disturbing and challenging confrontation you will ever have."

In David Bowie and Mick Rock, *Moonage Daydream*, 2005 [On the early 1970s] "Writers like George Steiner had nailed the term post-culture.... There was a distinct feeling that 'nothing was true' any more and that the future was not as clear-cut as it had seemed. Nor, for that matter, was the past. Therefore, everything was up for grabs. If we needed any truths we could construct them ourselves.... We are the future, now. And the one way of celebrating that was to create it by the only means at our disposal. With, of course, a rock 'n' roll band."

"The depressing realisation in this age of dumbing down is that the questions have moved from, 'Was Nietzsche right about God?' to, 'How big was his dick?'" *Esquire*, 2013

The Last Five Years documentary, BBC, 2017 "I wouldn't dream of getting on a space ship. It'd scare the shit out of me. I'm scared going down the end of the garden."

Comments on His Art

Sounds, 1970 "I look for sensation rather than quality, and heavy music seems to be full of musicians who have quality rather than musicians who for some reason can chill your spine. I suppose really I look for something in music that I look for in my own life."

Rolling Stone, 1971 "What the music says may be serious, but as a medium it should not be questioned, analyzed or taken seriously. I think it should be tarted up, made into a prostitute, a parody of itself. It should be the clown, the Pierrot medium. The music is the mask the message wears—music is the Pierrot and I, the performer, am the message."

Disc, 1972 "I was never naturally ahead of my time, I strived to be ahead. I hated every-day-ness and was living on adrenalin all the time."

Disc, 1972 "Marc Bolan opened things up for me—and for himself. Now it's down to old fashioned rock and boogie. I don't see what's so derisive about teeny-boppers. As far as I was concerned, the mind was at a most active stage at the age of about 14. Marc will progress at the same speed as his fans. He'll change along with them ... I admire Marc Bolan—he's terrific. He's a grafter. Me and Marc used to try to outdo each other—not in a nasty way. We were just wary of each other. It's inevitable we'd be into the same bag. He's very much an individual and so am I."

Circus, 1976 "I'm something of a grasshopper, and I tend to flit from one thing to another. That's probably one of my biggest faults."

Sunday Times Magazine, 1980 "I'm not playing a part constantly any more, the way I used to. I used to be very protective—very protective—of what I

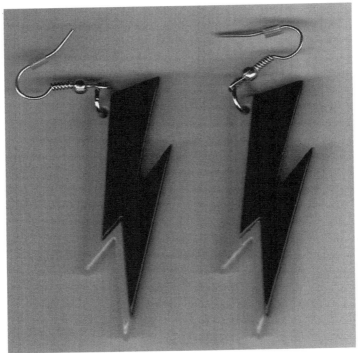

Aladdin Sane Lightening Flash earrings   *Amanda Mills collection*

considered to be my 'real' self. I would dress it up or disguise it to the point where I was beginning to lose it myself."

In Miles, *Bowie in His Own Words*, 1980 "Adolf Hitler was one of the first rock stars. Look at some of the films and see how he moved. I think he was quite as good as Jagger ... he worked an audience.... He was a media artist.... He used politics and theatrics and created this thing that governed and controlled the show for those twelve years. He staged a country."

In Miles, *Bowie in His Own Words*, 1980 "I do tend to stand on the outside sometimes. I don't know whether it's a failing or whether it's an advantage. My own feeling is that I hope very much that an outsider's viewpoint is as beneficial, if not more beneficial, than that of somebody who is completely involved."

In Miles, *Bowie in His Own Words*, 1980 "I fell for Ziggy too. It was quite easy to become obsessed night and day with the character. I became Ziggy Stardust. David Bowie went totally out the window. Everybody was convincing me that I was a Messiah ... I got totally lost in the fantasy."

In Miles, *Bowie in His Own Words*, 1980 "All I try to do in my writing is assemble points that interest me and puzzle through it and that becomes a song and other people who listen to that song must take what they can from it and see if information that they've assembled fits in with anything I've assembled and what do we do now.... All I can do is say, 'Have you noticed that and what does it mean?'"

In Barry Miles and Chris Charlesworth, *David Bowie Black Book*, 1980 "The chauvinism between various art forms—theatre and film, film and music—it's all so silly because the creative force is operative in all those things. I think it might be evident that I never completely leave one for the other—there's no barrier. I decided that when I was a painter and sculptor before I started making music, that I would apply my painting to music. I still do. Having broken down that barrier it seems easy to apply it to everything."

In Kevin Cann, *David Bowie: A Chronology*, 1983 "I wasn't at all surprised Ziggy Stardust made my career. I packaged a totally credible plastic rock star—much better than any sort of Monkees fabrication. My plastic rocker was much more plastic than anybody's."

New Musical Express, 1984 "I'm terribly intuitive—I always thought I was intellectual about what I do, but I've come to the realisation that I have absolutely no idea what I'm doing half the time, that the majority of the stuff that I do is totally intuitive, totally about where I am physically and mentally at any moment in time and I have a far harder time than anybody else explaining it and analysing it."

In David Buckley, *Strange Fascination*, 1999 "I am totally apolitical.... It is not my position for the kind of artist I am . . . to adopt any given policy or stance politically because my job is an observer of what is happening."

GQ, 2002 "I suppose for me as an artist it wasn't always just about expressing my work; I really wanted, more than anything else, to contribute in some way to the culture I was living in."

GQ, 2002 "You know, what I do is not terribly intellectual. I'm a pop singer for Christ's sake."

Livewire, 2002 "I had to resign myself, many years ago, that I'm not too articulate when it comes to explaining how I feel about things. But my music does it for me, it really does. There, in the chords and melodies, is everything I want to say. The words just jolly it along. It's always been my way of expressing what for me is inexpressible by any other means."

Livewire, 2002 "Strangely, some songs you really don't want to write. I didn't like writing 'Heathen.' There was something so ominous and final about it. It was early in the morning, the sun was rising and through the windows I could see two deer grazing down below in the field. In the distance a car was driving slowly past the reservoir and these words were just streaming out and there were tears running down my face. But I couldn't stop, they just flew out. It's an odd feeling, like something else is guiding you, although forcing your hand is more like it."

60 Minutes, 2002 "I'm just an individual who doesn't feel that I need to have somebody qualify my work in any particular way. I'm working for me."

David Bowie conference pass Limerick University, Ireland, 2012   *Author's Collection*

60 Minutes, 2003 "I was never particularly fond of my voice. I thought that I wrote songs and wrote music and that was sort of what I thought I was best at doing. And because nobody else was ever doing my songs, I felt, you know, I had to go out and do them."

60 Minutes, 2003 "I think generally, I just cannot really envision life without writing, and producing records, and singing. I think, in short, it's as cornball as that. You know? It really is what I do. And I'm so glad I chose that to be my profession. It's been just terrific."

The Word, 2003 "All my big mistakes are when I try to second-guess or please an audience. My work is always stronger when I get very selfish about it."

Uncut, 2003 "I was basically an extremely shy person. I really was. I found it hard to get it up for a conversation with anyone. I was very reticent, and felt incredibly insecure about my own abilities of communication on a one-to-one level. So that flamboyant front was very useful to me. It gave me a platform: I talked to people as Ziggy. Some of me came through, but it was kinda twisted through the persona of Ziggy, who was a crazed mirror, one of those funny fairground mirrors. David Jones was in there somewhere. But not much."

In David Bowie and Mick Rock, *Moonage Daydream*, 2005 "For me and several of my friends, the seventies were the start of the twenty-first century. It was Kubrick's doing on the whole. With the release of two magnificent films, *2001* and *A Clockwork Orange*, within a short period, he pulled together all the unarticulated loose ends of the past five years into a desire of unstoppable momentum."

In David Bowie and Mick Rock, *Moonage Daydream*, 2005 "Cooper was all gallows, Frankenstein make-up and Boa constrictors. Not long after seeing him, I started wearing the drag queen feather boa as a rather feeble visual pun."

In David Bowie and Mick Rock, *Moonage Daydream*, 2005 [Speaking about the U.K. music scene in 1970] "At that moment in time, rock seemed to have wandered into some kind of denim hell. Street life was long hair, beads, leftover beards from the Sixties, and, God forbid, flares were still evident.... In fact, all was rather dull attitudinizing with none of the burning ideals of the Sixties."

Esquire, 2013 "I've always felt bemused at being called the chameleon of rock. Doesn't a chameleon exert tremendous energy to become indistinguishable from its environment?"

Comments on Success and the Music Business

Sounds, 1970 "My perspectives about this whole business are vastly different from other people's. If I knew what appealed to the vast majority of people I'd be in it for a whole different reason, I'd do lots of gigs and cultivate people."

RAM, 1975 "Whatever thing I was doing at the time, I adopted a character for it. I've said that so many times now. I'm getting used to trotting it out. I might look like Zsa Zsa Gabor next month, or Marlon Brando, you never can tell, 'cause I don't know what I will feel like then. If anything, maybe I've helped establish that Rock and Roll is a pose."

In Rex Reed, *Valentines and Vitriol*, 1978 "I'm an instant star. Just add water and stir."

Q, 1990 "Fame itself... doesn't really afford you anything more than a good seat in a restaurant."

In Mark Paytress, *The Rise and Fall of Ziggy Stardust*, 1998 "The rock business has become so established, and so much like a society, that I have revolted against it... I won't take it seriously and I'll break its rules... that's why I felt naturally inclined to take the piss out of it."

ten

Brixton 10 Pound note. Legal tender in the UK

Author's Collection

Esquire, 2013 "I never knew too many rock people. I would get to a place, some nightclub or other, and see all these famous rockers bonding. And I remember feeling completely on the outside. I regret that sometimes."

Esquire, 2013 "Fame can take interesting men and thrust mediocrity upon them."

32

"Not Sure If You're a Boy or a Girl"

Gay, Bi, Straight—Who Cares?

In the early 1970s, when David Bowie came to prominence via the hugely successful performative vehicle that was his Ziggy Stardust character, a large part of the intrigue, appeal, and even scandal that resulted was the product of Ziggy's inherent and celebrated androgyny. The blurring of gender lines through the purposeful and provocative commingling of traditional gender signifiers had the surefire capacity to shock a nation to its core back in 1972. Look! That man is wearing makeup and women's clothing and has carefully coiffed hair! While the kids, especially young boys, relished the opportunity to experiment with their look through a massively expanded palette of possibilities, their parents tut-tutted, their teachers drank ever-stronger tea at morning recess and developed nervous twitches, and Max Factor and Helena Rubenstein smiled broadly and checked their account balances. Yes, it was gender playtime, thanks to David Bowie (and Marc Bolan of T Rex, who many would justifiably argue kicked things off by wearing glitter under his eyes when he performed the hit "Hot Love" on TV's *Top of the Pops* in March 1971).

While the 1960s had unleashed the so-called sexual revolution, with the advent of the pill and the subsequent notion of free love and so on (and this was a big draw card for the countercultural generation), rock music—and the attendant youth society—before the 1970s was still drawn clearly along male and female lines. Sure, men had long hair and bell-bottoms, and ponchos were the domain of all, but nobody had taken gender and played with it, suggesting it was a malleable thing that could be experimented with. David Bowie was the first to commit fully to that, and when he did so, he was literally in boots (platform of course) and all. Certainly, Mick Jagger had adopted somewhat feminine attire in the late 1960s as the master showman at the front of the stage for the Rolling Stones, but there was never any suggestion in his stage demeanor—full of strutting and posing and "come hither" moves aimed at the ladies in the Stones' audience—that at the core of it he was anything other than 100 percent male. Ziggy Stardust's image, however, and the characteristics of his very being were intrinsically, purposely, cheek-suckingly blurry in that regard. On stage, Bowie's superb control over his gestures and his movements (the result of his mime training with Lindsay Kemp) meant that he never came across as a "bloke" or as a "brickie in eyeliner," as the band members of U.K. glam-rock band Sweet were once called. Their glam-era gender play was skin deep at best (great band though they were), whereas in Bowie's case, his "bending" went far deeper, and the result was that he came across as both masculine and feminine at the same time. His thin, slight body structure helped immensely in this portrayal. There was no broad chest, excessive body hair, or bulging thighs and biceps to destroy the illusion of his being between genders. Hence, the term *gender bender* quickly came into vogue as an oft-repeated descriptor used with respect by his legions of fans and as an insult by his many haters.

In the first half of the 1970s, speculation regarding Bowie's sexuality and gender afforded him as much publicity as did issues regarding his music. While much of this speculation was the result of the manner in which he purposely juxtaposed male and female gender signifiers, the most definitive statement was the declaration he made in 1972 in the popular music paper *Melody Maker*. With himself on the cover dressed as Ziggy Stardust, Bowie stated categorically to journalist Michael Watts, "I'm gay and always have been, even when I was David Jones," an utterance that—as certainly seems to have been the intention—resulted in enormous publicity. Just a few years later, Bowie told *Playboy*, "It's true—I am a bisexual. But I can't deny that I've used that fact very well." To this day, speculation remains rife as to the validity of these statements, fueled largely by the many retractions he made later in his career, including to Chris Charlesworth of *Melody Maker* just four years after his revelation in the same magazine: "That was just a lie. They gave me that image so I stuck to it pretty well for a few years ... I've never done a bisexual action in my life, onstage, record or anywhere else." Similarly, he told *Rolling Stone* in 1983 that the *Melody Maker* confession was "the biggest mistake I ever made." But then, such intentional fogginess and public mind changing were regular features of David Bowie's "keep-'em-guessing" tactics.

In his study titled *The Changing Room: Sex, Drag and Theatre*, Laurence Senelick may be correct in stating that, "for Bowie, this was simply one expedient guise of many." Senelick further refers to Bowie's image during the Ziggy Stardust years as a portrayal of "synthetic androgyny," and Ruth Padel describes him as "Ziggy Stardust, an alien hermaphrodite messianic pop deity." Ken McLeod meanwhile suggests that Bowie employed "bisexual/asexual symbolism," whereas David Buckley rightly summarizes, "It is not easy to simply accept that all this was mere play-acting and that Bowie was, in fact, just a straight man into experimentation. Although at the time, with gay liberation chic, with even straights coming out as gay, the fact of the matter is that Bowie was, to a degree, bisexual." During the Ziggy Stardust concerts, Bowie would perform mock fellatio on Mick Ronson's guitar. Buckley describes the act: "Bowie dropped to his knees, seized Ronson's buttocks and engaged in the first lewd act on a Gibson Les Paul performed on the British stage." This act, caught on camera on the very first occasion that Bowie and Ronson performed it, subsequently was published in many popular music magazines, proving extraordinarily controversial and newsworthy at the time. Bowie, conscious as ever to benefit from such opportunities for publicity, retained it as an integral part of his concerts from then on. While, arguably, some of his younger audience may not have read sexual overtones into this theatrical action—after all, he may have simply been playing the guitar with his teeth as Jimi Hendrix had done before him—the most common reading by the more mature audience at least was that it provided compelling evidence in support of Bowie's earlier *Melody Maker* "confession."

Bowie freely admitted to plenty of sexual experimentation at this time. Certainly, he and mime mentor Lindsay Kemp were lovers, and rumors endure to this day about an affair with Mick Jagger. Ex-wife Angie Bowie, acrimoniously divorced in 1980, wrote much about their varied and voracious sex life in her aptly named scandal-filled memoir *Backstage Passes: Life on the Wild Side with David Bowie* (1993). On balance, it would appear that David Bowie was into sexual experimentation in the late 1960s and early 1970s but settled into a heterosexual lifestyle from then on.

Does It *Really* Even Matter?

But, ultimately, the truth regarding Bowie's sexual preferences and practices during the 1970s—when the debate raged most strongly—and beyond is of little consequence. It is the speculation created around the issue that is important both in terms of ever-welcome publicity and, of even more impact in a societal sense, in terms of the empowerment that it provided to those for whom Bowie represented a model of acceptance, bravery, and pride in being different.

Within Bowie's lyrics, there are many examples of sexual ambiguity. For example, in "Rebel Rebel" from the *Diamond Dogs* album, he sings, "Got your mother in a whirl. She's not sure if you're a boy or a girl." While in "Lady Stardust" from *The Rise and Fall of Ziggy Stardust and the Spiders from Mars*, he sings, "Lady Stardust sang his songs of darkness and disgrace."

Reference to sexual activity—both homosexual and heterosexual—is also frequently embedded in Bowie's lyrics during the glam-rock era. In "John, I'm Only Dancing," Bowie assures his male lover that he is only flirting with the opposite sex: "John, I'm only dancing—she turns me on but I'm only dancing. She turns me on—don't get me wrong, I'm only dancing."

Later, in his music videos, he provided some magic and now iconic moments of gender play. To name but two sublime examples, we see gender play in "Boys Keep Swinging" (1979) and the more recent "The Stars (Are Out Tonight)" (2013).

In presenting himself as gay, gender ambiguous, bisexual, and a "gender bender"—whatever description is leveled at him—Bowie set himself against the prevailing machismo of the stereotypical rock star à la Roger Daltry, Robert Plant, and others. These uber-macho "cock rockers," as they came to be called, were testosterone-fueled "men's men," who claimed the rock stage for their own, very male kingdom. Women were hugely welcome to the party, of course, and an intrinsic part of the deal for some rockers (groupies could be flaunted like trophies à la Gene Simmons of KISS), but they were hardly what you might call empowered by the cock rockers. Bowie's smooth and calculated effeminacy, however, mocked the very essence of what these artists stood for, opening up the rock stage and the rock audience to all comers. As Buckley puts it, "Bowie's Ziggy Stardust character queered pop, challenging the machismo of cock rockers such as the Stones and Led Zeppelin, and helped to deconstruct the whole rock edifice. . . . Bowie positioned himself at a tangent to these constructs of masculinity."

The Personal Messages of Gratitude

Gay, bi, straight—whatever David Bowie was, the positive impact he made through his groundbreaking gender play left a legacy for generations. Some randomly chosen examples of gender-related fan tributes from Twitter and Facebook posted in the days immediately following his death include the following:

"Goodbye, David. You probably saved the lives of millions of gay/trans/odd/ extraterrestrial kids. RIP."

"Bowie inspired countless people to take personal risks which led them to their own forms of self-actualization. In the same way Holly, Candy, and Jackie—the Warhol Superstars—helped to liberate many trans feminine persons of that era, David Bowie liberated the gay, the bisexual, and the androgyne."

"David Bowie showed this queer kid from Baton Rouge that gender outlaws are cool. Androgyny=rock&roll, not a reason to kill myself."

"As a young little queer boy struggling to fit in #David Bowie showed me that 'just fitting in' wasn't the only option. He was an inspiration."

The Legacy

After David Bowie died on January 10, 2016, writers acknowledged his gender-blurring legacy. Four days after Bowie's death, in a piece in *Billboard* titled

"David Bowie, Sexuality and Gender: A Rebel Who Changed the Face of Music," Barry Walters put it succinctly, truthfully, and simply when he wrote, "Bowie led the way in contextualizing pop through LGBT identity." In the *Telegraph* the day following his death, Kaite Welsh enthused, "Decades after Bowie confused the public with his eyeliner and dresses, the messy, liminal place between two genders is now being celebrated, with a new generation of people making their own identities, dropping gendered pronouns and inventing new titles—creating their own world just like he did. The joy Bowie found in blurring gender boundaries is what these people—and millions of others—will remember. And boy, did he make it look like fun."

What David Bowie began at the beginning of the 1970s has him marked down as a trailblazing gender pioneer without peer in rock music.

Part 3

The Legacy

33

Changing Lives

David Bowie—How He Influenced Millions of Fans

F ans of David Bowie—the real hard-core ones—are like no other group of fans in the history of popular music. Why? Because David Bowie himself was like no other artist in the history of popular music. He not only went beyond popular music itself, mining interdisciplinary territories like no one else ever did or could, but also operated on multiple levels, with intelligent, relevant, and empowering messages that impacted on his fans in a far deeper emotional and psychological way than those of other artists. You didn't *have* to be there at the beginning in the early 1970s when he, in the guise of the game-changing Ziggy Stardust, moved the goalposts of popular music and introduced a whole generation to the power of self-transformation, piercing the myth of a single, fixed, and unchangeable personality. Those of us who were there and absorbed his message(s) as we admiringly and gratefully wore out our copies of *The Rise and Fall of Ziggy Stardust and the Spiders from Mars, Aladdin Sane, Pinups,* and *Diamond Dogs* cherish the fact that we were there, of course. But such was David Bowie's sustained potency and relevance, not to mention the value of his stylistic diversity that afforded him the opportunity to recruit new groups of fans as styles came and went, that the Bowie train was one that could be joined at any time over the course of five decades.

Speaking personally for a moment, as a lecturer in a university school of music, there are students not yet twenty years old who were still in school when Bowie died and who are as avid in their Bowie fandom as I am. David Bowie's blueprint for fearless creativity, for embracing change, and for self-improvement through the arts resonates as powerfully for them in 2020 as it did for me in 1973. Bowie's parting gift, *Blackstar*, is their version of *The Rise and Fall of Ziggy Stardust and the Spiders from Mars*. Or *Low*. Or *Scary Monsters*. Game changing, eye and ear opening, and convention challenging, Bowie's work remains relevant to today in a way that no other sixty-nine-year-old musician could ever achieve. So it doesn't matter if you were there at the beginning and worked forward chronologically as his career unfolded or came

Fan art by Martina Leonard

Author's Collection

in later and explored his works backward. It's all still there to be explored, to be absorbed, and to be learned from.

David Bowie: Tour Guide

The lives of so many people have been empowered through being David Bowie fans and following him on his eclectic, ever-changing, and frequently challenging journey. In perhaps the simplest and clearest expression of his motivation that he ever gave, he told interviewer Charlie Rose in 1998, "What really gets me off is to be able to introduce people to new things. I love the feeling of introducing a new subject or something, especially to younger people, that maybe excites them, and gets them going on something, and it influences them to do something—you know, opening up some kind of world . . . I always felt it was a gift when anybody ever took me anywhere, or showed me a new way of doing things . . . and I love doing that back."

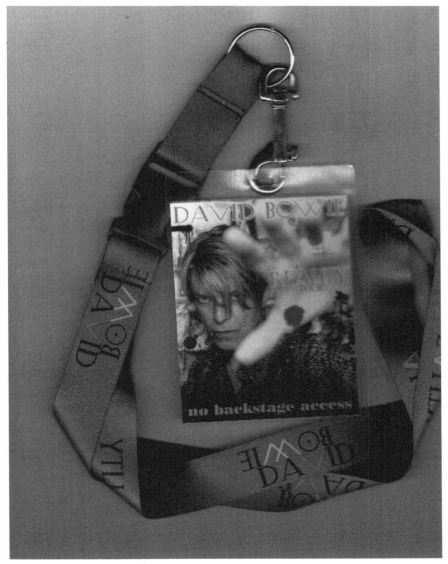

Reality Tour souvenir   *Author's Collection*

David Bowie's massive impact on the popular culture of the twentieth century—and into the twenty-first—is the singular reason that so many books are written about him. The number is staggering, far outweighing that of any other artist of his generation or since, and while *David Bowie FAQ* is the latest, there will undoubtedly be many, many more that will follow in this book's wake. For most rock stars, any books written about them will occupy the biography and music categories, and that will be the full extent of it. In the case of David Bowie, however, the multiple categories in which you will find books written about him reflect the complexity and breadth of what he achieved. In addition to publications from popular publishers (understandably the norm for popular music), more and more books are being written about David Bowie by academics and being published by academic presses. A thing called "Bowie studies" now exists, and textbooks that examine the artist from multiple disciplines are being created to allow students a way into understanding how he was able to make the impact he did. Music, performing arts studies, gender studies, film and media studies, celebrity studies—the list goes on and on. Since David Bowie's death, interest in all facets of his legacy has grown, not shrunk. This is both remarkable and fitting. No other artist has built a career on inviting those on the outside to come inside (and used himself as an example), on espousing egalitarian values, and—crucially— on making sexy such qualities as intelligence, deep thought, respect for the wider arts, and a search for betterment in both global and personal fields of endeavor. In a field (rock music) where dumbing things down, appealing to base instincts, and summing up tribal sensibilities is often in vogue, David Bowie continually went the other way and asked his fans to *think*. And not just to think for a moment and discard but to think deep and long.

This is how he affected so many people with a depth that no other artist has achieved. Sure, other artists exist who have the ability to change lives for the better and undoubtedly do so. But setting him apart, David Bowie managed it en masse. Despite often being on the fringes, whether in musical style, image, or message, he still managed to operate within the mainstream, and this meant that his appeal and impact went much further than has been the case for other artists. As a case in point, no other artist in history could ever have released an album such as *Low* (1977)—still considered by many to be his masterpiece—and had millions of fans faithfully follow his off-the-chart risky stylistic shift who had no previous experience of the ambient and electronic world he was about to immerse them in on those two sides of radical vinyl. *Low* achieved a number two placing on the U.K. album charts and number eleven in the United States. Debate raged, bouquets and brickbats abounded, music critics tugged at their forelocks and chewed their pens to find descriptors they'd never used before, and fans discovered a new world. It's just like Bowie said in the interview quoted earlier in this chapter and is

Reality Tour concert ticket

worth reiterating: "I love the feeling of introducing a new subject or something, especially to younger people, that maybe excites them, and gets them going on something, and it influences them to do something—you know, opening up some kind of world."

For millions, David Bowie did exactly that, whether it was new music, a new way to think about personality and personal growth, or the realization that they were not, after all, the freaks and outcasts they'd been led to believe they were.

"Never Look Back, Walk Tall, Act Fine"

Has there ever been a more empowering line of lyrics than this one from the song "Golden Years" from the *Station to Station* album of 1976? This kind of empowering encouragement is how David Bowie changed lives. By leading with himself as an example, he demonstrated how to be fearless, innovative, flexible (in the extreme), and tolerant of others and how to embrace—even seek out—difference instead of fearing it. Expressed here in a lyric, these seven words are much more than the sum of their parts, epitomizing as they do not only his approach to his career but also how he lived his life. To lapse briefly into a personal memory, I recall as a music undergraduate in the early 1990s being given advice by one of my professors, an Englishman named Dr. Patrick Little. He suggested that when I and my student cohort were to take a forthcoming three-hour end-of-year exam, the passing or failing of which would render the year's study a success or a failure, we wear our very best clothes into the examination room. "If you look good, you will perform at your best," he advised. How very David Bowie–like, I thought at the time and many times since during my own career. Hadn't Bowie's invention of and temporary absorption into Ziggy Stardust proved that very point to him? "Never look back, walk tall, act fine," indeed.

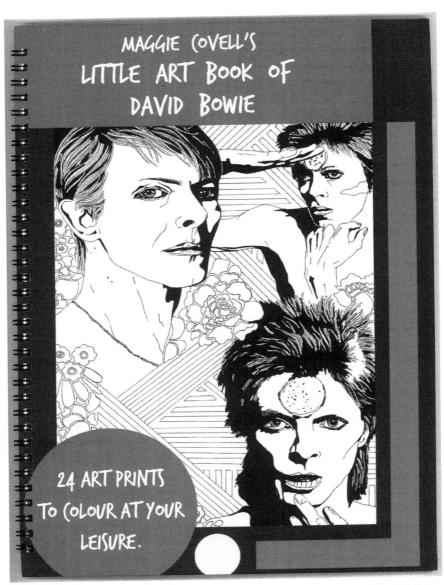

Fan Art Coloring Book by Maggie Covell

34

Apocalypse Anyone?

How David Bowie United a Fearful Generation

Within a handful of albums early in his career, spanning 1969 to 1974 and culminating in his apocalyptic masterpiece *Diamond Dogs*, David Bowie gave voice to the concerns of a new generation of fans for whom the idealism and lofty promises of the 1960s were irrelevant and for whom the underlying threat of unchecked technological advancement burned strongly. In so doing, he established a thematic cornerstone in his work that would be retained throughout his career, sometimes addressed more blatantly than at other times but ever present right until his final album, *Blackstar*, in 2016.

The 1970s Nuclear Threat

When David Bowie came to prominence in the early 1970s, nuclear war, indeed nuclear annihilation of the entire planet, seemed a very real possibility to a generation brought up on a diet of Cold War tension. There it was in prime time on the TV news in our lounges and living rooms every night. Nuclear stockpiling, warmongering rhetoric, and an always tangible East/West unease meant Bowie's generation of fans held a deep-seated and ingrained fear that one day a finger would descend on a big red button—to be quickly mirrored on a distant continent—resulting in mutual destruction. Who struck first would be a moot point; a fast death would come to the millions within the strike zones, while a slow death from radiation poisoning would be the fate of the "lucky" survivors of that initial exchange. Paranoia abounded, and fear-inducing phrases such as "Reds under the bed" were uttered. As Isaac Deutscher had suggested as far back as 1955 in his essay "1984: The Mysticism of Cruelty," "The chief predicament of contemporary society is that it has not yet succeeded in adjusting its way of life and its social and political institutions to the prodigious advance of its technical knowledge. We do not know what has been the impact of the atomic and hydrogen bombs on the thoughts of millions."

In *Cold War Modern: Design 1945–1970* (2008), writer and coeditor (with Jane Pavitt) David Crowley discussed a photographic image of Earth, titled

Earthrise, taken in 1968 by the astronauts of Apollo 8. He suggested, "The contrast between the luminous and indisputably living surface of the blue planet [Earth] swathed in clouds and the dusty surface of its satellite [the moon] prompted a wave of sentiment, with commentators stressing the fragility of the Earth in an age when militarism and affluence, twin buttresses of the Cold War, prevailed. The protective atmospheric layer that supported life on Earth was evidently thin when compared with the dark vacuum of empty space."

The Establishment of a Theme

This Cold War nuclear tension was part and parcel of a wider "fear-of-technology" theme that was explored by David Bowie throughout his career. His breakthrough 1969 hit "Space Oddity" epitomized with absolute clarity this thematic cornerstone, while the album that spawned it contained several other examples. In the lyrics of "The Cygnet Committee," for example, Bowie paints a frightening view of a technologically driven conflict in the future, where technology-gone-wrong decimates the human population: "The silent guns of love will blast the sky . . . I see a child slain on the ground as a love machine lumbers through desolation rows ploughing down man, woman." At the same time, he acknowledged the failure of the very human-centric and idealistic raison d'être of the counterculture: "[We] stoned the poor on slogans such as 'Love Is All We Need.'" This failure is revisited in "Wild-Eyed Boy from Freecloud": "And the missionary mystic of peace/love stumbled back to cry among the clouds."

Acknowledgment of and enthusiasm for Bowie's highlighting of such tension between the natural world and technological advancement is evident in a review by Tony Palmer, published in the *Observer* newspaper at the time of the album's release: "When he turns his eye to the absurdities of technological society, he is razor-sharp in his observations . . . at a time when we cling pathetically to every moonman's dribbling joke, when we admire unquestioningly the so-called achievements of our helmeted heroes without wondering why they are there at all."

At its worst, the notion of technology ruling over humans threatened the ultimate destruction of humanity, with humans left at the mercy of their own creations. In Stanley Kubrick's film *2001: A Space Odyssey* (1968), for example, Hal, the onboard computer, calculatedly kills the astronauts who accompany him into space. As he has frequently acknowledged, Bowie borrowed Kubrick's title and thematic content for his breakthrough hit, "Space Oddity." In the song, the technology that bore Major Tom into space just as easily abandons him, as related in the line "And I think my spaceship knows which way to go," sung as Major Tom and his ship drift apart.

Similarly, through the course of the song "Saviour Machine," a fictitious "President Joe" rises to power, promising to save the world. Ultimately, however, he lets the populace down, handing power over to a supposed utopian supercomputer that then proceeds to turn on its human creators: "The world held his hand, gave their pledge. So he told them his scheme for a saviour machine. They called it the prayer, its answer was law. Its logic stopped war, gave them food. How they adored till it cried in its boredom, 'Please don't believe in me, please disagree with me. Life is too easy, a plague seems quite feasible now, or maybe a war. Or I may kill you all.'"

Had human beings gone too far and overreached themselves in their thirst for technological advancement? As Bowie warned in the track "Memory of a Free Festival," "Man has pushed beyond his brain." In response to an interview question regarding the origins of "Space Oddity," as reprinted in the compilation by Miles *Bowie in His Own Words* (1980), Bowie acknowledged, "The publicity image of a spaceman at work is an automaton rather than a human being and my Major Tom is nothing if not a human being. It comes from a feeling of sadness about this aspect of the space thing. It has been dehumanised so I wrote a song-farce about it to try and relate science and human emotion. I suppose it's an antidote to space-fever, really."

David Bowie effectively removes the sense of awe surrounding space technology by referring to Major Tom's spaceship as a tin can. He undercuts the widely trumpeted, enormous technological triumph of putting a man in space by highlighting instead an all-too-human interest in the trivialities of celebrity: "And the papers want to know whose shirts you wear."

Ziggy Stardust's Apocalypse

On *The Rise and Fall of Ziggy Stardust and the Spiders from Mars* (1972), the theme of humankind technologically overreaching and the resultant disaster returns. While we never hear what the specific threat to Earth is—a threat that will result in annihilation in just five years' time according to the opening track—with nuclear disaster very much the flavor of the decade, it is the first likelihood that springs to the listener's mind.

As Ziggy stands alone on the album cover on the wet concrete of a nondescript, urban, industrial London street, his countenance purposeful and alert despite a studied casualness, he is presented as a kind of futuristic frontier hero, his guitar slung at his side like a sword or firearm in a pose reminiscent of statues of military heroes the world over. His diminution in the frame— never again on one of his album covers will he be so dwarfed and overshadowed—highlights the enormity of the task ahead of him; he is alone and small, pitted against the daunting city and the dangerous challenges of the night. But, even more dangerously, he is standing against the challenges and pitfalls of the space-age advancements in technology.

Space as a modern version of the American western frontier has been a commonly used analogy—in the arts, certainly, but also in politics. John F. Kennedy, for example, in his presidential acceptance speech of 1960, incorporated it as a key element as he looked toward the decade to come, stating, "I stand tonight facing west on what was once the last frontier . . . and we stand today on the edge of a new frontier—the frontier of the 1960s. A frontier of unknown opportunities and perils; a frontier of unfulfilled hopes and threats. . . . Beyond that frontier are the uncharted areas of science and space, unsolved problems of peace and war . . . I am asking each of you to be pioneers on that frontier." Daniel Deudney suggests, "Space is humanity's high frontier. Like all frontiers, space has produced unexpected treasures, generated strong enthusiasts, spawned wild speculations, and been enshrouded in myth and false promise." In popular entertainment also, space has been trumpeted as the ultimate, modern frontier, illustrated superbly through the well-known spoken voice-over from the theme of the popular U.S. science-fiction television series *Star Trek*: "Space—the Final Frontier."

Bowie's jumpsuit and boots on the cover of *The Rise and Fall of Ziggy Stardust and the Spiders from Mars* are similar in style to clothing worn by astronauts in pop culture science-fiction representations, such as Kubrick's *2001: A Space Odyssey* and television series such as *Lost in Space* and *Buck Rogers*, thus providing a strong visual inference. The album's title is clearly pure science fiction, and in conjunction with song titles on the back cover that include "Moonage Daydream," "Starman," "Lady Stardust," "Ziggy Stardust," and "Star," space is a prominently highlighted element. Providing yet further support, the back-cover picture of Bowie in a phone box is highly reminiscent of the peculiarly British form of space transport—a police phone box called the Tardis—favored by the time lord Doctor Who, the central character in the BBC science-fiction television series *Dr. Who*. Nicholas Pegg's view is that the cover conveyed the "adventitious impression that the guitar-clutching visitor to this unglamorous twilit backstreet has just touched down from another dimension altogether." Bowie, or Ziggy, might well have materialized on the spot much in the manner of the *Star Trek* crew teleporting down to the surface of an alien planet or Doctor Who's Tardis materializing amid who knows what or where. As Philip Cato so candidly puts it, "Bowie looking like a stranger from an unknown land, leaning against the wall, Gibson hanging nonchalantly against hip, outside K. West furriers on a deserted and rain-swept London backstreet, was just so fuckin' out of this world."

The whole notion of the *Ziggy Stardust* album is one of Earth needing salvation. But Ziggy, the androgynous, alien Starman who comes to Earth to save us, turns from hero to antihero as he succumbs to the earthly delights of sex, drugs, and rock 'n' roll and winds up a washed-up shadow of his former self by the end of the album. Mankind's last chance has gone.

Aladdin Sane's Apocalypse

On the next album, *Aladdin Sane*, war and apocalypse are blatantly located in the bracketed dates (1913–1938–197?) that accompany the title track. The first two dates indicate the years immediately prior to the start of World Wars I and II, and thus the 197? is a clear invitation to the viewer to speculate that by the end of the decade, the world will once again be at war. A single line in the song, in particular, supports this theme: "Passionate bright young things, takes him away to war." Other lyrics on the album that directly support this theme are sparse. During "Watch That Man," the album's opener, however, Bowie sings, "the bodies on the screen stopped bleeding" among other lyrics that set up a scene that mirrors the actions of live-for-today-for-tomorrow-we-all-may-die revelers in prewar Berlin, people desperately in pursuit of pleasure and seeking a last taste of the good times before disaster strikes.

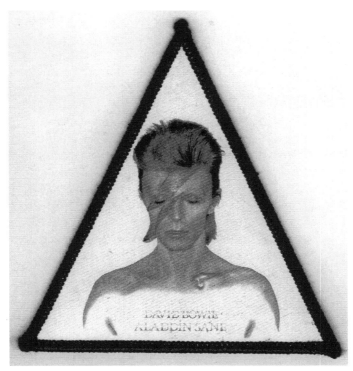

Aladdin Sane cloth patch   *Author's Collection*

Diamond Dogs: David Bowie's Ultimate Apocalypse Album

While the works discussed thus far in this chapter tapped into a generation's well-justified technological fears, it is on *Diamond Dogs* (1974) that Bowie gives them unadulterated full rein. *Diamond Dogs* is simply his ultimate apocalypse album. He borrows in part from George Orwell's *Nineteen Eighty-Four* to tell the story of a postapocalyptic world inhabited by packs of mutant survivors roaming a ruined cityscape as self-governing, wild animal hybrids, half man and half dog. Law and order has fallen, and it is everyone for themselves—an oft-visited scenario in postapocalyptic fiction. Denied the rights by the author's widow to create a work fully based on Orwell's novel, Bowie utilized bits and pieces that he'd already formed to that end and created his own thematically allied work instead.

Nineteen Eighty-Four was a highly significant critical and commercial success for Orwell, and although obviously a work of science fiction, it was nevertheless seen by many to be thematically analogous to real-world events of the twentieth century. In 1955, Deutscher had suggested, "Few novels written in this generation have obtained a popularity as great as that of George Orwell's *1984*.... The novel has served as a sort of an ideological super-weapon in the cold war." The book has a central theme of conflict between superpowers and an allied potential for apocalypse, offering its own fictional portrayal of a cold war between immensely powerful protagonists and thus mirroring the prevailing climate of mutual distrust and political hostility between the United States and the Soviet Union. As Scott Lucas has it, "This was a case of a text being in the right Cold War place at the right Cold War time." Certainly, such tension as existed in the middle decades of the twentieth century ensured that the theme of Orwell's novel was a topical subject and one ripe for a revisit by Bowie. As Deutscher went on, "At the onset of the atomic age, the world is living in a mood of Apocalyptic horror."

The second, third, and fourth tracks on side 2 of *Diamond Dogs* have song titles drawn directly from Orwell's novel, respectively: "We Are the Dead," "1984," and "Big Brother." The first of these, "We Are the Dead," is a line taken verbatim from the pivotal point in the novel where Winston Smith and Julia are captured. "1984" is, obviously, the title of the novel itself, while "Big Brother" refers to the party leader of the totalitarian state, Oceania, in which the events of Orwell's story take place.

Despite the obvious and acknowledged Orwellian influences, *Diamond Dogs* in its entirety is quite clearly Bowie's own vision of a dystopian, technology-gone-wrong future and not anyone else's. At the time of the album's release, Bowie's management and publishing company, MainMan, issued a promotional advertisement that confirms the work's apocalyptic nature. In part, it states that the album "conceptualises the vision of a future world with images of urban decadence and collapse." As biographer David Buckley put it in 2004, Bowie "created his own future urban nightmare environment, Hunger City, a sort of post-nuclear, technologically primitive hell."

While the image of Bowie as a half-man, half-dog freak dominates the cover, the implication that his hybrid state has come about as the result of some cataclysmic event, such as a nuclear war, sits in complete unison with the album's atmospheric, filmic, scene-setting opener, the spoken "Future Legend." All of the danger, dysfunction, degradation, fear, and horror that could be depicted with the spoken word is set against a background soundscape seemingly plucked straight from a horror movie, and all of this is brought to bear in the album's potent opener. By the time song 2, the title track, kicks in to introduce the mutants in full flight hustling in the mean backstreets of Hunger City, the listener has been completely drawn in, and every "what-would-it-be-like" fantasy and nightmare they'd ever had suddenly makes sense in the fantasy world that Bowie has conceptualized and presented.

In 1985, the author of *David Bowie: Theatre of Music*, Robert Matthew-Walker, offered an insightful reading of the album cover that addressed Bowie's human–canine state. He observed, "Even without listening to the album . . . it is possible to discern in the album's presentation a clear indication of temporality . . . the cover for this album depicts David's face and upper torso as part of an animal, joined to the bottom half of a dog's body. Even the shape of the hands and fingers have the appearance of paws, whilst close behind this monstrous figure are two female shapes, echoing the human-canine aspect of the front. This may not be quite as irrelevant as possibly it first appears. No one needs reminding of the warnings given to humankind of the likely effects on survivors of a nuclear war. Mutations might be among them. With the album's glimpse into the future, Bowie has taken this mutant nightmare to a logical if frightening conclusion."

The Continuation of the Theme

On the album immediately following *Diamond Dogs*, *Young Americans* (1975), David Bowie dramatically changed both musical style (shifting from glam to soul) and theme in one of the biggest U-turns of his career. Nevertheless, the critiquing of humankind's fascination for and overreliance on technological advancement would return time and time again in his career, establishing it as one of his primary thematic concerns. It would begin again the very next year with *Station to Station*, where the pulsing, mechanical motorik beat of experimental German bands such as Neu!, Can, or Kraftwerk were at the forefront of the Thin White Duke's epic title track. Later on the album, in "TVC15," the lyrics tell another variation on technological dominance as

Bowie's girlfriend succumbs to his television set, his mechanical friend that he watches every night. Over a honky-tonk piano accompaniment—unexpected given the nature of the musical style of side 1—Bowie relates how he brings his girlfriend home one night only to see the TVC15 swallow her: "I brought my baby home . . . she sat around forlorn. She saw my TVC15, and then baby's gone. She crawled right in, oh my."

On *Low* (1977), especially, technology effectively wins the battle, with the ambient electronic musical world that Bowie and Eno jointly invent laying waste to the traditional dominance of the human voice in popular music. Bowie's record company, RCA, was horrified as one of their flagship artists turned the industry on its head. The sounds made by computers and machines relegate the sounds made by humankind to a distant second place, and human sounds are completely absent for much of the album. As Charles Shaar Murray accurately put it in his review in *New Musical Express* at the time, *Low* consisted of "music and sounds so synthetic and depersonalized as to imply that the instruments did the playing after the band had gone home." The triumph of technology begins even before the vinyl is placed on the turntable, with the postapocalyptic image on the album cover that carries the implication of recent cataclysm, most likely nuclear war. The angry, orange sky gives every impression of a world in flames, and this hue is reflected in Bowie's hair. Even the lettering of the album title is orange, while the artist's name is rendered in yellow.

The triumph of technology theme continues on the following *"Heroes"* and, to a lesser extent, on the subsequent *Lodger*—considered by many to be the final album of Bowie's so-called Berlin trilogy. On the former's militaristic opening track of side 2, "V2 Schneider," there is a clearly evident allusion to Germany's deadly V-2 rockets of World War II, the world's first long-range ballistic missiles. In Bowie's hands, the reference becomes symbolic of the potential for technological advancement to threaten and destroy its creators.

Doomsday, Post-Millennium

In Bowie's first album of the new century, the very well-received *Heathen* (2002), the first sounds heard on the album are sparse and bleak, belonging to the slow, heavily atmospheric, and scene-setting "Sunday," which once again visits a postapocalyptic world. The opening lines are once again descriptive in a filmic way: "Nothing remains. We could run when the rain slows. Look for the cars or signs of life." Some critics assumed the song was written in the aftermath of 9/11; however, Bowie confirmed that it was written prior to this catastrophic terrorist event. Nevertheless, the lyrics seem completely apt for the images screened all over the world of the twisted smoking wreckage of New York's Twin Towers. Advanced technology in the form of jet airliners had been used as weapons against humankind, a fact in keeping with Bowie's ongoing problematizing of the human-versus-technology conundrum.

The title track of 2013's surprise album *The Next Day* contained the poignant line "They can't get enough of that doomsday song," a self-knowing acknowledgment of one of his own most important thematic staples. Through his ongoing presentation of doomsday themes throughout his career, Bowie has helped innumerable fans acknowledge and face their own fears, epitomizing the function of the best art in helping people make sense of the troubled and confusing world in which they live. This cornerstone trait continued on until the very end with *Blackstar*.

If apocalypse-level destruction, dysfunction, threat, and loss of order and the breakdown of society can be depicted in music, then *Blackstar* is the exemplar. So admirably experimenting and trying out new ideas right to the very last, here Bowie engages a completely new band of avant-garde jazz musicians to realize his vision. Headed by saxophonist Donny McCaslin, it's not jazz as we know it but more an eclectic hybrid with elements of whatever takes Bowie's fancy. In turns beautiful, ugly, jarring, challenging, and confrontational, *Blackstar* is to *Let's Dance* what a bicycle is to a pigeon. Completely eschewing the conventions of popular music, just as he did in 1977 with *Low*, the textures, unexpected breakouts, bursts of electronica, and avoidance of traditional form(s) result in a work analogous with the state of the world. This quality of the work was not missed by critic Jody Rosen, who, in her review of *Blackstar* for *Billboard*, commented that the seven songs on the album "serve up a veritable Grand Guignol of dread, death, even dismemberment.... It's tempting to say Bowie is channeling the zeitgeist, filling songs with the fury and foreboding of the scourged world of 2016.... On the other hand, for Bowie, such subject matter is nothing new. From the ill-fated astronaut of 'Space Oddity' to the lovers cowering beneath flying bullets in 'Heroes,' much of his greatest music has been streaked with violence and doom."

In Bowie's hands, the violence and doom of the works mentioned here—but also to be found elsewhere in his legacy—do not induce depression or resignation in the minds and ears of his listeners. As it presumably was for himself, working such issues out through his music is both cathartic and empowering. "Don't accept this!" is his message. Bravo, David Bowie.

35

Like-Minded Artists

How Do Madonna, Prince, and Lady Gaga Compare?

Any popular music artist eventually finds him- or herself being compared to others as either a precursor or a contemporary. It is a natural thing for both fans and critics alike to look for commonalities and threads of continuity. The unique nature of the ever-changing David Bowie, however, renders most comparisons irrelevant or flawed from the outset. He was very much a trendsetter, not a follower. Through his many innovations and his unique actor's approach to both popular music and stardom, David Bowie had a large and lasting effect on the industry, changing it from the inside, not only through his own work but also by the influence he had on others who followed him. It is only after the fact, so to speak, that those who might bear valid comparisons can be found. Three of the artists who bear the most obvious commonalities with him are Madonna, Prince, and Lady Gaga. Like Bowie, all three established themselves as being more than "just" musicians, becoming fashion icons, multimedia artists, and, to varying extremes, changelings. Like Bowie, all at times faced accusations of style over substance, and some of their musical changes proved difficult for fans and critics alike to accept. Nevertheless, their impact on and empowerment of their fans went far beyond that of average star/fan relationships, just as had been the case with Bowie.

Madonna

At a concert in Houston, Texas, in 2016, just days after David Bowie's death, Madonna performed his 1974 hit "Rebel Rebel" against a backdrop of his images as a tribute to the man who hugely inspired and influenced her. While introducing the song, she told the cheering audience, "I want to pay tribute to a man who inspired my career. If you haven't heard about David Bowie, then look him up, motherfuckers. He was one of the geniuses in the music industry, one of the

Ray of Light album by Madonna, 1998   *Author's Collection*

greatest singer-songwriters of the twentieth century, and he changed my life when I went to see him in concert in Detroit. He showed me that it was OK to be different. And he's the first Rebel Heart that I laid eyes on."

This was not the first time Madonna had acknowledged the impact Bowie had on her life. She previously had expressed her fond admiration for David Bowie in an even more public forum when she gave an acceptance speech on his behalf on his induction into the Rock 'n' Roll Hall of Fame in 1996. On that occasion too, she reminisced about seeing him perform in the first-ever rock concert that she'd attended, at age fifteen, in Detroit's Cobo Arena. She recalled that after watching Bowie that day—against the wishes of her parents, who subsequently grounded her for the rest of the summer—she "came home a changed woman."

It's clear that Madonna learned many lessons from David Bowie. She too has a changeling nature and has played with image, gender, sexuality, musical style, and even interdisciplinarity (especially acting) in ways comparable to Bowie. In many aspects, her work has been extremely important. Just as Bowie inspired her and numerous people of her generation with his contention that being different was a strength and not a weakness and that change was to be pursued rather than avoided, Madonna has passed on the baton/message to a whole new generation that was too young to hear, experience, and absorb it the first time around. Particularly inspiring for young women during her heyday, she too has empowered her fans in a similar way to her mentor. That social impact, then, along with the fact that she has kept and fully utilized her autonomy and creative freedom in an industry that often tries to bully and shoehorn artists into boxes, is perhaps where the closest comparisons to David Bowie lie. In addition, she has excelled as a writer and producer.

One would be hard pressed to argue that Madonna's musical output has had anywhere near the same groundbreaking quality and stylistic breadth as Bowie's. She is not the singing talent that Bowie was nor the songwriter he was—a great nose for pop hooks though she certainly possesses. There have been stylistic variations in her work, with various albums described by critics as pop, folk, acoustic, dance, disco, electronica, and more. But there is nothing like the quantum leaps one can observe in Bowie's work, from *Hunky Dory* to *Diamond Dogs* to *Young Americans* to *Low* to *Let's Dance* to *Earthling* and, ultimately, to *Blackstar*, to name-drop just some of Bowie's stylistic extremes. But this aside, for the reasons outlined above, Madonna clearly is of a similar ilk to her girlhood hero. Her own success owes much to her recognition and adoption of Bowie's masterful blueprint. She is well deserving of the comparisons even if, perhaps arguably in the eyes of her admirably devoted fans, not measuring up in purely musical terms.

Prince

Following David Bowie's death at the beginning of 2016, Prince began including "Heroes" in his live sets, something he continued to do right up until his own unfortunate and unexpected demise. Indeed, the final time he performed "Heroes" was in his April 14 concert at the Fox Theatre, Atlanta, just one week before his own death on April 21. His touching and intimate piano and vocal renditions of Bowie's classic song in these concerts (check out the fan footage on YouTube) were not his first public performances of Bowie's music. At the Essence Festival in New Orleans in July 2014, for example, he joined Nile Rodgers onstage to perform "Let's Dance" before following up with his own headlining set. Prince attracted criticism on the online fan community website Prince.org and elsewhere for making no public announcement following

Controversy album by Prince, 1981

Bowie's unexpected death amid a tidal wave of such celebrity tributes. But then, notoriously reclusive and private, he never was one to make such gestures, and besides, the "Heroes" tributes in the concerts that followed removed any doubt with regard to the respect that the diminutive star had for his elder.

While Madonna, Lady Gaga, and indeed Bowie himself were all very open about their influences and would candidly name-drop those to whom they felt indebted, this was not the Prince way. Yet Prince's performative methodology; self-management of his career; investment in fashion, gender, and sexuality; and championing of the outsider bear such close comparisons to the precedents that Bowie had set that it seems a sure bet that Bowie had been an integral part of Prince's own raison d'être. In a tribute piece to both fallen artists published in the *Washington Post* the day after Prince's death, writer Dan Zak addressed this synergy between the two. Under the title "The Quality That Made Prince and David Bowie Immortal," he wrote, "The pale alien from

Brixton and the black man from Minneapolis had something in common, in that they had nothing in common with anyone. They stripped masculinity of its insecurities. They were beyond labels, immune to the generics of genre. They were born into a world that expects certain things and they spent their careers defying those expectations."

The Prince biography published on allmusic.com suggests further, musical similarities. Written by Stephen Thomas Erlewine, it notes, "With each album he released, Prince showed remarkable stylistic growth and musical diversity, constantly experimenting with different sounds, textures, and genres.... Occasionally, his music was inconsistent, in part because of his eclecticism, but his experiments frequently succeeded; no other contemporary artist blended so many diverse styles into a cohesive whole." Such an appraisal is typical of those written about David Bowie—indeed, this could just as easily *be* a Bowie overview—and demonstrates the common territory held between the two. But once again, head-to-head, if one is to compare the stylistic breadth of both men's musical journeys, it is Bowie's that is the far more expansive and musically daring. But to highlight and labor this fact would do Prince a disservice because—as with Madonna—with such artists it is never *just* about the music. It is about the empowerment of others; the example of inclusiveness and border crossing that they provided for their generation(s) is of prime importance. In that regard, once again, Prince and David Bowie are bona fide brothers in arms.

Lady Gaga

Born in 1986 and therefore a full twenty-eight years younger than Madonna and Prince (both born in 1958), Lady Gaga has often been linked to David Bowie. One of the most successful recording artists in the world today, with numerous awards and accolades particularly across music and acting spheres, she is described on Wikipedia as a "singer, songwriter, and actress ... known for her unconventionality and provocative work as well as experimenting with new images"; such descriptors immediately suggest common ground. Yet there are further similarities. On his breakthrough album, *The Rise and Fall of Ziggy Stardust and the Spiders from Mars* (1972), Bowie critiqued the notion of fame and celebrity, and these themes were also addressed by Gaga on her enormously successful, career-defining debut album, *Fame* (2008). Drugs, sexual and gender identity, love, and alienation were all visited within her album's overarching theme, mirroring Bowie's thematic palette. In both cases, these were albums written, performed, and released by would-be stars, projecting and imagining the real thing before having experienced it. Soon afterward, both artists released albums that further critiqued the notion of fame and celebrity but this time in

The Fame Monster album by Lady Gaga, 2009   *Author's Collection*

the light of having achieved it and experienced both the good and the bad sides. Bowie's was *Aladdin Sane* (1973), and Gaga's was *The Fame Monster* (2009). Plus, of course, on *Young Americans* (1975), Bowie came up with his hit critique on the matter in the chart-topping song "Fame."

When quizzed by National Public Radio (npr.org) about her tribute to David Bowie at the Grammy Awards ceremony in 2016, Lady Gaga responded by saying, "I feel like my whole career is a tribute to David Bowie." Like Madonna, Lady Gaga attributes much of her career and even her fundamental approach to her art to the trailblazing Londoner and is able to—as Madonna did in her recollection of attending Bowie's concert in Detroit—pinpoint a single moment of enlightenment that changed the course of her life. As she further explained in the same interview, her big moment was when she first laid eyes on the *Aladdin Sane* album cover: "I was 19 years old, and it just changed my perspective on everything, forever. It was an image that changed my life. I remember I took the vinyl record out of the casing and I put it on my vinyl player.... 'Watch That Man' came on and, I mean, that was just the beginning of my artistic birth. I started to dress more expressively. I started to go to the library and look through more art books. I took an art history class. I was playing with a band."

Just as Bowie proved to be a lightning rod for the marginalized and alienated, so too Lady Gaga fulfills the same function for many of her fans. She makes their sense of feeling different and unaccepted overt with her continual referencing of "monsters." Monsters, of course, is a heavily loaded term that for centuries has been applied to those deemed society's misfits and freaks. In addition to labeling herself as one, she refers to her fans as little monsters as well, thereby creating a close and intimate bond with them that goes beyond most star/fan relationships and is reminiscent of the hordes of little "Bowie-ites" of the early 1970s who would dress up like their hero and find acceptance amid their like. Throughout Bowie's career, from the "And I looked and frowned and the monster was me" proclamation in "The Width of a Circle" (from *The Man Who Sold the World*) to the freak show cover of *Diamond Dogs*, the self-analyzing of the *Scary Monsters (and Super Creeps)* album, and far beyond, monsters and freaks were Bowie's stock-in-trade as well. As he told interviewer Sir Tim Rice in 1980 when questioned about his motivation for taking on the role of the extremely disfigured John Merrick in the Broadway play *The Elephant Man*, "I have an eclectic thing about freaks and isolationists and alienated people."

As with Madonna and Prince, Lady Gaga's musical palette is nowhere near as expansive as Bowie's. While this is completely understandable given her far shorter career span thus far, it also seems unlikely she would ever stray far from her synth-pop core and become the musical tourist that Bowie was. But, again, this is rather to miss the point. Lady Gaga has picked up David Bowie's baton in terms of fan empowerment and the embracing of multiple disciplines. Whether her expansive talents, changeling qualities, and allied multifaceted fields of endeavor will enable her to achieve the extraordinary career longevity of Bowie, Madonna, and Prince remains to be seen. But, thus far, she has successfully carried their baton into the first two decades of the twenty-first century.

David Bowie: The First of His Kind

All three of these artists are trailblazers in their own right and intrinsically have expanded the boundaries of popular music to intersect with fashion, film, gender and sexuality, the politics of alienation, and so on, exposing and changing the very nature of celebrity in the process. Bowie was the first of his kind, and his blueprint was adopted by the other three. There can, of course, only be one first-of-a-kind, and this in no way lessens or devalues the achievements of Madonna, Prince, and Lady Gaga. Undoubtedly, others will follow, and the world of entertainment will always be so much the better for such multitalented, multifaceted, and courageous artists. Their most telling point of difference and the proof of their depth lies in what they mean to their fans compared to "normal" pop stars who produce catchy music but offer little more than that. In introducing his interview with David Bowie in the *Telegraph* in December 1996, Mick Brown remarked, "Throughout the Seventies, David Bowie did not have fans. He had acolytes, disciples, obsessives; teens and 20s who would buy every record, watch every move, copy his clothes, his haircuts—the upswept flaming bush of Ziggy Stardust, the soul-boy quiff of Young Americans—his attitude."

Bouquets and Brickbats

What Reviewers Have Said about David Bowie through the Years

Always an artist who polarized—especially during the 1970s and 1980s—
Bowie's critics frequently matched critical acclaim with vehement derision. The retrospective reading of a selection of Bowie reviews reveals some
perceptive observations made early in his career before he became a star,
some rave reviews and caustic put-downs after stardom had been achieved,
and then a growing across-the-board admiration for his later, especially
post-millennium, work.

The 1960s

First studio album, *David Bowie*, released June 1, 1967, on Deram Records: "A
remarkable, creative debut album by a nineteen-year old Londoner who wrote
all 14 tracks and sings them with a sufficiently fresh interpretation to make
quite a noise on the scene if he gets the breaks and the right singles." Anon., *Disc
and Music Echo*, June 1967

Single release "Rubber Band" and "The London Boys," 1967: "I do not think
Rubber Band is a hit. What it is is an example of how David Bowie had pro-
gressed himself into being a name to reckon with.... Listen to this record and
then turn it over and listen to The London Boys, which actually I think would
have been a much more impressive topside. But both are worth thinking about."
Anon., *Disc and Music Echo*, December 1967

Second studio album, *David Bowie* (United Kingdom), released November
4, 1969 (aka *Man of Words/Man of Music* in the United States and later *Space
Oddity* on the album's rerelease in the wake of the success of the *Ziggy Stardust*
album), on Philips Records: "The lyrics are full of the grandeur of yesterday,
the immediacy of today, and the futility of tomorrow. This is well worth your
attention." Anon., *Music Now!*, November 1969

Second studio album, *David Bowie*: "His love reveries are dreary, self-pitying and monotonous. But when he turns his eye to the absurdities of technological society, he is razor-sharp in his observations." Tony Palmer, *The Observer*, 1969

The 1970s

Third studio album, *The Man Who Sold the World*, released November 4, 1970, on Mercury Records: "This remarkable young man (who poses in feminine attire in the sleeve picture) has, as usual, written all his own material for this nine-track album. The lyrics mostly mirror the current unrest of the world." Allen Evans, *New Musical Express*, April 1971

Third studio album, *The Man Who Sold the World*: "Bowie's music offers an experience that is as intriguing as it is chilling, but only to the listener sufficiently together to withstand its schizophrenia." John Mendelsohn, *Rolling Stone*, February 1971

Fourth studio album, *Hunky Dory*, released December 17, 1971, on RCA Records: "With his affection for using intriguing and unusual themes in musical settings that most rock 'artists' would dismiss with a quick fart as old-fashioned and uncool, he's definitely an original, is David Bowie, and as such will one day make an album that will induce us homo superior elitist rock critics to race about like a chicken with its head lopped off.... Until that time, *Hunky Dory* will suffice hunky-dorily." John Mendelsohn, *Rolling Stone*, January 1972

Fourth studio album, *Hunky Dory*: "David Bowie is a million different people and each one is a bit more lovely than the one before. But for Christ's sake don't think he's a gimmick or a hype! Instead, enjoy him as he is; a surreal cartoon character brought to life for us all to enjoy.... It's very possible that this will be the most important album from an emerging artist in 1972, because he's not following trends—he's setting them." Danny Holloway, *New Musical Express*, January 1972

A prediction made six months before the breakthrough album *The Rise and Fall of Ziggy Stardust and the Spiders from Mars* was released: "Everyone just knows that David is going to be a lollapalooza of a superstar throughout the entire world this year, David more than most. His songs are always ten years ahead of their time, he says, but this year he has anticipated the trends: 'I'm going to be huge, and it's quite frightening in a way,' he says." Michael Watts, *Melody Maker*, January 22, 1972

Fifth studio album, *The Rise and Fall of Ziggy Stardust and the Spiders from Mars*, released June 6, 1972, on RCA Records: "Of course there's nothing Bowie would like more than to be a glittery super-star, and it could still come to pass. By now everybody ought to know he's tremendous and this latest chunk of fantasy can only enhance his reputation further." James Johnson, *New Musical Express*, June 1972

Fifth studio album, *The Rise and Fall of Ziggy Stardust and the Spiders from Mars*: "Bowie's bid for stardom is accelerating at lightning speed." Michael Watts, *Melody Maker*, July 1972

Sixth studio album, *Aladdin Sane*, released April 13, 1973, on RCA Records: "David Bowie was last year's Ziggy Stardust, this year's Aladdin Sane and probably next year's Pinocchio." Nick Kent, *New Musical Express*, April 1973

Seventh studio album, *Pinups*, released October 19, 1973, on RCA Records: "Although many of the tracks are excellent, none stands up to the originals." Greg Shaw, *Rolling Stone*, December 1973

Seventh studio album, *Pinups*: "Pin-Ups slowly, but surely, dies a death ... [it] fails to live up to its promise." Ian MacDonald, *New Musical Express*, 1973

Eighth studio album, *Diamond Dogs*, released April 24, 1974, on RCA Records: "Once more into the apocalypse.... The 'mood' is the ultimate in punk SF post-atomic doom—where 'after dark' is forever, rock 'n' roll mutants are *real* mutants, and the glitter won't come off your face because it *is* your face." Ian McDonald, *New Musical Express*, May 1974

Eighth studio album, *Diamond Dogs*: "D-d-d-decadence, that's what this album is all about, thematically and conceptually.... [He] pretentiously likes to think of himself as the prescient chronicler of a planet falling to pieces, so this is again a quasi-Orwellian concept album about a future world where the clockwork orangutans skulk like dogs in the street while the politicians etc. and blah blah blah ... I'm getting a bit tired of his broken-larynxed vocals; they're so queasily sincere they reek of some horrible burlesque, some sterilely distasteful artifice. It's the same old theatrical delivery of pretentious lyrics." Lester Bangs, *Creem*, August 1974

Ninth studio album, *Young Americans*, released February 21, 1975, on RCA Records: "The main item on the menu is none other than ye olde Loneliness Of The Long-Distance Superstar—an odd one for Bowie considering he built a sizeable proportion of his reputation on exploring his divorce from stardom, being outside looking in on fame ... it sounds virtually nothing like the Bowie we've all come to love or loathe." Ian MacDonald, *New Musical Express*, March 1975

Ninth studio album, *Young Americans*: "Bowie has just changed his props ... this tour it's black folk." Lester Bangs, *Creem*, 1975

Tenth studio album, *Station to Station*, released January 23, 1976, on RCA Records: "DAVID BOWIE, never one to maintain continuity in his work or in his life, has become more elusive than ever in the past year.... Will the Philly bump 'n' hustle which he rightly calculated as his springboard to American chart success remain his stock-in-trade a while longer, leaving his staunch Ziggy-era fans alienated through another release? With *Station To Station* (the RCA album's

The Next Day studio album cover, released March 2013   *Author's Collection*

original title was *Golden Years*), Bowie answers the question with an emphatic 'No.'" Richard Cromelin, *Circus*, March 1976

Tenth studio album, *Station to Station*: "*Young Americans* was a successful experiment, but rather than creating another entrapping persona, he had simply created an audience for his work that was apart and very different from his *Ziggy* army. So his task became not the creation of yet another persona, but the unification of an audience he'd divided by success. That's where the new album, *Station To Station*, fits in." Ben Edmonds, *Phonograph Record*, January 1976

Eleventh studio album, *Low*, released January 14, 1977, on RCA Records: "[*Low* consists of] . . . music and sounds so synthetic and depersonalized as to imply that the instruments did the playing after the band had gone home." Charles Shaar Murray, *New Musical Express*, January 1977

Eleventh studio album, *Low*: "Bowie has gone right out on a limb with this album. He'll probably lose a bunch of fans, but I admire him for having the courage to put it out. He could have cruised on churning out *Ziggy Stardust Part 22* forever, instead, he battles on, donning new styles and guises, widening his scope and improving all the time. And that's part of the reason he's so exciting . . . you never know what he'll get up to next but can rest assured he won't stay trapped in the same bag, regardless of how successful it may be." Kris Needs, *ZigZag*, February 1977

Twelfth studio album, *"Heroes,"* released October 14, 1977, on RCA Records: "What to make of *"Heroes"* I dunno. I never know what to make of Bowie albums. I just absorb them, they're hateful to analyse." Tim Lott, *Record Mirror*, October 1977

Twelfth studio album, *"Heroes"*: "That's it then, a strange, cold sometimes impenetrable album, but Bowie makes all these unlikely ingredients work. Bits fail but so what? He could live in luxury for the rest of his days and just churn out another *Ziggy* every year. Instead he's on the move, going places he ain't gone before. Good for Bowie." Kris Needs, *ZigZag*, October 1977

Twelfth studio album, *"Heroes"*: "David Bowie is the most inconsistently appealing genius in rock. With his chameleon ability to change from disco to space-rock to romantic ballads to astringent mechanomusic, Bowie has demonstrated that he can master and present music any way he cares to." Ira Robbins, *Crawdaddy!*, January 1978

Thirteenth studio album, *Lodger*, released May 18, 1979, on RCA Records: "Another year, another record. Even when playing at superstars, it was always hard to escape the sense of Bowie as tourist." Jon Savage, *Melody Maker*, May 1979

Thirteenth studio album, *Lodger*: "The LP is easy to listen to because it rarely challenges the listener; it only baits you with slick and highly embossed surfaces. It is not really a departure from *Low* and *'Heroes,'* but a rejection of their serious nature. . . . You can't help liking parts of it, but if you really liked *Low*, liked 'Heroes,' and generally like the challenging side of Bowie's previous works, you can't help feeling cheated and dismayed by this one." Paul Yamada, *New York Rocker*, July 1979

The 1980s

Fourteenth studio album, *Scary Monsters*, released September 12, 1980, on RCA Records: "Learning to live with somebody's depression: the man in the clown suit stops running, finds self in back-against-wall situation, attempts to deal with same." Charles Shaar Murray, *New Musical Express*, September 1980

Fourteenth studio album, *Scary Monsters*: "Slowly, brutally and with a savage, satisfying crunch, David Bowie eats his young." Debra Rae Cohen, *Rolling Stone*, December 1980

Fifteenth studio album, *Let's Dance*, released April 14, 1983, on EMI Records: "With this album, Bowie seems to have transcended the need to write endlessly about the dramas of being D*A*V*I*D B*O*W*I*E and about all his personal agonies.... Powerful, positive music that dances like a dream and makes you feel ten feet tall." Charles Shaar Murray, *New Musical Express*, April 1983

Sixteenth studio album, *Tonight*, released September 1, 1984, on EMI Records: "This album is a throwaway, and David Bowie knows it." Kurt Loder, *Rolling Stone*, November 1984

Seventeenth studio album, *Never Let Me Down*, released April 27, 1987, on EMI Records: "I guess you could say *Never Let Me Down* did just that; let me down. Maybe it'll make a good primer for first-time Bowie students. Maybe they'll go back to *Aladdin Sane*, *Diamond Dogs*, *Young Americans*, even *Scary Monsters*." Roy Trakin, *Creem*, August 1987

Seventeenth studio album, *Never Let Me Down*: "It used to be easy. Once a year or so, David Bowie would choose a new persona, pick up a fresh batch of pop-culture reference points, borrow a new musical style and release a new album. Then we'd all sit around and figure out who he was this time.... *Never Let Me Down* isn't so cut and dried. It's an odd, freewheeling pastiche of elements from all the previous Bowies ... [that] doesn't bode as well for Bowie's present, or his future." Steve Pond, *Rolling Stone*, June 1987

The 1990s

Eighteenth studio album, *Black Tie White Noise*, released April 5, 1993, on Arista Records: "The 1980s was not a happy decade for David Bowie.... Now he has rediscovered the insistent electro-dance rhythms and sensual synth and sax textures with which he seduced critics and fans alike during the latter part of the 1970s ... and if any collection of songs could reinstate his godhead status, then this is it." David Sinclair, Q, May 1993

Eighteenth studio album, *Black Tie White Noise*: "In a strange way, when Bowie was weird, he defined our normalcy. It was inevitable that, when he straightened out, he'd lose our attention.... Once he sang 'I'm an alligator,' and it was easy to believe him. Now he's reduced to begging 'wait ... don't lose faith,' and even that moment of pitiful honesty isn't his, because Morrissey wrote the best song in sight. The hunter has finally been caught by the game." Dave Thompson, *The Rocket*, May 1993

Nineteenth studio album, *The Buddha of Suburbia*, released November 8, 1993, on Arista Records: "The Buddha Of Suburbia, in many respects, is David Bowie's most important album of the 90s. Not the best (that is still Earthling), but this is the one that shook Bowie out of simply trying too hard after simply not trying hard enough a decade previously. It's rough, and has an air of the deliberately unfinished about it. Had it not been linked with Hanif Kureishi's exemplary dramatisation of his book and Bowie called it something like Strangers, it would have been retrospectively given a great deal more air and talked about being the belated follow-up to Low and 'Heroes.'" Daryl Easlea, BBC Review, 2007

Twentieth studio album, *1. Outside*, released September 26, 1995, on RCA Records: "No-one who's been listening to rock for less than a dozen years can remember a time when Bowie was good.... With this record, he's hard again; his mojo be working, big-time." Charles Shaar Murray, *Mojo*, October 1995

Twentieth studio album, *1. Outside*: "David Bowie has made a career of being anything and everything other than himself. But Outside ... is way too much of a good thing. Bowie's almost pathological fear of dropping all the masks ... has driven him into multiple-personality overdrive and forced melodrama. The music ... feels shoehorned into the script with frustrating rigidity." David Fricke, *Rolling Stone*, October 1995

Twentieth studio album, *1. Outside*: "Those legions who came in on *Let's Dance* will most certainly be left completely and utterly bewildered. Perhaps though, that's entirely the point." Tom Doyle, Q, October 1995

Twenty-first studio album, *Earthling*, released February 3, 1997, on RCA Records: "Bowie lets the songs tell the story. Gone are the spoken interludes and overblown avant-garde flourishes that marred Outside; instead, the tracks on Earthling are linked only by the power of the turbocharged guitars, the energy and intensity of the skittering drum-and-bass rhythms, the spiritual-technological tug of war in the lyrics and Bowie's signature baritone croon." Mark Kemp, *Rolling Stone*, February 1997

Twenty-first studio album, *Earthling*: "Where most junglists dab just a pale wash of synthesized strings or the cooings of soft-soul vocalists onto their rhythm beds, Bowie and his band splash samples around with abandon, then pour further layers of rock-hard instrumental playing onto that. He'll undoubtedly come in for some stick for using young folks' musical forms, but wouldn't it be wonderful if all 50-year-old rockers retained such an interest in the future?" Andy Gill, *Mojo*, March 1997

Twenty-second studio album, *"Hours...,"* released October 4, 1999, on Virgin Records: "His past selves have proved a difficult act to follow ... after the artful *1. Outside* and the indecent noise terror of *Earthling, 'hours...'* crowns a trilogy that represents significantly more than a mere coda to a once-unimpeachable career ... the album's despairing subtext is all too apparent. What's more, it suits Bowie just fine." Mark Paytress, *Mojo*, November 1999

The 2000s

Twenty-third studio album, *Heathen*, released June 11, 2002, on ISO/Columbia Records: "Packed with fantastic songs, liberally sprinkled with intriguing touches.... It would be wrong to herald *Heathen* as a complete return to 1970s form.... But those were records made by a decadent gay saxophone-playing cokehead alien Pierrot with an interest in fascism and the occult. *Heathen* is the work of a multi-millionaire 55-year-old father of two." Alexis Petridis, *The Guardian*, May 2002

Twenty-third studio album, *Heathen*: "David Bowie has exquisitely hip taste.... A loose theme runs through these songs, covers included: the search for guiding light in godless night. But the real story is *Heathen*'s perfect casting: Bowie playing Bowie, with class." David Fricke, *Rolling Stone*, May 2002

Twenty-fourth studio album, *Reality*, released September 16, 2003, on ISO/Columbia Records: "*Reality* is a proper album, with a beginning, a middle and an end. It's direct, warm, emotionally honest, even, and the surfeit of pleasingly deceptive musical simplicity allows the irony of the central concept—that there is no such thing as reality anymore—an opportunity to filter through." Daryl Easlea, BBC.com, 2003

Twenty-fourth studio album, *Reality*: "There's a restlessness to much of the music that not only makes for a great album but suggests that Bowie is struggling more than ever for answers." Steve Morse, *Boston Globe*, September 2003

The 2010s

Twenty-fifth studio album, *The Next Day*, released March 8, 2013, on ISO/Columbia Records: "*The Next Day* is the comeback Bowie fans feared would never happen.... There are loads of musical and lyrical references to his past, as Bowie broods over the places he's gone and the faces he's seen. But he's resolutely aimed at the future." Rob Sheffield, *Rolling Stone*, February 2013

Twenty-fifth studio album, *The Next Day*: "It is an enormous pleasure to report that the new David Bowie album is an absolute wonder: urgent, sharp-edged, bold, beautiful and baffling, an intellectually stimulating, emotionally charged, musically jagged, electric bolt through his own mythos and the mixed-up, celebrity-obsessed, war-torn world of the 21st century." Neil McCormick, *The Telegraph*, February 2013

Twenty-fifth studio album, *The Next Day*: "This is a record that while happy to acknowledge Bowie's titanic past and borrow, magpie-like from it, is anything

Blackstar studio album cover, released January 2016   *Author's Collection*

but navel-gazing, self-referential or reverent, instead leaping forward with a restless energy to tomorrow." Emily Mackay, *New Musical Express*, March 2013

Twenty-sixth studio album, *Blackstar*, released January 8, 2016, on ISO/Columbia: "When David Bowie returned from exile with 2013's 'The Next Day,' an album that wistfully referenced his late-'70s art-rock heyday, it felt like this eternal futurist was starting to look back. Wrong, earthlings! Released on his 69th birthday, 25th album 'Blackstar' spins the spaceship back around and points it at the moon. Bowie's formidable record of reinventing himself with each new album remains intact.... Warped showtunes, skronking industrial rock, soulful balladeering, airy folk-pop, even hip-hop—it all has a place on this busy, bewildering and occasionally beautiful record." Sam Richards, *New Musical Express*, January 2016

Twenty-sixth studio album, *Blackstar*: "One of the most aggressively experimental records the singer has ever made.... This album represents Bowie's most fulfilling spin away from glam-legend pop charm since 1977's Low. Blackstar is that strange, and that good." David Fricke, *Rolling Stone*, December 2015

37

Bowie's Awards

Nominations, Acceptances, and Polite Refusals

Where It All Began: The Ivor Novello Special Award

In 1970, David Bowie received the first major accolade of his career—if a seemingly and uncharacteristically conventional and old-fashioned one—when he received an Ivor Novello Special Award for Originality for "Space Oddity" (1969). Awarded annually by the British Academy of Composers and Songwriters to honor excellence in songwriting and composition, other notable recipients over the award's six decades of recognizing excellence (1956–current) have included Bryan Adams, Adele, Adam Ant, Emma Bunton, Nick Cave, Eric Clapton, Adam Clayton, Phil Collins, Ray Davies, Cathy Dennis, Dizzee Rascal, Noel Gallagher, Bob Geldof, Barry Gibb, Maurice Gibb, Robyn Gibb, David Gilmour, Thom Yorke, Amy Winehouse, Robbie Williams, Pete Townshend, U2, Roger Taylor, Rod Stewart, Neil Sedaka, Ed Sheeran, Nile Rodgers, Tim Rice, and Smokey Robinson.

While most David Bowie fans are aware of this early industry recognition for the originality of "Space Oddity" and the fact that it was his first major award, it was not his first award per se, as on July 25, 1969, he had taken part in the Malta International Song Festival and had been awarded "Best Production" for the song "When I Live My Dream."

David Bowie would receive another four Ivor Novello award nominations during his career, and he would take out the awards for three of these. Three of these other four nominations were in 1984 and were for the same song: the worldwide smash hit "Let's Dance." The categories that "Let's Dance" was nominated for were "International Hit of the Year," "The Best Rock Song of the Year," and "The Best-Selling A Side of the Year," and he was successful in being awarded the first two of these nominations. In addition, in 1990, he was given the highest accolade possible: the award for having made an "Outstanding Contribution to British Music."

"Just 'Cause You Nominate Me, It Doesn't Mean I'll Accept Your Award, Thanks"

Unlike, arguably, the majority of celebrities, who seem both content and delighted to receive with open arms every accolade that is proffered in their direction in order to further inflate their status and longevity, David Bowie was not one to accept awards that he felt were fatuous or for which he felt undeserving. This is a highly admirable quality and an approach underlined very publicly and emphatically when in 2000 he famously turned down the offer of a CBE (Commander of the Order of the British Empire) title, which the Queen awards to those deemed to have made "a distinguished, innovative contribution to any area" of British life. In declining the award, he commented, "I seriously don't know what it's for." Similarly, in 2003, he was offered an even higher award, a knighthood, which would have given him the title of Sir David Bowie. This offer from the Queen—the highest such accolade possible in the United Kingdom—was in recognition for "having [made] a major contribution" to British life that was considered "inspirational and significant . . . over a long period of time." Again he declined, stating to a largely incredulous press, "I would never have any intention of accepting anything like that. It's not what I spent my life working for."

A Summary of Other Awards

Happy to accept awards that related far more directly to his art, primarily his music and acting, David Bowie would be the recipient of many other accolades in addition to the Ivor Novellos that reflected both industry and fan recognition of his talents. These included four BRIT (British Phonographic Industry) awards from ten nominations, for "Best Male Solo Artist" (1984 and 2014), "Outstanding Contribution" (1996), and an "Icon" award bestowed posthumously at the 2016 awards ceremony; five Grammy awards from nineteen nominations, including a Lifetime Achievement award (2006), a Daytime Emmy award (2003), a GQ award (2000), four MTV Video Music awards (1984 [twice], 1986, 2016), an iHeartRadio Much Music Award (1998), eleven NME (New Musical Express) awards (1973 [twice], 1974 [three times], 1977, 1978,

1981, 1983 [twice], 2016), a Q award (1995), a Saturn award (1976), a WB Radio Music award (1999), and a Webby award (2007).

When Academia Came Knocking

In 1999, David Bowie had an honorary doctorate bestowed on him by the prestigious Berklee College of Music. In a wide-ranging and ever-amusing acceptance speech, he acknowledged his widespread influences, paying particular gratitude to his friend and idol John Lennon and rattling off a string of names from across a broad stylistic palette, including John Coltrane, Harry Partch, Eric Dolphy, the Velvet Underground, John Cage, Sonny Smith, Anthony Newley, Florence Foster Jenkins, Johnnie Ray, Julie London, the Legendary Stardust Cowboy, Edith Piaf, and Shirley Bassey. He also tipped his hat to some of his many talented collaborators, including Reeves Gabrels (Berklee alumni) and Brian Eno. The primary message contained in his speech was to encourage the assembled brightly gowned academics, fellow graduates, and their friends and families to experiment and to think outside the box in their artistic endeavors. In his emotive conclusion, he then paid tribute to music itself, sharing what he had gained from his involvement in the art form and willing on his audience to do likewise: "Music has given me over forty years of extraordinary experiences. I can't say that life's pains or more tragic episodes have been diminished because of it. But it's allowed me so many moments of companionship when I've been lonely and a sublime means of communication when I wanted to touch people. It's been both my doorway of perception and the house that I live in. I only hope that it embraces you with the same lusty life force that it graciously offered me. Thank you very much and remember, if it itches, play it."

Unsurprisingly, given his enormous success and his unsurpassed longevity, David Bowie received a multitude of awards and accolades throughout the world over the course of his career, and it's certain that numerous more minor and obscure ones exist than have been listed here. Many of these, such as reader's and listener's polls, for example, required no acceptance or otherwise from the man himself—they were simply bestowed. But the major ones that required a process of nomination followed by either acceptance or a polite refusal on Bowie's part were very carefully considered by the artist. That he did not regard himself worthy—or else simply considered it inappropriate—of receiving the ultimate award available to British citizens and becoming Sir David Bowie speaks volumes about his careful evaluation of the nature, intention, and implications of such awards and accolades. Not for him was the lure of joining the ranks of rock star "Sirs," such as Sir Paul McCartney, Sir Elton John, Sir Cliff Richard, and Sir Mick Jagger (the latter accepting his knighthood much to the incredulity and annoyance of bandmate Keith

Richards, who felt Jagger should have declined, telling *Uncut* magazine, "It's not what the Stones is about, is it?"). For David Bowie, becoming a Sir was one thing, but industry recognition and awards were quite another matter. These truly meant something to him. Given his fierce intellect, his thirst for knowledge in all manner of fields, his lifelong curiosity about the universe, and his nonstop probing into the human condition that he expressed through his art right until the very last, the honorary doctorate bestowed on him by such a highly regarded institute as Berklee too must have meant a great deal. Never one for trivialities, his willingness to accept the honor spoke volumes. Sir David Bowie? No. Dr. David Bowie? Yes (albeit convention decrees that the recipients of honorary doctorates may use the term only with considerable restrictions). His acceptance speech is readily available to be viewed on the Internet. His pleasure at accepting the honor shines throughout.

38

The Bowie Legacy

A Summary of What He Left Behind

The Musician

David Bowie's legacy has multiple levels across multiple disciplines. Most obviously, he was, of course, one of the most gifted, most consistent, and all-around greatest musical artists of the twentieth (going well into the twenty-first) century. His epic songs number too many to list in this limited summary and include the floating brilliance of "Space Oddity," so contemporaneous with the historical triumph of the Apollo 11 moon landing and the space fever that existed in the late 1960s as the space race of the Cold War held the world transfixed; the exemplar of the songwriter's craft that was "Life on Mars," with its yearning for deliverance and self-betterment; the youth anthem "Rebel Rebel," which tied up with a bow the entire glam-rock phenomenon of the early to mid-1970s and summed up generational alienation; and the telling critique of the flawed fragility of the human condition with its inherent division and estrangement that was "Heroes." These songs and many more are now top-shelf examples in the history of popular music of the power and potential of the song as an art form that could move mountains.

Without precedent, he was capable of taking on any existing musical style, immersing himself in and familiarizing himself with its recognizable hallmarks, and making it his own, whether the soul perfection of the songs on *Young Americans*, the sublime dance pop of *Let's Dance*, or the drum 'n' bass powerhouse that was *Earthling*. He had the ability to distill the very essence of a chosen style and create masterpieces with it that equaled or bettered the efforts of other artists who existed at the very heart of such styles and never stepped outside them. Even more remarkably, however, David Bowie was responsible for leading popular music in new directions in which it otherwise would not have gone, the groundbreaking experimental sounds of the *Low* and *Blackstar* albums arguably being just two notable examples.

Very often, this brilliantly executed changeling quality has led critics and fans alike to refer to David Bowie as a chameleon, but such a descriptor is an error. Chameleons change color in response to a perceived threat; their motivation is reactionary. David Bowie changed by choice and at will, not as a response to fear or threat.

Interdisciplinarity

Further, David Bowie was responsible for merging popular music with other art forms, including film and theater. No other popular musician has made as great an impact on the world of movies as he did. David Bowie brought theatricality writ large to the rock stage—theatricality of real depth and substance rather than mere showbiz pizzazz. During the early 1970s, he punctured the 1960s myth of authenticity that still prevailed and in which any sign of artifice was abhorred.

Such was his intrinsic interdisciplinarity that to describe David Bowie as simply a rock star is actually to do him a disservice. At his very core, he was a multidisciplinary artist with the mind-set of an actor who, through his own fearless actions, drew attention to the fact that one did not have to remain fixed in one medium alone. Armed with an appropriate skill set, such as he was, he showed that an artist could "shop around" and use whatever medium he or she chose.

The Power of Ch Ch Change

David Bowie is a fine example and therefore a blueprint, a role model, and an exemplar—there are many apt descriptors that could be used here—of a fearless artist prepared to embrace change instead of being scared of it. Many artists across many fields find success with a particular style that they make their own and from that point on are reluctant to change for fear of losing their audience. In contrast, David Bowie made the very act of change *his* style. But this is a lesson that doesn't apply simply to his impact and influence on other

Novelty Million dollar bill

Author's Collection

artists; it goes much wider than that. Such was his worldwide appeal that his example of embracing change instead of resisting it is one that resonates with fans every bit as much as with other artists. As he espoused as early as 1972 with the creation of his Ziggy Stardust character, life *can* imitate art. He made artifice both acceptable and extraordinarily useful as a tool for self-improvement. That is, if you believe in yourself and can find the strength within to look and act in a self-chosen, self-made reinvention of yourself—of how you *want* to be rather than how you have been or are currently being—then those qualities that you foster and portray through pretense can become your real qualities given time. Confidence and self-belief can be manufactured and worn like a mask using Bowie's theater-derived tactics, but once you've shown that brand of confidence and you know that you can improve yourself in the ways that you wish to, what started out as a veneer of confidence gradually becomes the real thing. Simply, you can transcend whatever life has handed to you and reinvent yourself in your own idealized image. David Bowie's methodology is a blueprint for taking control of one's life.

Self-Improvement through David Bowie

David Bowie made the lives of many, many people better, people who felt marginalized, estranged, and alienated for any number of reasons, including gender, physical appearance, psychological, generational, political, and more. This fan empowerment goes far beyond the achievements and social impact of your average music star who might give people some nice melodies to hum along to but that's about it. With no disrespect intended, it's unlikely that Phil Collins or Rod Stewart ever changed the lives of their fans. Drawn like moths to a light, fans were attracted to David Bowie's purposely overblown and heavily painted expressions of difference through which he gloriously thumbed his nose at societal notions of normality and acceptance; his fans felt better understood and less alone in his company. This was sheer empowerment in action. Because David Bowie's message throughout his career was one of embracing difference(s) instead of treating it as a negative thing, as happens throughout the world, he drew millions of people to him, people who saw in him a kindred spirit. In that sense, he was a motivational artist.

The Sexiness of Smarts

Another legacy is the sheer intelligence that David Bowie brought to bear in his work. A very intelligent, extremely well-read man with a continual thirst for knowledge, the depth of his knowledge was at all times clearly evident in his work, and as a result he made being smart sexy and desirable in a medium where (feigned) indifference to—or outright dismissal of—cerebral depth was at times the prevailing norm. He introduced to popular music a succession of unlikely and extremely weighty topics drawn from the social sciences and, with them, associated characters, such as the likes of Friedrich Nietzsche and Aleister Crowley (both appear in the song "Quicksand" from the *Hunky Dory* album [1971] through the references, respectively, to the Supermen and to the Golden Dawn). He also introduced concepts such as the Kabbalistic Tree of Life (references to two of the ten elements, "Kether to Malkuth," are found in the title track of the *Station to Station* album [1976]). In addition, his knowledge was sufficient to be able to discuss and debate such issues with any interviewer game enough to venture there and risk exposing his or her own lack of knowledge of such topics. Of all the decades of interviews with rock musicians that are available to be reread across multiple media, David Bowie's interviews stand out in this regard. An intimate knowledge of what and, more to the point, *why* he was doing what he did at any given time in his career set him apart from his peers.

The Sexiness of Self-Belief

David Bowie's legacy can best be summed up in his own words in the Nietzschean line from the extraordinarily self-appraising "Quicksand" from the *Hunky Dory* album. The line is a perfect slogan for self-belief: "Just a mortal with potential of a superman." It describes David Bowie, who demonstrated by example that anyone else with drive and talent can be likewise. Such self-belief and self-empowerment was a primary component of the artist's work.

Ticket to *David Bowie Is* exhibition, Melbourne   *Author's Collection*

Fan Tributes

In April 2018, I put a call out via Facebook to all Bowie fans wherever on the globe they might be, inviting them to send me short tributes. I wasn't sure what to expect in terms of a response, but I was simply inundated. Those tributes that are reprinted here represent the very tip of the iceberg, as fans clamored to record their love and respect.

"I love Bowie and 38 years ago I was pacing my mum's hallway to 'We Can Be Heroes' as I was moving my baby boy down ready to come into the world. A homebirth happy baby was born. Cheers Bowie!" Sarah Mcdougall

"You have always been a great inspiration to me David. From a young age, my dream was to be one of your backing singers!! True story. Thank you for your artistry and your constant reinventions. You were a bloody cool bloke (and I loved how you returned to a jazz influence). RIP xxx." Karin Lou Reid

"A major influence on prog rock—Fripp and Belew of King Crimson on guitars at various points (and revitalising Crimson in the process!) as well as Rick Wakeman of Yes on so many albums and singles." Rob Burns

"He was the greatest of guides." Martin Phillipps

"Journey begins: 1972 Bowie picked on me. Listen to Ziggy. The Rock n' Roll star knew about Belfast, my city; but he took me to Mars. 1983 Murrayfield for some Serious Moonlight, 1987 Slane's Spider and 2003 for a Reality check; The Disco King's renaissance in Dublin. Middle age but we never get old. 2016 and a Blackstar took him across the universe (with John). An Earthling no more. Hello Spaceboy, everyone says Hi (from Ireland)!" Paul McCulloch

"I lost my virginity to Putting Out Fire (with gasoline)." Lisa Scott

"Back in 1972 I discovered The Second Hand Record Shop in Dunedin. We were allowed to go to town on Friday nights on our own but had to catch the 9pm bus home. I walked in and immediately spotted the *Ziggy Stardust* album. The cover drew me in and I bought it. My first album. When I actually played it I LOVED IT!! I had discovered David Bowie! None of my friends at the time got it like I did. I played it loud wearing headphones. I loved Bowie for his cool hair, his many costumes, the way he moved, his elegance, and his unreal music. He showed me that you can be yourself, even if no one else gets it. He showed me it was ok to experiment with different looks, to be brave and dress how you feel. It's ok not to fit the mold, in fact it's cool. Love your work forever David Bowie. xx." Dallas Cunningham

"David Bowie has two different colored eyes. Some wolves have two different colored eyes. My theory, aliens spliced the dna of David Bowie with a wolf which is why he loved making songs about space." Jimi De Deker

"Bowie is one of the reasons I love music so much and it's just beginning." Stevie Power, age thirteen

"David Bowie was a major part of the soundtrack of some very important years in my life." Milton Sangrouber

"Since discovering him at the age of fourteen, Bowie has been a consistent navigator throughout my life. While his music and audiovisual works have enriched my soul, his approach to creativity and collaboration have taught me how new cultural forms, ideas and identities can be formed through processes such as cultural alchemy, performativity and chance composition. Bowie also actively demonstrated the transformative impulse of critical thought, transgression and discomfort." Lisa Perrott

"He was the bright light that lit the path. Go this way, not that way." Alison May

"He changed the way I see not only music but life. And he is still, with everything he left behind." Paul Cathro

"I grew up surrounded by music, thankfully very good music, but I found Bowie all by myself, and it was a revelation, uplifting and reassuring. His beautiful eclectic works of art, with his intelligence and humour, was exactly what I needed at the time, and every time since then. Eternally grateful for what he has given the world." Tahlia Hopkins

"I met with David Bowie in 1978 in Baton Rouge, Louisiana: a private gathering post-concert all nighter in a kitsch bar. Then Bowie asked me to chauffeur him. Bodyguard, David Bowie, my boyfriend and me in my Mercedes. To Japan in 1982. The die was cast. Japan and Bowie, my theme song." Helene Thian

"My first ever album was The Rise and Fall of Ziggy Stardust and the Spiders from Mars. I followed the instruction on the back cover TO BE PLAYED AT MAXIMUM VOLUME. A life changing moment." Scot Cameron

"To me Bowie is all of creativity, innovation, art, music, writing, superstar, icon, hero, savior, inspiration, solace, changeling, artistic eye candy, bloke down the pub and much more. The power of Heroes still brings a tear to my eye forty years after first hearing it." Ian Loughran

"David Bowie has always been there as a reference point as I've moved through different phases and genres, beyond music, in the ether, at times cryptic, always inspiring." Richard Wallis

"For me, Kooks has meant a lot as a parent, letting my kids know her weird parents love her to bits and have her back, that it's ok to be true to yourself and that you don't always have to follow the rules!" Sarah Gallagher

"David Bowie's impact on my life has been immeasurable, but the best way I can describe it was that the man and his music turned my head when I was a teenager, and it's never been the same. Whether the albums or films were stellar, or less-than-stellar it has never mattered: there was always something that spoke deeply to me, and increased my fascination. Thank you, David Jones, for your creations, whether musical or whatever, I will treasure them always." Amanda Mills

"I think many of us probably first knew David Bowie as someone who signified a space where alternatives to hetero-masculinity were possible. What Bowie did in the early seventies by crossing boundaries of sex and sexuality, he was to do in later work with musical genres and, ultimately, with performance of all kinds. I will always value his attempt to bring musical vocabularies in conversation with one another. He expanded the possibilities of art in general and contemporary music in particular." Shelton Waldrep

"David Bowie inspired my musical identity in the 1970s. I was a Ziggy fan, and also had all the earlier albums. Posters on the bedroom walls, dyed hair with an iconic 'Ziggy' hairstyle, and a consumer of everything Bowie. A live show happened for me in 1983 with the Serious Moonlight Tour at Milton Keynes Bowl. Bowie on stage, early sounds and new songs—this was the zenith for me." Henry Johnson

"David, your music saved me. You taught me to write. To beat imposter syndrome by posing most sincerely. But since you introduced me to Newton, I am losing my footing over loose shale, and in here, with the television voices, struggling to come down. Starman, he gets under your skin." Dene October

"Major Tom, Ziggy Stardust, Aladdin Sane, the Thin White Duke: all vivid markers in my life from teenager to cover band muso and radio producer. I saw David Bowie 'in the flesh' twice. From about 10 metres away at Auckland Railway Station in 1982, while working as a minor (uncredited) crew member on the film *Merry Christmas, Mr. Lawrence* and, along with over 50,000 others, at the very last Glass Spider Concert in 1987. Vale, Starman." Barry McConnachie

"It was a somewhat late awakening, but the time it came I knew I had seen the light. They say stars keep shining way after they die, but yours I'm sure will never fade away. Thank you David for sound-tracking my life; we'll meet again as stardust one day." Ana Leorne

39

"The Stars Are Out Tonight"

Celebrity Tributes to David Bowie

When David Bowie passed away so unexpectedly on January 10, 2016— his illness had been carefully concealed from all but his closest family, friends, and musical collaborators—the outpouring of love and respect displayed across all media and from all levels of society was unprecedented. The immediacy of social media ensured a plethora of heartfelt reactions from all over the world from those still reeling from the shock of the news, and many of the messages came from top-line celebrities, be they luminaries in the arts, sportspeople, or politicians—all manner of fields—thereby reflecting David Bowie's reach and impact on all and sundry.

Duncan Jones (David Bowie's son): "So proud! Heart bursting for you. :)" Twitter, January 11, 2016

Iggy Pop: "David's friendship was the light of my life. I never met such a brilliant person. He was the best there is." Twitter, January 11, 2016

Brian Eno: "David's death came as a complete surprise, as did nearly everything else about him. I feel a huge gap now . . . I received an email from him seven days ago. It was as funny as always, and as surreal, looping through word games and allusions and all the usual stuff we did. It ended with this sentence: 'Thank you for our good times, Brian, they will never rot.' And it was signed 'Dawn.' I realise now he was saying goodbye." *New Musical Express*, January 11, 2016

Paul McCartney: "Very sad news to wake up to on this raining morning. David was a great star and I treasure the moments we had together. His music played a very strong part in British musical history and I'm proud to think of the huge influence he has had on people all around the world. I send my deepest sympathies to his family and will always remember the great laughs we had through the years. His star will shine in the sky forever." Instagram, January 12, 2016

Gail Ann Dorsey (bassist and backing vocalist): "So much of my life wouldn't have happened. I wouldn't know where I would be, but he completely, single-handedly altered the course of my life." *Rolling Stone*, January 25, 2016

Bowie Symposium poster, Limerick, Ireland, 2012 . Bowie dolls created by Tanja
Stark. Poster design by Joe Gervin   *Author's Collection*

Madonna: "Talented. Unique. Genius. Game Changer. The Man who Fell to Earth. Your Spirit Lives on Forever!" Facebook, January 11, 2016

Al Yankovic: "I feel like the wind has been knocked out of me—I was not ready for this. RIP Bowie." Twitter, January 11, 2016

Debbie Harry: "Who doesn't love Bowie? A visionary artist, musician, actor, a completely renaissance man ... I can't say enough things about David Bowie to show how much I love him." *Rolling Stone*, January 11, 2016

Sting: "The first time Trudie and I met David was during the Serious Moonlight Tour somewhere in the U.S. We were watching the show from the side of the stage, Trudie heavily pregnant with our daughter Mickey. David bounded over to us between songs, kissed Trudie's bump and asked when she was due. 'January,' she said, somewhat taken aback. 'Ah, a Capricorn like me!' David told us with that irresistible smile of his. 'I've got to get back, I'll see you later!' he said, running on stage just in time to catch the first line of 'Let's Dance.' "We were totally captivated by his energetic charm, his extraordinary music, his art and his unique spirit, and we felt as though he'd actually blessed our baby! That was over 30 years ago. We've never forgotten it—we will never forget him." *Toronto Sun*, January 13, 2016

Kanye West: "David Bowie was one of my most important inspirations, so fearless, so creative, he gave us magic for a lifetime." Twitter, January 11, 2016

Alice Cooper: "It's hard to know exactly what to say when you hear of someone's passing. I know that I have certainly lost one of my life-time Rock and Roll theatrical comrades in David Bowie. We both started in theatrical Rock N Roll at the same time, and in some cases we challenged each other to go farther and push the envelope. The loss of David Bowie will be hard to swallow for everyone. He leaves behind a rich history of musical and cultural experimentation and invention that will rarely be seen again, if ever. He was one of a kind. The man that fell to Earth has gone back to the planet that he came from. Condolences to his family and fans." Facebook, January 12, 2016

Russell Crowe: "RIP David. I loved your music. I loved you. One of the greatest performance artists to have ever lived." Twitter, January 11, 2016

M.I.A.: "RIP David Bowie—someone who was connected to the source." Twitter, January 11, 2016

Justin Timberlake: "I can never express into words how you will continue to inspire me.... Thank you for showing a pimple-faced, curly-mopped kid that DIFFERENT was THE THING TO BE. A GENIUS for the ages and the ages to come." Twitter, January 12, 2016

Ricky Gervais: "I just lost a hero. RIP David Bowie." Twitter, January 11, 2016

Chris Cornell: "David Bowie was an inspiration. As a songwriter, he had this intense vitality throughout his entire career. He made aging as a recording artist seem totally doable in a vital way.... When *Scary Monsters* came out, I saw him performing on a talk show, and I saw the 'Ashes to Ashes' video where he dressed in some strange European clown costume. That had a huge impact on me. Because my first interpretation of him was the red-haired, androgynous Ziggy Stardust character, and seeing him like this made me think, 'Oh, you can be whoever you want. You can live a hundred lives. You can create you and you can recreate you, and it's viable.' He was the one that proved that that works." *Rolling Stone*, January 12, 2016

Pharrell Williams: "David Bowie was a true innovator, a true creative. May he rest in peace." Twitter, January 11, 2016

Alison Moyet: "David Bowie. Our greatest, gone and here forever. A world's heart breaks." Twitter, January 11, 2016

David Beckham: "A creative genius and influence over us all. Rest In Peace STARMAN." Instagram, January 11, 2016

Tina Turner: "A piece of my heart has broken. Not only was David a passionate supporter of my career but more importantly a very special person in my life. An icon. Irreplaceable loving friend. I am missing him greatly." Facebook, January 13, 2016

Gene Simmons: "David Bowie, you will be sorely missed. Bowie's 'Changes' and the Ziggy story songs were a major influence for me." Twitter, January 11, 2016

Keith Richards: "I'm deeply saddened by such a sudden shock. David was a true original in everything he did and, along with many others, I'm going to miss him. Another goodbye to another good friend." Facebook, January 13, 2016

Kelly Clarkson: "So bummed 2 hear about David Bowie passing. I have loved him since I saw The Labyrinth as a kid! Great music & a super innovative artist!" Twitter, January 12, 2016

Sadiq Khan (mayor of London): "Terrible news to hear Brixton born David Bowie has died. No one in our age has better deserved to be called a genius." Twitter, January 11, 2016

Moby: "Goodbye my friend. You gave us everything. Thank you for the music and the dinners and the laughter and the friendship. I will always love you." Facebook, January 11, 2016

Tony Visconti: "He always did what he wanted to do. And he wanted to do it his way and he wanted to do it the best way. His death was no different from his life—a work of Art. He made Blackstar for us, his parting gift. I knew for a year this was the way it would be. I wasn't, however, prepared for it. He was an extraordinary man, full of love and life. He will always be with us. For now, it is appropriate to cry." Facebook, January 11, 2016

Michael Stipe: "Right now, it feels as if the solar system is off its axis, as if one of our main planetary anchors has lost its orbit. That said—I am certain that wherever Bowie is now—I want to be there someday." Facebook, January 13, 2016

Brian Viglione (Dresden Dolls): "What words can you possibly say to adequately describe the feeling of loss of such a soul who inspired so many of us

and gave so much of himself to his work and music. We love you David Bowie."
Facebook, January 11, 2016

Elvis Costello: "The right words would be written in ink on card, not to be seen suddenly and brutally, like the news. In acknowledgement, the lights on this particular, peculiar little theatre will be lowered for a while. With deepest gratitude and respectful condolences to the family and friends of a truly great artist, beautiful melodist and elegant gentleman." Facebook, January 13, 2016

Adam Lambert: "Bowie was one of the bravest artists of the century. A true Icon." ... "I love how Bowie challenged people's perception of gender stereotypes and what an outsider truly was. He was SO ahead of his time." Twitter, January 11, 2016

Brian May: "Never predictable, never classifiable, immensely lateral thinking and fearless, he stands as one of Britain's greatest musical creators. I'm certainly proud to have worked with him. RIP David." *Daily Mirror*, January 11, 2016

Florence Welch (Florence and the Machine): "David Bowie was a huge influence on me throughout my life. The original star-man returned to the stars.... Thank you for everything you brought us. RIP David Bowie xx." Twitter, January 11, 2016

J. K. Rowling: "I wish he could have stayed on earth longer. RIP." Twitter, January 11, 2016

Reeves Gabrels (cowriter, coproducer, and guitarist): "It is my deepest hope that David is remembered as a man and an artist and not turned into a once-upon-a-time symbol of controversy by the media, a saucy soundbite by the tabloids or a silkscreen on a t-shirt worn by baby boomers and hipsters alike trying to create the appearance of cool without ever looking below the surface. It would be wonderful if music fans took this opportunity to listen. Now is the time to go deep. There is a life's work waiting there to be heard." *Mojo*, February 8, 2016

Ken Scott (producer of the *Hunky Dory* and *Ziggy Stardust* albums): "The lack of fear that he showed, even in his death, that's something that went through his whole musical life. I think there was a certain amount of fear when we started *Hunky Dory*, but as things started to come together, and it was obvious it was working, that fear started to disappear. From then on, he felt more and more sure and less and less fearful. That's why he could go from one genre to another. Most artists, if they're successful, they stick to that plan, because they're worried that they'll suddenly lose their fans. But David's attitude was always, 'I'm going to do what I want to do and hope they come along with me, but if they don't, they don't.' That's truly unique and totally courageous, especially in music." Quartz Media, January 15, 2016

Peter Gabriel: "I was shocked to learn of David Bowie's death this morning ... we will miss him badly." Twitter, January 12, 2016

Nile Rodgers (producer): "Your life changed my life. Love forever." Twitter, January 12, 2016

Lady Gaga: "Well, the moment that I saw the *Aladdin Sane* cover for the first time, I was 19 years old, and it just changed my perspective on everything, forever.... It was an image that changed my life. I remember I took the vinyl record out of the casing and I put it on my vinyl player.... 'Watch That Man' came on and, I mean, that was just the beginning of my artistic birth. I feel like my whole career is a tribute to David Bowie." *Billboard*, February 22, 2016

Justin Welby (Archbishop of Canterbury): "I'm very, very saddened to hear of his death. I remember sitting listening to his songs endlessly in the '70s particularly and always really relishing what he was, what he did, the impact he had. Extraordinary person." BBC Radio 4, January 11, 2016

Trent Reznor: "It feels like the loss of a mentor.... For me, every Bowie album has its own set of memories. Back in the heyday of records, I'd go over to my friend's house and listen to his collection of records in his basement. *Scary Monsters* was the first one I related to. Then I went backwards and discovered the Berlin trilogy, which was full-impact. By the early Nineties, as I found myself onstage with an audience, I was in full-obsession mode with Bowie. I read into all the breadcrumbs he'd put out—the clues in his lyrics that reveal themselves over time, the cryptic photographs, the magazine articles—and I projected and created what he was to me. His music really helped me relate to myself and figure out who I was. He was a tremendous inspiration in terms of what was possible, what the role of an entertainer could be, that there are no rules." *Rolling Stone*, January 26, 2016

Amanda Palmer (Dresden Dolls): "There's something going on right now that has never happened before, since rock 'n' roll did not exist for this generation of people before us. We're watching Lou Reed dying, Bowie dying and Lemmy dying. It feels weird to look at my newborn baby and go: 'Oh my God, these people are all going to be distant history to you.' We've lived through this thing and we're now seeing the end of an era. We were there to witness this thing happen and the world changes so fast; you start taking it a little bit less for granted when you see the perfected completion of an entire career.... David Bowie is now a finished story. And that just seems so strange." *New Musical Express*, February 5, 2016

German Foreign Office: "Good-bye, David Bowie. You are now among #Heroes. Thank you for helping to bring down the #wall." Twitter, January 11, 2016

Boy George: "As a teenager growing up in Suburbia, I was very much the odd one out and Bowie was the light at the end of a very grey tunnel. He validated me and made me realize I was not alone. Listening to his early songs I felt he was speaking directly to me when he sang, 'We're painting our faces and dressing thoughts from the skies, from paradise.' Bowie painted a mythical landscape where otherness and individuality reigned supreme . . . I always dreaded this day. I hoped he was immortal. I was sure of it. Today feels like the end of everything!" *Daily Mail*, January 12, 2016

John Taylor (Duran Duran): "Seriously, what could you say to the man who changed everything, and made anything possible?" Twitter, January 12, 2016

Lorde: "I've never met a hero of mine and liked it. It just sucks, the pressure is too huge, you can't enjoy it. David was different. I'll never forget the caressing of our hands as we spoke, or the light in his eyes. That night something changed in me—I felt a calmness grow, a sureness. I think in those brief moments, he heralded me into my next new life, an old rock and roll alien angel in a perfect grey suit. I realized everything I'd ever done, or would do from then on, would be done like maybe he was watching. I realized I was proud of my spiky strangeness because he had been proud of his. And I know I'm never going to stop learning dances, brand new dances. It's not going to change, how we feel about him. For the rest of our lives, we'll always be crashing in that same car. Thankyou, David Bowie." Facebook, January 12, 2016

Cyndi Lauper: "Oh no I am so sorry to hear of David Bowie's passing. He was such a great artist and has lead the way for so many of us." Twitter, January 12, 2016

Billy Bragg: "Bowie was the only pop star from my schooldays who wasn't dismayed by punk. It inspired him and he inspired it. A truly transcendent artist." Twitter, January 11, 2016

Mike Garson (keyboards): "When I heard at 11 p.m. on Sunday, I was absolutely shocked. However as the shock took over my body, I recalled one conversation I never shared because I was too afraid to share it. But it always struck me with deep fear and power. We were on the bus touring in 1996 and he said, 'Mike, I went to this powerful psychic somewhere at the end of the 1970s or in the early 1980s. He said I was going to live to around 69, 70, 71.' I said, 'Oh, my God.' He said, 'It wasn't like this guy was a wacko. I believe him and I know it's true.' So it was always in my mind as we were getting close to that. When I got the call, that thought clicked in at the same time the shock took over. . . . But the talking about it helps because I'm thinking of the joyful moments we shared over all those years." *Rolling Stone*, January 29, 2016

Elton John: "I am still in shock. Never saw it coming. My deepest condolences to Iman and the family. An amazing life. An amazing career." Twitter, January 12, 2016

David Cameron (British prime minister): "I grew up listening to and watching the pop genius David Bowie. He was a master of re-invention, who kept getting it right. A huge loss." *Daily Mirror*, January 11, 2016

Major Tim Peake (astronaut—sent from the International Space Station): "Saddened to hear David Bowie has lost his battle with cancer—his music was an inspiration to many." Twitter, January 11, 2016

Woody Woodmansey (drummer in the Spiders from Mars): "As an artist he was unique. He wanted to shake things up and make life more exciting, more interesting for audiences and himself and he managed to do that continually throughout his career. His legacy is the music, the films, in fact all the various mediums he employed to create effects that were true for him." QuaysNews .com, December 9, 2016

Carlos Alomar (guitarist): "Working with David, and specifically working on his Berlin trilogy, has carried me to where I am now—specifically with the way we worked with electronic music. The act of saying, 'If I'm an artist, I can present my music to my fans and not present it to my record company' was very important.... [On the *Low* album:] During those years, nobody did anything like that. It was unexpected. The record company guy would say, 'What are we supposed to do with this?' And the answer is, 'Herald a new genre,' as David did. We had a period of new-age music, new-wave music, electronic music, rock & roll, blue-eyed soul, plastic soul, glam-rock, punk. These are all genres of music that have solidified under the umbrella of one man. Who does that?" *Rolling Stone*, January 11, 2016

40

Signing Off

Blackstar and the Artist's Final Words

*B*lackstar, released on January 8, 2016, on the occasion of David Bowie's sixty-ninth birthday, was not quite the jump-out-from-behind-the-door-and-go-boo! surprise that its predecessor, *The Next Day* (2013), had been. Its arrival had been announced on his official website, davidbowie.com, well ahead of time, back in October 2015. Nevertheless, *Blackstar* was still an album of surprises, full of Bowie-esque pushing of—or complete disregard for—boundaries and therefore a most fitting way for David Bowie to bow out.

Blackstar album, 2016   *Author's Collection*

A Poignant Observation

On January 7, the day before the album's official release and just three days before David Bowie died on January 10, writer Ryan Dombal prefaced his review, on the hugely popular Pitchfork.com, in the following eerily poignant manner: "David Bowie has died many deaths yet he is still with us." Dombal was correct, of course, but only just. Still, his complete lack of knowledge of how ill David Bowie was at the time of the album's release is symptomatic of the universal ignorance of his condition. If *The Next Day* had been a stupendous industry coup in terms of keeping his comeback album totally under wraps (after a ten-year silence, during which almost everyone believed he'd retired without announcing the fact), then the blanket concealment of his grave illness at the time of the release of *Blackstar* was every bit as big a coup. Dombal went on to preface his review thus: "He is popular music's ultimate Lazarus: Just as that Biblical figure was beckoned by Jesus to emerge from his tomb after four days of nothingness, Bowie has put many of his selves to rest over the last half-century, only to rise again with a different guise. This is astounding to watch, but it's more treacherous to live through; following Lazarus' return, priests plotted to kill him, fearing the power of his story. And imagine actually *being* such a miracle man—resurrection is a hard act to follow."

Alas, unlike the many bereavements experienced by David Bowie's performance personas over the years, this time there would be no resurrection. Still, as if foretelling the future, the eloquent and insightful Dombal further predicted that "Bowie will live on long after the man has died."

The Album

The music of *Blackstar* does its level best to defy description, with the terms *avant-garde*, *art rock*, *experimental*, and *jazz* being prevalent in reviews. While these descriptors are justifiably the nearest touchstones available to anyone wishing to map out its eclectic heart, they are too limiting and barely do the album's seven tracks justice because other influences abound too, including Nu-jazz, drum 'n' bass, acid house, industrial, and hip-hop, to just scratch the surface. The lyrics, meanwhile, are among the most poignant, searching, unsettling, and even angry that the artist ever recorded—and that is saying something given that throughout most of his career, he was one of the most provocative artists in rock music and certainly the most challenging of the artists in the elite superstar category. Here, his attention is quite clearly and understandably focused on the subject that must have been uppermost in his mind throughout the project: his own mortality. If this sounds like bleak material, then think again. The music is too multilayered, intelligent, and demanding of the listener to allow anything like the complacency required for doom and gloom. David Bowie wants anything but pity from his audience, and self-pity is nowhere evident. Musically and lyrically, *Blackstar* remains prickly and confrontational, more a walk through dangerous woods than a walk in the park. It is a salient lesson for all artists in how to remain questioning, vital, and relevant right to the very end. *Blackstar* fully deserves the application of the overused term *epic*.

Tony Visconti was the album's coproducer (with Bowie). He told *Rolling Stone*, "Making Blackstar wasn't a haphazard affair, we knew every minute we were making something akin to constructing a Gothic cathedral." Dispensing with his long-standing musical collaborators, David Bowie instead used as his instrumental core a quartet of New York jazz musicians who he'd heard in a club in Greenwich Village and who were highly regarded in a local sense but unknown to a wider or popular music audience. Saxophonist Donny McCaslin (also the bandleader), keyboardist Jason Lindner, bassist Tim Lefebvre, and drummer Mark Guiliana (augmented where required by other local musicians) are at the heart of *Blackstar*.

On Working with David Bowie

In an interview with *Billboard* conducted just days after David Bowie's death, the band recorded some of their thoughts on being the last musicians to work with the great musical icon.

Lefebvre recalled that Bowie "was a lovely human being, deeply erudite and caring, and absolutely one of the funniest people I've ever met.... [It was] a joy to be in his presence, and create some music."

Lindner stated, "I'm deeply saddened, stunned, mystified and completely awed by the power of David Bowie's creativity and determination to produce all he did in the single year I've known him. It's humbling to have been invited to share in the process leading to *Blackstar*, and to witness his brilliance and benevolence."

Guiliana expressed gratitude: "Thank you from the bottom of my humble heart for letting me into your life, and in doing so changing mine. It was an absolute honor to create with you. I am forever grateful."

McCaslin said, "I am so deeply saddened by today's news. Working with David Bowie on *Blackstar* was a life-changing experience for me, and a gift beyond measure. David was fully present and engaged in the creative process from the moment he entered the studio until he left. He was always gracious, generous, and funny. I will always be inspired by him, am grateful to have known him, and am holding his family and friends in my heart."

The Album Cover: Where Is David?

For the first time ever, David Bowie's image is absent from an album cover. As described in an article by Andy Gill titled "David Bowie and Blackstar: The Reclusive Rock God Is Still a Star Man," published in the *Independent* on January 8, 2016, "If The Next Day's cover image presented Bowie partly obscuring his past, here he's wiped it out completely." While the cover of *The Next Day* (2013) replicated the *"Heroes"* (1977) cover but with a black square obliterating the artist's face, the sleeve of *Blackstar* features simply a (black) star and the word *bowie* created from fragments of the star shape. Over the course of Bowie's career, the calculated and carefully constructed images he projected on his album covers frequently communicated almost as much to an audience as the music contained on those albums. Bowie was a master of synergizing both sound and vision. Here, on *Blackstar*, his absence could not be more loaded. He knew he would soon be, quite literally, absent and that *Blackstar* would be the last album he ever created. Sure enough, just two days after its release, this situation was to transpire.

The Hidden Surprises

The surprises on *Blackstar* do not begin and end with the music and his photographic absence, however. The jet-black vinyl cover features a cutout star that reveals the record beneath it with an all-black picture label. When the record is removed, the black paper behind the cutout reveals a hidden picture. Held up to a light source, a star field emerges from the foldout sleeve, something it took fans more than four months to discover after the record's release. The designer, Jonathan Barnbrook, who also designed the covers for *Heathen*, *Reality*, and *The Next Day*, has since claimed there are many other surprises hidden in the record's artwork, and no doubt these too will gradually emerge as time goes on.

Blackstar: David Bowie's Parting Gift

Tony Visconti, David Bowie's friend and collaborator of many decades standing, expressed his thoughts through a Facebook post as the world became aware of Bowie's demise. He declared, "He always did what he wanted to do. And he wanted to do it his way and he wanted to do it the best way. His death was no different from his life—a work of Art. He made Blackstar for us, his parting gift. I knew for a year this was the way it would be. I wasn't, however, prepared for it. He was an extraordinary man, full of love and life. He will always be with us. For now, it is appropriate to cry."

What Does It Mean?

The album's evocative title has been the subject of much speculation. There are several potential meanings of *Blackstar*. In ancient Judaic belief, the term is another name for Saturn, while it is also a theoretical alternative (as a gravitational entity) to a black hole in space. Given David Bowie's lifelong fascination with science fiction and space, either—or both—meaning seems likely.

Elvis Presley recorded a little-known song of the same title in 1960. The song is about death, and its lyrics include, "Every man has a black star—a black star over his shoulder. And when a man sees his black star he knows his time, his time has come." Presley's movie *Flaming Star* was originally to be titled *Black Star*, and the song was to be the title track. On the name change, however, the song was rerecorded as "Flaming Star" and the original shelved until it surfaced in a boxed set that included such rarities and non-released material some thirty years later. David Bowie was a self-acknowledged ardent fan of Presley's and shared the same birthday as the sneering, hip-swiveling rock 'n' roll icon.

In further speculation, journalist Michael Azerrad pointed out in a tweet that *black star* is a medical term used by radiologists for a type of cancer lesion. Subsequent articles in *New Musical Express*, the *Guardian*, and the *Telegraph*—to name but three—further explored this possibility. As David Bowie suffered from liver cancer, however, and the term is associated with breast cancer, this possibility is not overly likely.

Reception and Performance

At the Fifty-Ninth Grammy Awards, *Blackstar* won "Best Alternative Music Album," "Best Engineered Album, Non-Classical," and "Best Recording Package." In addition, the title single received accolades, taking out the categories of "Best Rock Performance" and "Best Rock Song." Further, *Blackstar* was awarded "British Album of the Year" at the 2017 Brit Awards, while the influential and highly respected website Metacritic named it the most critically acclaimed album of the year.

Blackstar charted very highly in the album charts of many countries across the world. It hit the number one spot in Australia, Austria, Belgium, Canada, Croatia, the Czech Republic, Denmark, Finland, France, Germany, Holland, Ireland, Italy, New Zealand, Norway, Poland, Portugal, Russia, Scotland, Spain, Sweden, Switzerland, the United Kingdom, and the United States. Far from being a result of some sort of worldwide wave of nostalgia for all that Bowie had achieved earlier in his lengthy career, the success of *Blackstar* rested on its own considerable merits and proved beyond doubt that David Bowie was an artist at the peak of his game when he passed away.

Selected Bibliography

David Bowie is one of the most talked-about and written-about artists of the twentieth and twenty-first centuries. Books about him have been published in the popular press since the early to mid-1970s, while in the last two decades in particular, the considerable ranks of these are now being joined by more serious and academic works as the innovative and interdisciplinary aspects of the art he produced become more and more widely recognized and renowned. Since Bowie's death, the number of publications in both realms has increased markedly. In contrast to most of those artists one might consider to be his peers, there is just *so* much to write about and pore over. Undoubtedly, many more publications are yet to come. In addition, there are literally thousands of magazine and newspaper articles and online features. Simply, David Bowie has been big news for decades, and the mind-blowing number of words written about him is a direct reflection of that fact. The following list is anything but exhaustive but contains a combination of the better, more interesting, more unusual, and more well-written works, many of which were consulted in the preparation of this book.

Auslander, Philip. *Performing Glam Rock: Gender & Theatricality in Popular Music*. Ann Arbor: University of Michigan Press, 2006.

Bell, Edward. *Unmade Up ...: Recollections of a Friendship with David Bowie*. London: Unicorn Publishing, 2017.

Buckley, David. *David Bowie: The Complete Guide to His Music*. London: Omnibus Press, 2004.

———. *Strange Fascination: David Bowie, the Definitive Story*. London: Virgin Publishing, 1999.

Cann, Kevin. *Any Day Now: David Bowie, the London Years 1947–1974*. London: Adelita, 2010.

———. *David Bowie: A Chronology*. London: Vermillion, 1983.

Chapman, Ian. *Experiencing David Bowie: A Listener's Companion*. Lanham, MD: Rowman & Littlefield, 2015.

Dogget, Peter. *The Man Who Sold the World: David Bowie and the 1970s*. London: Bodley Head, 2011.

Duncan, Paul, ed. *David Bowie: The Man Who Fell to Earth*. Cologne: Taschen, 2017.

Frith, Simon. "Only Dancing: David Bowie Flirts with the Issues." In *Zoot Suits and Second Hand Dresses: An Anthology of Fashion and Music*, edited by Angela McRobbie, 132–40. Boston: Unwin Hyman, 1988.

Gilbert, Pat. *Bowie: The Illustrated Story*. Stillwater, MN: Voyageur Press, 2017.

Gilman, Leni, and Peter Gilman. *Alias David Bowie*. London: Hodder and Stoughton, 1986.

Hebdige, Dick. *Subculture: The Meaning of Style*. London: Methuen, 1979.

Hoskyns, Barney. *Glam: Bowie, Bolan and the Glitter Rock Revolution*. London: Faber and Faber, 1998.

Jones, Dylan. *David Bowie: A Life*. New York: Crown Archetype, 2017.

Matthew-Walker, Robert. *David Bowie: Theatre of Music*. Bourne End: Kensal Press, 1985.

Néjib. *Haddon Hall: When David Invented Bowie*. London: SelfMadeHero, 2017.

O'Leary, Chris. *Rebel Rebel*. Alresford: Zero Books, 2015.

O'Neil, Terry. *When Ziggy Played the Marquee*. Woodbridge: ACC Art Books, 2017.

Paytress, Mark. *The Rise and Fall of Ziggy Stardust and the Spiders from Mars*. New York: Schirmer Books, 1998.

Pegg, Nicholas. *The Complete David Bowie*. London: Reynolds & Hearn, 2002.

Perone, James E. *The Words and Music of David Bowie*. Westport, CT: Praeger Publishers, 2007.

Pitt, Kenneth. *Bowie: The Pitt Report*. London: Omnibus Press, 1985.

Rock, Mick, and David Bowie. *Moonage Daydream: The Life and Times of Ziggy Stardust*. Guildford: Genesis Publications, 2002.

Sandford, Christopher. *Bowie: Loving the Alien*. London: Warner Books, 1996.

Stevenson, Nick. *David Bowie: Fame, Sound and Vision*. Cambridge: Polity Press, 2006.

Thompson, Dave. *David Bowie: Moonage Daydream*. London: Plexus, 1987.

Trynka, Paul. *Starman: David Bowie, the Definitive Biography*. London: Sphere, 2011.

Waldrep, Shelton. *The Aesthetics of Self Invention: Oscar Wilde to David Bowie*. Minneapolis: University of Minnesota Press, 2004.

Welch, Chris. *David Bowie: We Could Be Heroes*. New York: Thunders Mouth Press, 1999.

Wilcken, Hugo. *Low*. New York: Continuum, 2005.

FAQ Selected Listening

The following list of albums comprise David Bowie's official studio releases and live albums ordered chronologically as his career unfolded. For the uninitiated, being faced with the enormous quantity of David Bowie music in all its various forms can be simply overwhelming: there is just so much of it to be found. Greatest-hits packages, boxed sets, bootlegs, bonus releases with digitally remastered versions, outtakes, alternative arrangements, live albums released decades after the fact, and so on have therefore been omitted in the interests of encouraging those who are not yet familiar with David Bowie's original output to discover this body of work in a way that approximates the experiences of his lifelong fans across five-plus decades. Once this body of work has been experienced, delving into the plethora of other material available is an enormous but pleasurable undertaking.

David Bowie, released on June 1, 1967, Deram Records.

David Bowie (aka *Man of Words/Man of Music* and *Space Oddity*), released on November 4, 1969, Philips Records.

The Man Who Sold the World, released on November 4, 1970, Mercury Records.

Hunky Dory, released on December 17, 1971, RCA Records.

The Rise and Fall of Ziggy Stardust and the Spiders from Mars, released on June 6, 1972, RCA Records.

Aladdin Sane, released on April 13, 1973, RCA Records.

Pinups, released on October 19, 1973, RCA Records.

Diamond Dogs, released on April 24, 1974, RCA Records.

David Live, released on October 29, 1974, RCA Records.

Young Americans, released on February 21, 1975, RCA Records.

Station to Station, released on January 23, 1976, RCA Records.

Low, released on January 14, 1977, RCA Records.

"Heroes," released on October 14, 1977, RCA Records.

Stage, released on September 8, 1978, RCA Records.

Lodger, released on May 18, 1979, RCA Records.

Scary Monsters, released on September 12, 1980, RCA Records.

Let's Dance, released on April 14, 1983, EMI Records.

Tonight, released on September 1, 1984, EMI Records.
Never Let Me Down, released on April 27, 1987, EMI Records.
Tin Machine, released on May 22, 1989, EMI Records.
Tin Machine II, released on September 2, 1991, London Records.
Black Tie White Noise, released on April 5, 1993, Arista Records.
The Buddha of Suburbia, released on November 8, 1993, Arista Records.
Outside, released on September 26, 1995, RCA Records.
Earthling, released on February 3, 1997, RCA Records.
"Hours...," released on October 4, 1999, Virgin Records.
Heathen, released on June 11, 2002, ISO/Columbia Records.
Reality, released on September 16, 2003, ISO/Columbia Records.
The Next Day, released on March 8, 2013, ISO/Columbia Records.
Blackstar, released on January 8, 2016, ISO/Columbia Records.

Index

Page references for illustrations are italicized.